SYMBOL AND RHETORIC IN
ECCLESIASTES

Society of Biblical Literature

Academia Biblica

Saul M. Olyan,
Old Testament Editor

Mark Allan Powell,
New Testament Editor

Number 2

SYMBOL AND RHETORIC IN
ECCLESIASTES
The Place of *Hebel* in Qohelet's Work

SYMBOL AND RHETORIC IN ECCLESIASTES
The Place of *Hebel* in Qohelet's Work

Douglas B. Miller

Society of Biblical Literature
Atlanta

SYMBOL AND RHETORIC IN ECCLESIASTES
The Place of *Hebel* in Qohelet's Work

Copyright © 2002 by the Society of Biblical Literature

Library of Congress Cataloging-in-Publication Data

Miller, Douglas B., 1955-
  Symbol and rhetoric in Ecclesiastes : the place of Hebel in Qohelet's work / by Douglas B. Miller.
      p. cm. — (Academia Biblica ; 2)
Includes bibliographical references and index.
  ISBN 1-58983-029-6 (pbk. : alk. paper)
  1. Bible. O.T. Ecclesiastes—Criticism, interpretation, etc. I. Title. II. Academia Biblica (Series) ; no. 2.
  BS1475.52 .M55 2002b
  223'.80447—dc21
                                        2002003084

07 06 05 04 03 02   5 4 3 2 1

Printed in the United States of America
on acid-free paper

To Adam Andrew, Aaron Thomas, and Daniel Joseph

Table of Contents

Acknowledgements

In addition to the obvious irony of proposing something new for a book whose author declares "there is nothing new under the sun" (Eccl 1:9), I must confess my trepidation at presenting a thesis which seems so distinctive from previous proposals for Ecclesiastes. Yet my feelings of dis-ease are relieved on two counts: first, I believe this proposal is consistent with and actually reinforces previous understandings of the book at numerous points, and second, I believe it makes an important contribution to appreciating the coherence and rhetorical purpose of Ecclesiastes. Any insight it may provide I offer to those whose awareness of the landscape far exceeds my own, and to the people of God who must ultimately test it in the life of faith and service.

To my dissertation advisor, C. L. Seow, I am indebted for insight and guidance. His generosity in making available to me the typescript of his Anchor Bible Ecclesiastes commentary prior to publication was especially appreciated. I am also indebted to other Princeton Theological Seminary faculty who served at various times on the dissertation committee: James F. Armstrong, Dennis T. Olson, and Julie A. Duncan, whose encouragement was particularly valuable in the early stages.

I am grateful for the staff and resources of Speer Library at Princeton Theological Seminary, without which important research would not have been possible. I am also grateful for the administrative support of Tabor College, particularly for faculty development grants and for release time which enabled me to complete the project.

I wish to thank Professor Saul Olyan, Hebrew Bible editor of SBL Academia Biblica, and Leigh C. Andersen of the Society of Biblical Literature for their editorial expertise. The camera-ready copy was printed with Nota Bene Lingua software, version 6.0. Thanks go to Matthew Klaassen of Nota Bene for his technical assistance.

I have taken the opportunity provided by this publication to update the bibliography. This was especially valuable in regard to the work of Michael V. Fox, an important interlocutor who recently revised his major work on Ecclesiastes, and C. L. Seow, some of whose work was originally available to me in prepublished form. I also revised the tables, supplemented the second appendix, and brought the argument into closer conformity with its summary in *Journal of Biblical Literature* 117 (1998): 437–54. I am grateful to the Catholic Biblical Association for permission concerning chapter 5, portions of which were published in modified form in *Catholic Biblical Quarterly* 62 (2000): 215–35.

To my parents, Wilbur and LeAnna Miller, both of whom have provided for my instruction in numerous ways over the years, I acknowledge my deep gratitude and love.

This book is dedicated to my children, Adam, Aaron, and Daniel, whose energy and joy kept me going after *hebel* while we were all experiencing plenty of the same.

Abbreviations and Symbols

Periodicals, Series, and Reference Works

AB	Anchor Bible
ABD	*Anchor Bible Dictionary*
ABL	*Assyrian and Babylonian Letters*, Harper
ABR	*Australian Biblical Review*
ABRL	Anchor Bible Reference Library
AEL	*Ancient Egyptian Literature*, Lichtheim
AnBib	Analecta biblica
ANET	*Ancient Near Eastern Texts Relating to the Old Testament*, Pritchard, 3d ed.
AOAT	Alter Orient und Altes Testament
ATD	Das Alte Testament Deutsch
BBB	Bonner biblische Beiträge
BBR	*Bulletin for Biblical Research*
BDB	Brown, Driver, and Briggs, *Hebrew and English Lexicon*
BHS	*Biblia Hebraica Stuttgartensia*, Elliger and Rudolph
Bib	*Biblica*
BKAT	Biblischer Kommentar, Altes Testament
BT	*The Bible Translator*
BWL	*Babylonian Wisdom Literature*, Lambert
BZAW	Beihefte zur Zeitschrift für die alttestamentliche Wissenschaft
CAD	*The Assyrian Dictionary of the Oriental Institute of the University of Chicago*
CBQ	*Catholic Biblical Quarterly*
CBQMS	Catholic Biblical Quarterly Monograph Series
CC	Continental Commentaries
DDD	*Dictionary of Deities and Demons in the Bible*, van der Toorn, Becking, and van der Horst

DJD	Discoveries in the Judaean Desert
EBib	Études bibliques
EncJud	*Encyclopaedia Judaica*
GBS	Guides to Biblical Scholarship
GKC	*Gesenius' Hebrew Grammar*
HALOT	*The Hebrew and Aramaic Lexicon of the Old Testament*, Koehler, Baumgartner, Stamm, and Richardson
HAR	*Hebrew Annual Review*
HAT	Handbuch zum Alten Testament
HKAT	Handkommentar zum Alten Testament
HRCS	Hatch and Redpath, *Concordance to the Septuagint*
HUCA	*Hebrew Union College Annual*
IBC	Interpretation Biblical Commentary
ICC	International Critical Commentary
IDBSup	*Interpreter's Dictionary of the Bible: Supplementary Volume*
Int	*Interpretation*
IRT	Issues in Religion and Theology
ITC	International Theological Commentary
ITQ	*Irish Theological Quarterly*
JBL	*Journal of Biblical Literature*
JCS	*Journal of Cuneiform Studies*
JNES	*Journal of Near Eastern Studies*
JSOT	*Journal for the Study of the Old Testament*
JSOTSup	Journal for the Study of the Old Testament: Supplement Series
JTS	*Journal of Theological Studies*
KAT	Kommentar zum Alten Testament
KHC	Kurzer Hand-Commentar zum Alten Testament
LCL	Loeb Classical Library
NEchtB	Neue Echter Bibel
NICOT	New International Commentary on the Old Testament
OTL	Old Testament Library
PEQ	*Palestine Exploration Quarterly*
PSB	*Princeton Seminary Bulletin*
RSR	*Recherches de science religieuse*
ScEccl	*Sciences ecclésiastiques*
SubBi	Subsidia biblica
TAPA	*Transactions of the American Philological Association*
TDNT	*Theological Dictionary of the New Testament*, Kittel and Friedrich
TDOT	*Theological Dictionary of the Old Testament*, Botterweck and Ringgren

THAT	*Theologisches Handwörterbuch zum Alten Testament*, Jenni and Westermann
VS	Verbum salutis
VT	*Vetus Testamentum*
VTSup	Vetus Testamentum: Supplement Series
WBC	Word Biblical Commentary
ZAW	*Zeitschrift für die alttestamentliche Wissenschaft*
ZDPV	*Zeitschrift des deutschen Palästina-Vereins*

Books of the Hebrew Bible

Gen	Genesis
Exod	Exodus
Lev	Leviticus
Num	Numbers
Deut	Deuteronomy
Judg	Judges
1–2 Sam	1–2 Samuel
1–2 Kgs	1–2 Kings
Isa	Isaiah
Jer	Jeremiah
Ezek	Ezekiel
Hos	Hosea
Joel	Joel
Amos	Amos
Jonah	Jonah
Mic	Micah
Hab	Habakkuk
Zeph	Zephaniah
Zech	Zechariah
Mal	Malachi
Ps(s)	Psalm(s)
Job	Job
Prov	Proverbs
Ruth	Ruth
Eccl	Ecclesiastes
Lam	Lamentations
Esth	Esther
Dan	Daniel
Neh	Nehemiah
1–2 Chron	1–2 Chronicles

Books of the Apocrypha and Pseudepigrapha

Bar   Baruch
4 Ezra   4 Ezra
Sir   Ben Sira
Wisd of Sol Wisdom of Solomon

Books of the New Testament

Matt   Matthew
Luke   Luke
Acts   Acts
Eph   Ephesians
Col   Colossians

Ancient Versions

Aq.   Aquila
Copt.   Coptic
DSS   Dead Sea Scrolls
LXX   Septuagint
LXX^A Codex Alexandrinus of the Septuagint
LXX^B Codex Vaticanus of the Septuagint
LXX^P Hamburger Papyrus of the Septuagint, Diebner and Kasser
MT   Massoretic Text
OL   Old Latin
Sym.   Symmachus
Syr.   Syriac
SyrH.   Syriac version of Origen's Hexapla
Tg.   Targum
Theod.   Theodotion
Vulg.   Vulgate

Dead Sea Scroll Texts

1QH   Qumran Cave 1 Thanksgiving Hymns
1QM   Qumran Cave 1 War Scroll
1QS   Qumran Cave 1 Rule of the Community
4Q184   Qumran Cave 4 Wiles of the Wicked Woman
4Q511   Qumran Cave 4 text fragment
4QJer^a Qumran Cave 4 portions of Jeremiah
4QJer^b Qumran Cave 4 portions of Jeremiah
4QQoh^a Qumran Cave 4 fragment of Ecclesiastes

Rabbinic Texts

'Abod. Zar.	*'Abodah Zarah*
B. Bat.	*Baba Batra*
B. Meṣi'a	*Baba Meṣi'a*
B. Qam.	*Baba Qamma*
Bek.	*Bekorot*
Ber.	*Berakot*
Eccl. Rab.	*Ecclesiastes Rabbah*
'Erub.	*'Erubin*
Giṭ.	*Giṭṭin*
Ḥul.	*Ḥullin*
Ketub.	*Ketubbot*
Lev. Rab.	*Leviticus Rabbah*
Sanh.	*Sanhedrin*
Šabb.	*Šabbat*
Yebam.	*Yebamot*
Zebaḥ.	*Zebaḥim*

Modern Translations

CEV	Contemporary English Version
GNB	Good News Bible
JB	Jerusalem Bible
KJV	King James Version
NAB	New American Bible
NASB	New American Standard Bible
NEB	New English Bible
NIV	New International Version
NJB	New Jerusalem Bible
NJPS	New Jewish Publication Society Translation
NKJV	New King James Version
NRSV	New Revised Standard Version
REB	Revised English Bible
RSV	Revised Standard Version

Miscellaneous

adj.	adjective
ANE	ancient Near East(ern)
Arab.	Arabic
Aram.	Aramaic
B.C.E.	before the Common Era

bis	twice
ca.	circa
C.E.	Common Era
cf.	*confer*, compare
ch(s).	chapter(s)
cj.	conjecture (uncertain reading)
Dtr	Deuteronomistic History
ed(s).	editor(s), edited by, edition
e.g.	*exempli gratia*, for example
emph.	emphasis
Eng.	English
esp.	especially
et al.	*et alii*, and others
etc.	*et cetera*, and the rest
Fs.	Festschrift
HB	Hebrew Bible
Heb.	Hebrew
ibid.	*ibidem*, in the same place
idem	the same
i.e.	*id est*, that is
Mid. Heb.	Middle Hebrew
MS(S)	manuscript(s)
n.	note
OB	Old Babylonian
pl.	plural; plate
p(p).	page(s)
ptc.	participle
rev.	revised
s.v.	*sub verbo*, under the word
trans.	translated by
txt em	textual emendation
Ugar.	Ugaritic
vb.	verb
viz.	*videlicet*, namely
vol.	volume
v(v).	verse(s)
x	no. of times a word or form occurs

Symbols

< >	text emended
[ ]	text broken

Chapter 1

INTRODUCTION

In recent decades there has been a surge of optimism regarding Ecclesiastes. Though its complexities are far from resolved, the possibility of a coherence to its message—a consistency to its thought and purpose—has been seriously entertained. Its compatibility with ancient Near Eastern wisdom writings has been reinforced. The sophistication of its use of language has been more greatly appreciated, and some scholars have even suggested a rationale for the apparent contradictions in the book.

However, efforts to understand the important lexeme *hebel*, traditionally translated as "vanity," could themselves be described as largely in vain. This term occurs nearly forty times in Ecclesiastes,[1] serving both as the book's motto and in many of its summary statements.[2] The material sense of *hebel* is generally recognized to be something akin to "vapor" or "breath." Yet Qohelet is not speaking of literal gas or steam.

"Completely *hebel*!" says Qohelet at the beginning of Ecclesiastes, "Completely *hebel*! All is *hebel*" (1:2). Frequently through the book, Qohelet comments that "this too was *hebel*," or "all is *hebel* and a chasing after wind." As the book concludes, it appears that Qohelet has made his case: "Completely *hebel*," repeats Qohelet, "All is *hebel*" (12:8). Then the voice of the epilogue,

---

[1] There are thirty-eight occurrences of *hebel* in the MT. Some would emend הכל to הבל at 9:2 (per LXX, et al.), and some would delete its second occurrence at 9:9.

[2] The most obvious way to read 1:2 is as a declaration which Qohelet then proceeds to defend. As Michael V. Fox notes, "The book's motto is a thesis that we can expect to see validated in the following monologue" (*A Time to Tear Down and a Time to Build Up* [Grand Rapids: Eerdmans, 1999], 163).

giving the last word, testifies that Qohelet is a careful thinker whose teaching is to be trusted (12:9–14). We therefore would expect that his use of *hebel* has likewise been deliberate and purposeful.

Yet, commentators and translators have found the term to be confusing, so that its interpretation has become perhaps the most crucial of many challenges involved with the book of Ecclesiastes.[3] Because of its central use in the book, the approach taken to *hebel* dramatically shapes the way the entire book is understood. If, for example, the reader takes "all is *hebel*" in 1:2 to mean "All is ephemeral and illusory,"[4] then perhaps Qohelet is pointing out life's limitations, a realistic counselor of life's hopeful as well as severe aspects. But if Qohelet is understood to say, "All is meaningless" (so NIV), or to declare, "Es ist eben alles Scheisse,"[5] then it appears Qohelet is making a thoroughly pessimistic statement about human experience.

Difficulties with *hebel* are reflected both by the general diversity of approaches taken to it, and by incongruity among the glosses offered for the term.

THE PROBLEM:
THREE APPROACHES TO *HEBEL* IN ECCLESIASTES

Essentially three divergent orientations to the meaning of *hebel* in Ecclesiastes have been adopted: abstract sense, multiple senses, and single metaphor.

Abstract Sense
Some scholars have attempted to determine a single, abstract meaning of *hebel* by which to do justice to its diverse applications in Ecclesiastes.[6] That is,

---

[3] F. Ellermeier, *Qohelet I/1. Untersuchungen zum Buche Qohelet* (Herzberg: Jungfer, 1967), 97, and Graham S. Ogden, "'Vanity' It Certainly Is Not," *BT* 38 (1987): 301–2, note the singular importance of this term. According to James Crenshaw, the concern to explain the book's inconsistencies has been the central focus of research during the past fifty years ("Qoheleth in Current Research," *HAR* 7 [1983]: 41–56). These inconsistencies significantly involve *hebel*.

[4] C. L. Seow, *Ecclesiastes* (AB 18C; New York: Doubleday, 1997), 42. For Seow's further explication of this term, see *Ecclesiastes*, 47, 101–2, 112–13, and "Beyond Mortal Grasp: The Usage of *Hebel* in Ecclesiastes," *ABR* 48 (2000): 1-16.

[5] Frank Crüsemann, "Die unveränderbare Welt," in *Der Gott der kleinen Leute* (Munich: Kaiser, 1979), 80, translated as "The Unchangeable World: The 'Crisis of Wisdom' in Koheleth," in *God of the Lowly* (trans. Matthew J. O'Connell; Maryknoll, N.Y.: Orbis, 1984), 57. Crüsemann states that "Koheleth is unable to find either meaning or reason for hope in the realities of his experience" (ibid.).

[6] The term "abstract" indicates a meaning whose reference set is very broad, the members of which have little in common. For example, cattle, corporate stocks, and gold

a single term, often a noun and its adjective complement, is chosen to represent the meaning which applies to *hebel* in every one of its occurrences.

Of recent major English Bible translations, NRSV and NKJV (vanity/vain),[7] REB and NJB (futility/futile), NEB (emptiness), and NIV (meaningless) have stayed with a single expression for each occurrence of the Hebrew word. Among commentators, W. E. Staples argues that "incomprehensible" fits the sense of *hebel* in each context, while for Graham S. Ogden *hebel* similarly "conveys the notion that life is enigmatic and mysterious." Edwin Good suggests that it means "incongruous" or "ironic," while H. L. Ginsberg offers "zero" as a gloss.[8]

The methodological issue has been set forth clearly by Michael Fox. First, he accepts the importance of a context-sensitive, or "semantics," approach to interpretation.[9] Next, he argues that the universal pronouncements that "all is *hebel*," which frame Qohelet's words in 1:2 and 12:8 and to which Qohelet refers within the book, are statements of the book's theme. As such, they suggest that there is some continuity of meaning through all of the *hebel* texts:

---

bullion may be categorized by the abstract term "wealth," which recognizes only a small element of commonality among all their differences. "Cattle" is a much less abstract term, although it still embraces a variety of elements in its "set" (cows of all breeds, sizes, colors, etc.). Terms for *hebel* discussed in this approach represent a broad variety of experiences, having relatively few common aspects. For example, both the period of youth and the futility of toil are called "vanity." This orientation is similar to the "Single Metaphor" approach (discussed below) in that both positions attempt to find a single gloss for *hebel*. Though the choice of terms in both approaches could be considered abstract, this section is titled "Abstract Sense" because its glosses are at a much higher level of abstraction and because many proponents disregard the possibility that *hebel* is used as a metaphor in Ecclesiastes.

[7] These follow the KJV and RSV, although the RSV makes one exception at 5:6, translating *hebel* as "empty" words. "Vanity" as a translation for *hebel* may be traced to LXX (mostly words such as ματαιότης, emptiness) and Vulg. (*vanitas*).

[8] W. E. Staples, "The 'Vanity' of Ecclesiastes," *JNES* 2 (1943): 95–104; Graham S. Ogden, *Qoheleth* (Readings—A New Biblical Commentary; Sheffield: JSOT Press, 1987), 22; idem, "'Vanity' It Certainly Is Not," 307; Edwin M. Good, "Qoheleth: The Limits of Wisdom," in *Irony in the Old Testament* (Philadelphia: Westminster, 1965), 182; cf. Timothy Polk, "The Wisdom of Irony: A Study of *Hebel* and Its Relation to Joy and the Fear of God in Ecclesiastes," *Studia Biblica et Theologica* 6 (1976): 7–9; H. Louis Ginsberg, *Studies in Koheleth* (Texts and Studies of the Jewish Theological Seminary of America 17; New York: Jewish Theological Seminary of America, 1950), 1. G. A. Barton (*The Book of Ecclesiastes* [ICC; Edinburgh: T & T Clark, 1908]) employs "vanity" or "vain" throughout.

[9] Kurt Galling had previously emphasized the importance of contextual indicators for discerning the "accent" (*Akzent*) intended by Qohelet ("Der Prediger," in *Die fünf Megilloth* [2d ed.; HAT 18; Tübingen: Mohr/Siebeck, 1969], 78–79).

Qohelet's thematic declaration that everything is *hebel* and the formulaic character of the *hebel*-judgments show that for Qohelet there is a single dominant quality in the world and that this quality inheres in the particular *hăbalim* [sic] that he identifies.[10]

Fox insists that an approach which offers a list of translation equivalents or uses a variety of different glosses to translate *hebel* in the book,

> gives us no hint that 1:2 and 12:8 generalize the conclusions reached in the course of Qohelet's investigation. If Qohelet were saying, "X is transitory; Y is futile; Z is trivial," then the summary, "All is *hebel*" would be meaningless. . . . To do Qohelet justice, we must look for a concept that applies to all occurrences, or, failing that, to the great majority of them. Then the summary statement "all is *hebel*" can use the word in the sense established in the particulars.[11]

Some commentators who would agree with Fox to this point have attempted to find a metaphorical rationale for a consistent *hebel* translation. Fox acknowledges that the "literal sense" of *hebel* "from which the others are derived" is "vapor" and surveys proposed metaphorical meanings of the term.[12] However, he insists (a third point) that no known metaphorical sense of *hebel* can accomplish the requisite continuity. As an example, he cites Eccl 8:14, and translates:

> There is a *hebel* that occurs on the earth: there are righteous people who receive what is appropriate to the deeds of the wicked and there are wicked people who receive what is appropriate to the deeds of the righteous. I said that this too is a *hebel*.[13]

The two pronouncements of *hebel* frame a fact: certain unjust situations exist. To call this situation "vaporous," Fox says, gives no information about it: "none of the qualities usually associated with vapors apply." Other possible glosses, such as "transitory," "*Nichtiges*" (emptiness), and "vain," whether or not they involve metaphor, are equally unsatisfactory for him.[14]

Therefore, he moves to as high a level of abstraction as is necessary to be

---

[10] *Time to Tear Down*, 35. Fox cites the NJPS and, in his earlier work (*Qohelet and His Contradictions* [Bible and Literature Series 18; Sheffield: Almond, 1989], 36) cites Loretz as an example, who lists "Forübergehenden, Gewichtlos-Leichten, des Wertlosen, Leeren, Macht- und Hilflosen, kurz, ein Wort für Nichtiges, Hinfälliges" (O. Loretz, *Qohelet und der Alte Orient* [Freiburg: Herder, 1964], 223).

[11] *Time to Tear Down*, 36.

[12] Ibid., 27–29.

[13] Ibid., 30.

[14] Ibid.

faithful to each occurrence of *hebel*, and yet also to make sense of *hebel* within the overall context of the book. He concludes that Qohelet uses the term to mean "absurd."[15]

The insight of the abstract sense approach is that, whatever the variety of contexts in which *hebel* is used throughout the book, we expect a consistency of meaning between their use there and the framing statements in 1:2 and 12:8 that "all is *hebel*."[16]

However, the position involves three difficulties. The first concerns the high levels of abstraction necessary to embrace all the contexts in which *hebel* is used in the book. As the examples mentioned above illustrate, there are quite a number of abstract terms which are plausible for *hebel*, and it is difficult to adjudicate the superiority of one proposed term over another. By the same process used to offer "incomprehensible," "vain," or "absurd" for *hebel*, one might argue just as well for "bizarre" or "frustration."[17]

A second and related difficulty for its proponents is that it typically shows little regard for the way *hebel* is used outside of Ecclesiastes. They propose a special and even unprecedented sense for the term. For example, Edwin Good assumes that Qohelet "uses words with meanings peculiar to himself."[18] Concerning *hebel*, he states:

> Qoheleth uses the term *hebel* to mean something very close to "irony" and ironic."Wherever he uses it, the subject is treated ironically.[19]

---

[15] *Time to Tear Down*, 30. Fox explains that by "absurd" he means the "disjunction between two phenomena that are thought to be linked by a bond of harmony or causality, or that *should* be so linked. . . . [T]he absurd is irrational, an affront to reason—the human faculty that seeks and discovers order in the world about us" (ibid., 31). However, that aspects of life are contradictory does not mean that things are completely unknowable. For Qohelet, *hebel* concerns much that he *does* know and which he evaluates as a bad sickness. For Fox, *hebel* "is oppressive, even tragic" (Michael V. Fox, "The Meaning of *Hebel* for Qohelet," *JBL* 105 [1986]: 410–13). His understanding may thus be distinguished from that of E. Good ("Limits": "incongruous/ironic") and that of André Barucq, who uses "*absurd/absurdité*" but more in the sense of mysterious and confusing (*Ecclésiaste* [VS 3; Paris: Beauchesne, 1968], 27–28, 55–56), as does Bruno Pennacchini, cited by Fox (*Time to Tear Down*, 34; Bruno Pennacchini, "Qohelet ovvero il libro degli assurdi," *Euntes Docete* 30 [1977]: 491–510). Roland Murphy is another who likes the term "absurd" with the sense of incomprehensible (*Ecclesiastes* [WBC 23A; Dallas, Tex.: Word, 1992], lix). Diethelm Michel uses "*absurd*" which he likens to "*sinnlos*" (*Untersuchungen zur Eigenart des Buches Qohelet* [BZAW 183; Berlin/New York: Walter de Gruyter, 1989], 44).

[16] This argument will be defended in Chapter 4.

[17] Not all contexts would work equally well with either of these, but there would be enough fit to make a case.

[18] E. Good, "Limits," 177.

[19] Ibid., 182. That is, labor, acquiring goods, piling up wealth, and wisdom all work

If Qohelet did employ *hebel* in a novel way, we would expect him to provide
assistance for his readers in order to avoid miscommunication. Yet advocates
of this position do not substantiate how he helps his audience move from
known uses of *hebel* to the more unusual employments of it which they
propose. In short, any proposal of this nature would be more persuasive if it
could show either how Qohelet helps his readers with the proposed novel
usage, or how the rationale for *hebel* is in continuity with *hebel*'s overall
established usage.[20]

For most proponents, a consequence of this "novel use" thesis is that, in
summary statements such as "all is *hebel* and chasing after wind," or "all is
hebel and a great evil," Qohelet is saying two different things in each case, e.g.,
"toil is meaningless *and* futile," and "injustice is meaningless *and* bad." It is
important to recognize that, in or out of Ecclesiastes, *hebel* is virtually always
accompanied by additional descriptive terms or phrases. Outside of
Ecclesiastes, these terms and phrases are recognized as complementing *hebel*'s
meaning in that context. The thesis of Qohelet's novel use for *hebel* supposes
that Qohelet associated words with *hebel* which were only tangentially realted
to his intended meaning for the term. That is not impossible, yet interestingly,
in most cases within Ecclesiastes, *hebel* is connected to subjects similar or
identical to those found with the term outside the book. Examples include the
transience of human existence (Eccl 6:12 and Ps 144:4) and the futility of
effort (Eccl 4:4 and Isa 49:4). A novel use for the term requires that Qohelet is
not using *hebel* to mean transience in Eccl 6:12 or futility in Eccl 4:4.

Third, without exception the abstract glosses offered are cast in a
negative direction. This is because much of what Qohelet evaluates by *hebel*
warrants such terms. But it then becomes unclear how someone as discouraged
about life as Qohelet is supposed to be can nevertheless repeatedly commend
joy and instruct his readers in wise choices.[21] For throughout the book, Qohelet

---

toward or assume certain things which are not so.

[20] Polk criticizes Edwin Good's position on this point ("Wisdom of Irony," 8–9).
According to Good ("Limits," 182), when Qohelet declares something to be *hebel*, he is
declaring it to be ironic. Polk, on the other hand, insists that *hebel* itself is a term of negative
judgment meaning "vanity," "emptiness," and so on; Qohelet sees the ironies of life and calls
them vanity. Through his admonitions to joy, Qohelet acknowledges the additional irony that
life nevertheless has good in it.

[21] As Daniel C. Fredericks puts it, "If Qoheleth is disenchanted with the human
condition to the extent that for him everything is futile or absurd, then he is indeed naive and
superficial to commend joy and wise behavior as often as he does" (*Coping with Transience:
Ecclesiastes on Brevity in Life* [The Biblical Seminar 18; Sheffield: JSOT Press, 1993],
32). Fredericks also notes the absence of common terms, such as אַיִן (nothing), רִיק
(emptiness), שָׁוְא (worthless), and תֹּהוּ (empty), which we might expect Qohelet to use in

urges his readers to be content, to cooperate with others, to enjoy their food, their work, their spouse, and to accept these as gifts of God. How then can we understand him to insist that "all" is "emptiness" or "zero?"[22]

Some who adopt this approach take Qohelet's *hebel*-declarations as a general assessment, within which he can still commend some things as better than others.[23] But this suggests that life is not really as bad as Qohelet has declared it to be—everything is really not so absurd, empty, or meaning-less—and does not resolve the other tensions which result from this position.

Finally, no proposal to date has been completely successful in its attempt to translate *hebel* by one abstract concept.[24] Every gloss offered for *hebel* in all of its contexts fails in one or more of them. For example, it seems forced to say with Fox in 6:4 that the person there "comes into *absurdity* and goes into darkness."[25] Something of emptiness is indicated here, or perhaps the inscrutable. Likewise, it seems unfitting in 11:10 to describe the time of youth as "meaningless" (NIV) since youth is being commended as something positive. The sense of urgency there requires that *hebel* is conveying something akin to brevity. In fact, Fox himself makes an exception and translates, "for youth and juvenescence are *fleeting*."[26] Eccl 6:12, which likewise indicates a connection between *hebel* and transience, raises a similar difficulty for this position. Such passages also demonstrate why "vanity" and "futility" are unsatisfactory when used to translate *hebel* throughout.

Those who acknowledge this difficulty often posit that Qohelet largely makes a distinctive use of *hebel*, such as to mean "vanity," but occasionally "relapses" into conventional uses of the term.[27] This resolves the tension

---

support of *hebel* if indeed he intended it to mean something akin to "vanity" throughout (p. 28), esp. since all are used at least once as synonyms of *hebel* elsewhere in the HB.

[22] Various theories of editors and insertions have been made for the book, but none discounts that the original author at some points makes exhortations of the type just noted.

[23] Several approaches to the thematic statements of 1:2 and 12:8 in particular are summarized in the discussion of the multiple senses approach below.

[24] Proponents of this position often argue that Qohelet is attempting to say something which strains the capability of his language. Some inconsistency on his part would thus be warranted.

[25] *Time to Tear Down*, 241. To do so, Fox insists that the one about whom *hebel* is designated in this verse is the one described in Eccl 6:3a and not the stillborn of 6:3b. See discussion in Chapter 4.

[26] *Time to Tear Down*, 316 (emphasis added), with explanation at 318–19. Roland Murphy (*Ecclesiastes*) also abandons a uniform gloss ("vanity") in 11:10, where he too gives "fleeting." K. Galling ("Der Prediger") employs *Nichtiges* (or forms thereof) for *hebel*, though at 9:9, "*flüchtigen Daseins*" (transient existence). Luther employed "*eitel*" and "*Eitelkeit*" until 6:4 where he used "*Nichtigkeit*."

[27] So Klaus Seybold, "הֶבֶל ;הֲבַל," *TDOT*, vol. 3, 318.

between the thematic statement of 1:2 and the diversity of *hebel* contexts by considering Qohelet to be inconsistent with his employment of *hebel*. A multiplicity of meanings suggests a second approach to this issue.

Multiple Senses

The diversity of contexts in which Qohelet uses *hebel* has motivated some translators to a calculated use of multiple terms in translation. Typically, a majority of the passages are treated uniformly, with terms such as "vanity/vain" (NASB, NAB, JB), "futility/futile" (NJPS), and "useless" (GNB). However, the remaining texts then employ an assortment of glosses: "emptiness" and "fleeting" (NASB); "fleeting" (NAB, JB); "nothing/ nothingness," "fleeting," "brief span," "frustration," and "illusory" (NJPS); and "not a thing/nothing at all," "no good," "doesn't mean a thing/no meaning," "nonsense," "not very long" (GNB).

Even more diverse, however, is the *Modern Language Bible* which renders *hebel* as "futility," "worthless," "fruitless," "useless," "emptiness," "profitless," "follies," "vain," "unproductive," "ineffective," "passing," and "transit." *Die Bibel in heutigem Deutsch* uses "*sinnlos*" or similar terms and phrases for most occurrences of *hebel*, but translates "*vergeblich*" in 1:14 and 2:15, "*Nichts*" in 6:4, and "*gehen schnell*" in 11:10, among others.

Among commentators, R. B. Y. Scott uses "breath," "vapor," "futility/futile," "empty/empty thing," "hollow mockery/thing," "transitory," "meaningless/makes no sense," "anomalies," "oblivion," and "fleeting," while James L. Crenshaw employs "futility/futile," "absurd/absurdity," "transient," "brief," "fleeting," and "empty."[28]

While it is true that in the sources cited several of these glosses are synonyms and reflect an essentially equivalent sense for *hebel*, a diversity still exists, and the willingness to use such a variety of terms reflects a distinctive orientation. R. N. Whybray summarizes:

> As a general rule Qoheleth appears to use [*hebel*] mainly . . . to emphasize the *futility* of various human activities or situations; but in some passages—e.g. 6:12; 9:9 (where it corresponds to RSV's 'vain'); 11:10—it may mean no more than "brevity."[29]

---

[28] R. B. Y. Scott, *Proverbs, Ecclesiastes* (AB 18; New York: Doubleday, 1965); James L. Crenshaw, *Ecclesiastes* (OTL; Philadelphia: Westminster, 1987). Others taking this approach include R. Gordis (*Koheleth—The Man and His World: A Study of Ecclesiastes* [3d ed.; New York: Schocken, 1968]), R. N. Whybray (*Ecclesiastes* [New Century Bible Commentary; Grand Rapids: Eerdmans, 1989]), and W. Zimmerli (*Das Buch des Predigers Salomo* [3d ed.; ATD 16/1; Göttingen: Vandenhoeck & Ruprecht, 1980 (1962)]).

[29] Whybray, *Ecclesiastes*, 36.

This is similar to the understanding of Walther Zimmerli,[30] and reflects the insight that Qohelet is using the term in more than one way.

However, this view fails to account for Qohelet's framing statements that "all is *hebel*" (1:2; 12:8; et al.).[31] If a shopkeeper were to announce that "all is on sale," then point to items throughout the store saying, "this is on sale," "that is on sale," "this too is on sale," and finally conclude by repeating "all is on sale," we would expect that something of common attribution was being said about each item in that store.

Various attempts have been made to eliminate the difficulty caused by the apparent universality of this *hebel* predication. Norbert Lohfink argues that *hebel* in these verses predicates only that which is in the immediate context and thus is not thematic for the book as a whole.[32] Others consign 1:2 and 12:8 to a later editor.[33] Both of these points will be addressed in Chapter 4. For now it is sufficient to say that the use of *hebel* as a leitmotif throughout the book and the repetition of "all is *hebel*" elsewhere (1:14; 2:17; 3:19) obviate the role of a later editor.[34] That is, if 1:2 and 12:8 were added by such an editor, it was done out of recognition of *hebel*'s thematic role.[35]

If the statement in 1:2 and 12:8 is appropriate for framing the book, Fox is correct to insist that "all is *hebel*" embraces *each* matter cited as *hebel* by Qohelet throughout the book. Qohelet thus appears to be saying *one thing* when he pronounces that "all is *hebel*," and yet the multiple senses approach interprets him as also saying certain *other* things by use of the same term. If *hebel* sometimes means "nothing," while at other times means "fleeting,"

---

[30] Zimmerli, *Predigers*, 243. For example, Zimmerli says: "Selbst die dem Menschen von Gott selber hier gewährte (und dort versagte) Genussfähigkeit und Freude wird für diesen nicht verfügbar, sondern bleibt im Bereich des Vergänglichen (2:24–26)" (ibid.). Zimmerli most often uses *eitel* to translate *hebel*, but also *Nichtigkeit* (and related terms), and (in one case) *flüchtigen* (9:9).

[31] That is, as discussed above with the abstract sense approach, the statements of motto which frame the book imply that Qohelet's uses of the term have something in common. He discusses a particular point, then summarizes that "this too (or "indeed") is *hebel*" in the process of demonstrating that "all is *hebel*."

[32] N. Lohfink, "Koh 1,2 'alles ist Windhauch'—universale oder anthropologische Aussage?" in *Der Weg zum Menschen* (ed. Rudolf Mosis and Lothar Ruppert; Freiburg: Herder, 1989), 201–16.

[33] So Ellermeier, *Qohelet*, 100.

[34] F. J. Backhaus, *Denn Zeit und Zufall trifft sie alle: Studien zur Komposition und zum Gottesbild im Buch Qohelet* (BBB 83; Frankfurt am Main: Anton Hain, 1993), 326, 330.

[35] Fox believes 1:2 and 12:8 contain a thematic summary added by a later editor, yet one who understood Qohelet's thought correctly: "Of course it is an oversimplification, but that's what summaries are" (*Time to Tear Down*, 162).

"frustration," and "illusory" (so NJPS), what is meant by "*all* is *hebel*"?[36]

It is not tenable that such diverse meanings are combined in any of the individual contexts, nor does it work to pick one of these glosses (e.g., "fleeting" or "illusory") as somehow including all the others in a summary way.[37] Qohelet declares certain things to be *hebel* which do not fit other of the categories proposed. He is not saying that a situation is *nothing* in which people do not find satisfaction in their wealth (5:9 [Eng. v. 10]).[38] Nor is he suggesting that toil motivated by envy is *transitory* (4:4–6). Likewise, it is not *illusory* when the righteous receive the reward of the wicked (8:10–14).

Those who would espouse this approach, then, must content themselves with the book's inconsistent use of *hebel*, and particularly with the problem of the framing thesis statements (1:2; 12:8). Such inconsistency in an author is possible, of course, but it raises questions about the quality of Qohelet's communication and the coherence of his thought.[39]

It is common for scholars who take this position to recognize the metaphorical dimension of *hebel*. For example, Gordis, who glosses with "vanity," "folly," "futility," "nothingness," and "fleeting breath," cites "unsubstantial" and "transitory" as the metaphorical sources of Qohelet's usage.[40] Scott, another who employs a variety of glosses, also understands the term to be used metaphorically and translates *hebel* as "breath" or "vapor" a dozen times, notably in the declarations of 1:2 and 12:8.[41] An appreciation for metaphor in the book has led to a third proposal for *hebel*.

Single Metaphor

This third approach reflects the insight that *hebel* serves as a live

---

[36] As Fox says, "Qohelet's thematic statement, 'Everything is הבל' implies that there is some meaning common to the various occurrences of the term. To define the word, as commentators commonly do, by offering a list of translation equivalents . . . is inadequate" (*Contradictions*, 35–36). Also Daniel Fredericks: "It would become hopelessly obscure if one were to take the phrase 'everything is breath' and have any number of options for interpretation and translation in each context" (*Coping*, 17).

[37] As Fox likewise insists, "The renderings suggested by the various translations and commentaries are . . . distinct qualities, not merely different nuances or colorations of one concept: what is fleeting may be precious, what is frustrating may be no illusion, what is futile may endure forever" (*Contradictions*, 36).

[38] That is, the context makes it clear that the set of circumstances surrounding the person with wealth is being commented upon and not the effort to obtain that wealth.

[39] It should be acknowledged that many proponents of this approach do not pretend that there is, or need be, such concord. They simply allow that Qohelet is being to some extent multifarious in his usage of this term.

[40] *Koheleth*, 205.

[41] Scott, *Proverbs, Ecclesiastes*, ad loc. See especially the comments in his

metaphor in the book.[42] Like the abstract sense approach, its proponents construe *hebel* as having one sense, or one primary sense, in all its uses. It thus differs from that of some advocates of the multiple senses position who propose that *hebel* is a metaphor but one with several different referents.

Two scholars, Daniel C. Fredericks and Kathleen A. Farmer, have recently argued that *hebel* has the single metaphoric sense of "transience" throughout Ecclesiastes.[43] Farmer draws attention to the virtual equation of *hebel* and רוּחַ in Eccl 1:14; 2:11, 17, 26; 4:4, 16; and 6:9. This suggests, she says, that the material referent (vapor or breath) should be contemplated for *hebel* in each case. Doing this will allow the metaphorical nature of the term to be appreciated.[44]

The distinctiveness of this alternative is evident in Farmer's treatment of Eccl 8:14 as compared to that of Fox.[45] In 8:10–14, Qohelet comments on those now dead who were wicked, yet were praised in the city while alive.[46] The failure of badness to be quickly judged contributes to human propensity in that direction. Despite this, Qohelet is confident that those who fear God will receive good, and that it will not be good for the wicked.

But the verse which immediately follows (8:14) seems to directly contradict the statements in vv. 12–13: the wicked and the righteous receive just the *opposite* of the treatment they justly deserve. Scholars have variously accounted for this reversal by proposing that vv. 12–13 were inserted by a later editor, or that these verses are a quotation or thesis upon which Qohelet wishes to comment. But, Farmer says, if we appreciate the metaphorical sense of *hebel*

---

introduction, pp. 201–2.

[42] A "live" metaphor is one which actively engages the mind in a comparison between the term's material sense and what is being described, which requires alertness to clues regarding the metaphor given by the author. However, most who understand *hebel* to have a metaphoric sense of "useless" or "vanity" do not emphasize such an active participatory role by the reader.

[43] Fredericks, *Coping*, and Farmer, *Who Knows What Is Good? A Commentary on the Books of Proverbs and Ecclesiastes* (ITC; Grand Rapids: Eerdmans, 1991). D. B. Macdonald, without comment, translates *hebel* consistently as "transitory" or "(case of) transitoriness" (*The Hebrew Philosophical Genius: A Vindication* [Princeton: Princeton University Press, 1936], 70–85). Two others who emphasize *hebel* as metaphor are Leo Perdue in his *Wisdom and Creation: The Theology of Wisdom Literature* (Nashville: Abingdon, 1994), 206–8, and John J. Collins in *Proverbs, Ecclesiastes* (Knox Preaching Guides; Atlanta: John Knox, 1980), 72. Perdue states that "the root meaning that underlies the term, and thus human existence, is ephemerality" (p. 207).

[44] Farmer, *Who Knows?* 143–46.

[45] Fox's treatment of this passage was summarized above.

[46] Verse 10 is difficult. Farmer's reading is one of several possible, none of which is an obstacle to Farmer's basic thesis.

here, we will recognize that Qohelet is describing this situation as merely short-term. "This is *hebel*" here means not, "This is absurd" (Fox), but rather "Such may be the case for a while, but later God's justice will prevail."[47]

Although nicely presented in her introduction, Farmer defends her thesis only selectively, not discussing the role of *hebel* in passages such as 4:7–12 and 6:1–6 where it would be more difficult to sustain.[48] Further, even the prime examples she cites, the passages in which *hebel* is joined with "chasing the wind," do not work so well with *hebel* translated as "fleeting" (1:14; 2:11, 17, 26; 4:4, 16; and 6:9).

It is certainly plausible to consider the *results* of such toil to be fleeting, and it is true that Qohelet occasionally uses "toil" (עָמָל) of labor's results rather than of the effort itself (cf. 2:18). However, in the texts just cited, Qohelet uses *hebel* of the (ineffective) effort itself.[49] For example, in 2:12-17 Qohelet complains that those who worked hard to achieve wisdom will die as do fools. It is not that the results of their effort is transient, but that their effort is futile.[50]

Fredericks, in *Coping with Transience*, likewise defends the proposal that *hebel* primarily means "transience" in Ecclesiastes. After noting other contexts in the HB where *hebel* means transient, Fredericks addresses its application in Ecclesiastes to life/death, toil, pleasure, and tragedy. He, like Farmer, does an excellent job of demonstrating the plausibility of the sense of transience in many of *hebel*'s contexts.[51]

---

[47] *Who Knows?* 181–83.

[48] It is important to acknowledge that Farmer's book is in a commentary series directed primarily toward a popular rather than to a scholarly audience.

[49] See discussion ad loc. in Chapter 4 of this study.

[50] In addition, Farmer would have it that when Qohelet says, "All/This is *hebel* and chasing after wind," he is saying, "The *results* of this toil are fleeting (*hebel*) and the *toil itself* is futile effort (chasing after wind)." It is dubious that the terms הַכֹּל (all) and זֶה (this) would have two different antecedents in the same statement: toil and toil's results. Farmer explains Eccl 1:16–17 as follows: "Wisdom itself tells [Qohelet] that the effort one needs to expend in order 'to know wisdom and to know madness and folly' cannot produce permanent results: 'This also is but a striving after wind'" (*Who Knows?* 155).

[51] As mentioned above regarding the proposal of Farmer, the subject of *hebel* in most עָמָל (toil) passages cannot be interpreted as *toil* itself by this proposal since Qohelet is not saying that effort is a transient matter. Unlike Farmer's explanation, for Fredericks both the *hebel*-phrase and the "wind" phrase function as synonyms. He argues that רְעוּת רוּחַ and רַעְיוֹן רוּחַ mean not "chasing wind," but "will of the wind" or "desire of the wind," a proposal which is both etymologically and syntactically possible (taking the genitive as subjective). Thus, "All/This is *hebel* and רַעְיוֹן/רְעוּת of the wind" means, "[All/This is] temporary and like the will of the wind" (*Coping*, 21, 29–31). In his extended discussion of עָמָל (*Coping*, 48–63), Fredericks uses the word "ephemeral" for *hebel*, a gloss which could be applied to *toil* itself (as futile) as well as to its *achievements* (as being short-lived). His use of "ephemeral" thus obscures the fact that Fredericks, like Farmer, interprets עָמָל as toil's results (transient) and

However, Fredericks must acknowledge that this sense for the term will not work in every passage. It appears out of place, for example, when used of verbosity (e.g., 5:6 [Eng. v. 7]). Also difficult are 4:7–8 (an irrational obsession with work), and 7:6 (the laughter of fools).

Suggesting that *hebel* may connote "futility" in such texts, Fredericks then continues:

> But [such cases] are few and should not invert the proportion toward a message of futility for the book as a whole. It is as if Qohelet assumes that we have learned that *life* is like a breath, brief in length. . . . But now he wants us to be aware of the fact that *every* experience within life is breath, everything will pass.[52]

Yet Qohelet is displeased about other things he calls *hebel* that would be quite satisfactory if they *were* fleeting. He declares the relinquishing of one's wealth to one who never worked for it to be *hebel* and a "great evil (רָע)" (2:18–23). Qohelet calls an irrational obsession with work *hebel* and an "evil (רָע) business" (4:7–8), and the usurpation of one's wealth by a stranger *hebel* and an "evil (רָע) sickness" (6:1–6). Finally, the reality that the wise die just like fools is another part of the badness (רָע) done under the sun (2:12–17; 9:3). These matters are *hebel*, but they cannot be considered transient from the perspective of a human lifetime.

Fredericks correctly notes that *hebel* in such texts cannot simply indicate "meaninglessness," a much too casual attribution for the magnitude Qohelet gives these problems. It is not adequate, however, for him to relate such texts to the theme of transience by describing them as matters "that at times only transience can remedy,"[53] for this acknowledges that they are *not* transient.

Nevertheless, Farmer and Fredericks make a two-fold contribution. First, they have renewed attention to the metaphorical nature of *hebel* in Ecclesiastes and have raised new possibilities for "transience" as a meaning for *hebel* in certain texts. Secondly, they have continued to wrestle with reconciling Qohelet's statement that "all is *hebel*" with the fact that in the book he gives positive, hopeful advice along with his negative assessments. If the book is coherent, it does not seem possible that Qohelet's primary thesis in 1:2 is a *completely* nihilistic one.[54] By offering transience as *hebel*'s primary focus,

---

not the toil itself.

[52] *Coping*, 24.

[53] Ibid., 31.

[54] Fredericks explains that his argument is not an attempt to remove all trace of cynicism or pessimism from Qohelet. However, he believes his view takes all that the book has to say about wisdom, toil, tragedy, and joy into a more coherent whole with the result that Qohelet comes across less embittered than in some other readings (*Coping*, 95).

Qohelet is made to lament that life and its good things pass so quickly, rather than insisting that all of life is absurd or meaningless.

Yet there are *hebel*-texts for which "transience" will not work, so that this proposal likewise falls short of reconciling the book with its thesis. Fredericks' acknowledgement that in at least some instances *hebel* may mean "futile" in Ecclesiastes makes his version, in effect, a type of the multiple senses approach.

Conclusion

Qohelet has not used *hebel* in its material sense of "vapor" or "breath." The challenge for any proposal concerning Qohelet's use of *hebel* is to reconcile the programmatic statements of 1:2 and 12:8 both with the diversity of contexts in which *hebel* is used and with his positive advice, while achieving some consistency with known uses of *hebel* elsewhere.

The abstract sense approach works hard to retain the unity of *hebel*'s employment in the book but ultimately fails with both the diverse contexts and the advice. The variety of proposals offered by its proponents, united only in their pessimistic orientation to the book, as well as discontinuity with known uses of *hebel* elsewhere, also discourages confidence in the method employed.

The multiple senses approach respects the particulars, but does not account well for the book's thesis statements. Finally, the proposals offered to date for a single metaphoric sense of *hebel* have the virtue of offering a meaning for the term which is less harsh and is thus more consistent with Qohelet's positive advice. However, as with the abstract sense position, no single metaphor has been found adequate for the range of *hebel*'s diverse usage.

There is, of course, nothing which requires Qohelet to be consistent with his use of terms. In fact, it may be worth considering whether such inconsistency is part of his rhetoric. Yet there is another possibility for the way *hebel* is used in Ecclesiastes, one which is in continuity with Qohelet's use of language overall, accounts for the book's thesis statements, is consistent with known uses of *hebel* elsewhere, and allows for Qohelet's sincere presentation of advice.[55]

---

[55] One should be ever mindful of the irony inherent in new-fashioned efforts to interpret a book which insists there is "nothing new under the sun." On the other hand, as Daniel Fredericks points out (Fredericks, *Coping*, 97), according to wisdom, "It is the glory of God to conceal a matter, but the glory of kings is to search things out" (Prov 25:2). For that which may have been concealed, then, there is justification for a royal enthusiasm with which one might argue a new proposal.

STATEMENT OF THESIS

The thesis of this study is that Qohelet employs *hebel* as a "symbol," an image which holds together a *set* of meanings, or "referents," that can neither be exhausted nor adequately expressed by any single meaning.[56] A number of different referents may be discerned for *hebel* in Ecclesiastes, each of which finds connection with some aspect of *hebel*'s material sense: its insubstantiality, transience, or foulness. Qohelet carefully constructs these metaphorical referents of *hebel* into a single symbol embodying them all in order to communicate the message that all human experience is *hebel* in one way or another.

Recognition of *hebel*'s symbolic function does not entail a lack of precision in Qohelet's use of the term throughout. There are indications that Qohelet has been very careful in his construction of the *hebel*-symbol and that he has shaped *hebel*'s use appropriately in each case.

In Chapter 2, a precise method for discerning the symbolic and metaphorical functions of *hebel* in Ecclesiastes will be described which involves the role of "guarding" terms and phrases in the text. Most often a single meaning or "valency" is indicated for *hebel*, while in other contexts two or more are indicated (multivalency). Only in the absence of such terms and phrases, which is rare (e.g., 1:2 and 12:8), will it be concluded that Qohelet is using *hebel* with reference to all its meanings (omnivalency).

CONGRUITY WITH QOHELET'S USE OF LANGUAGE OVERALL

The function of the term *hebel* proposed in this study is consistent with Qohelet's rich use of metaphor and his frequent use of terms with multiple senses. Among his metaphors are terms for darkness (2:14; 5:16 [Eng. v. 17]; 6:4; 11:8; 12:1–3), shadow (6:12; 7:12; 8:13), and light (11:7–8; 12:2). Other metaphors include dreams (5:2 [Eng. v. 3]; 5:6 [Eng. v. 7]), illness (5:12 [Eng. v. 13]; 5:15 [Eng. v. 16]), heart (1:13, 16, 17; 2:1, 3, etc., 42x), chasing after wind (1:14; 2:11; 4:16; 6:9, etc., 9x), and images, such as a house, found in the book's final poem (12:1–7).

It can be demonstrated from comparative ancient Near Eastern literature as well as from the Hebrew Bible itself that some expressions, such as those involving the "heart" and "under the sun/heaven," are stock idioms of the

---

[56] Philip Wheelwright, *Metaphor and Reality* (Bloomington: Indiana University Press, 1962), 92–110.

culture and "dead" metaphors.[57] However, others are very much live meta-phors, as is reflected in the diversity of their application and by terms the author associates with them to guide the reader's understanding.[58]

Qohelet's word devices also include analogy and simile (wisdom to folly//light to darkness, 2:13; crackling of thorns//laughter of fools, 7:6), synecdoche (eye and ear, 1:8; eating and drinking, 2:24), hyperbole (nothing new under the sun, 1:9; 6:10; no one remembers anyone else, 1:11; 2:16; 9:5), and personification (the sun hurries, 1:5; the heart observes wisdom, 1:16, and guides Qohelet, 2:3) to give some examples of each.

Particularly interesting for the present thesis is Qohelet's use of antanaclasis, or the repetition of a word with a different meaning.[59] One example is the two different Hiphil forms of נוח in Eccl 10:4:

> If the anger of the ruler rises against you, do not leave (נוח) your post, for calmness will appease (נוח) great offenses.[60]

While some reported occurrences of antanaclasis are debatable,[61] in other cases it is more certain that Qohelet is putting a given word or root to a variety of uses.[62] Some of his favorite words are used in several different ways (although not technically antanaclasis in every case since their contexts are not immediately juxtaposed). For example, טוֹב (good, 52x in Eccl) and רָעָה/רָע (evil, 31x) correspond to each other in at least three types of use within the book. The following examples are representative:

---

[57] The phrase "under the sun" or "with the sun" occurs in Phoenician, Elamite, Aramaic, and other texts including the *Gilgamesh Epic*; cf. Ps 72:5. See discussion in Seow, *Ecclesiastes*, 104–6.

[58] A "stock" or "dead" metaphor is one which has a consistent singular meaning. Very little contextual assistance is necessary for it to be understood. A "live" metaphor, since it has the potential for more than one meaning, is highly dependent upon contextual clues for good communication.

[59] J. M. Sasson, "Wordplay in the OT," *IDBSup* (Nashville: Abingdon, 1976), 968–70; see also Anthony R. Ceresko, "The Function of *Antanaclasis* (mṣʾ 'to Find'//mṣʾ 'to Reach, Overtake, Grasp') in Hebrew Poetry, Especially in the Book of Qoheleth," *CBQ* 44 (1982): 551–69, and the literature cited there

[60] Sasson, "Wordplay," 970.

[61] For example, Sasson cites as an example the repeated phrase וְאֵין לָהֶם מְנַחֵם in Eccl 4:1, following the NEB translation which gives "no one to comfort them" and "no one to avenge them" respectively.

[62] N. Lohfink argues for such an instance in Eccl 5:17–19, the term מַעֲנֶה. From the root ענה II, this is usually understood to mean "to keep busy, occupy." However, ענה I, "to answer, reveal," if understood in 5:17–19, would recall the issues raised in 3:10–15, and suggest that "God answers, speaks, reveals himself by the joy of the heart" ("Qoheleth 5:17–19—Revelation by Joy," *CBQ* 52 [1990]: 625–35; the quotation is from p. 634).

טוֹב	רָעָה/רָע
pleasure (2:1; 11:9)	pain (7:3; 11:10)
positive evaluation (2:3; 11:7)	negative evaluation (5:12 [Eng. v. 13], 15 [Eng. v. 16]; 9:3)
positive things generally (5:10 [Eng. v. 11]; 11:6)	destruction of good things (5:12 [Eng. v. 13], 13 [Eng. v. 14]; 7:14; 9:3)

Not only is the diversity interesting for each of the terms mentioned above, but it is also notable how closely together some of these diverse uses are found. Additional examples of words Qohelet uses with a variety of meaning include the following (with representative examples):

חֹשֶׁךְ (6x) and the root חשׁך (2x)	absence of light (2:13); absence of wisdom (2:14); oppression (5:16 [Eng. v. 17]; 12:2–3); the unknown[63] (6:4 [bis])
רוּחַ (24x)	wind (1:6; 11:4); life breath (11:5); emptiness (1:14, 17; 6:9); spirit (7:8 [bis], 9); anger (10:4)
חֳלִי (2x)	sickness (5:16 [Eng. v. 17]); neg. evaluation (6:2). Cf. חוֹלָה (illness): neg. evaluation in 5:12 [Eng. v. 13], 15 [Eng. v. 16]

Such literary dexterity is part of Qohelet's style. Also interesting are the occasions in which intentional multivalency may be involved in a single use of a term. For example, in 8:8, the text appears to read well for two different senses of רוּחַ: "wind" and "life-breath." In 11:8 and 12:2–3, the noun חֹשֶׁךְ and the root חשׁך (respectively) may incorporate both the meaning "oppression" and the meaning "death." Another example is שַׁחֲרוּת in 11:10. This term may mean either "dawn" or "black hair," either of which would fit the context.[64] In 6:7, נֶפֶשׁ refers to the dissatisfaction of *people* but also specifically to their *appetite*, and it may also allude to Sheol (Death's appetite). Finally, צֵל (shadow) may be used metaphorically to indicate either protection or brevity (6:12; 8:13), whereas in 7:12 a traditional saying about the protection afforded by wisdom and money may allude ironically to its transience.

These examples reinforce the report of the epilogist that Qohelet was

---

[63] Or possibly death.

[64] Both meanings for the term, a *hapax legomenon*, have etymological justification.

teaching the people knowledge, weighing, studying, and arranging many מְשָׁלִים (proverbs, and other speech forms), seeking out pleasing words, and seeking to write words of truth plainly (Eccl 12:9–10). Given the extent of Qohelet's creative use of literary devices, it should not be surprising that his thesis statement (1:2) involves *hebel*, a term capable of several senses, which Qohelet employs with multivalency.

CONGRUITY WITH OTHER ISRAELITE LITERATURE

Just as Qohelet's symbolic use of *hebel* is consistent with his overall use of language, so it is notable that symbol is a literary device evident in the broader Israelite tradition as well. Particularly is this true of the wisdom literature, but two other studies may serve as a prelude to that discussion.

Ben Ollenburger's investigation of the Zion tradition, primarily concerning the Psalms and Isaiah of Jerusalem, exemplifies the use of a literary-cultural tensive symbol. In *Zion, the City of the Great King: A Theological Symbol of the Jerusalem Cult*,[65] he demonstrates that the Zion symbol involved the presence of Yahweh among his people, specifically as "king," and the exclusive prerogative of Yahweh to defend and provide security for this people. The Zion tradition partakes of several motifs: (1) the divine mountain, (2) the river of paradise, (3) the conquest of chaos, (4) the defeat of the nations, and (5) the pilgrimage of the nations.[66] The pre-Israelite myth was made to connect with Jerusalem, and additional motifs were developed subsequently. The status of Zion as a powerful central symbol within Israelite theology and politics is reflected within Israel's literature of worship and prophecy.

Tree imagery is the special study of Kirsten Nielsen in *There Is Hope for a Tree: The Tree as Metaphor in Isaiah*.[67] She investigates the role of trees in Isaiah, and makes passing comment on the tree as ancient Near Eastern cult symbol. However, the frequency and diversity of the imagery used by the prophet suggests a multivalency characteristic of literary symbols. It is especially important for its ability to represent both judgment and hope. For example, Isa 1:30 has: "For you shall be like an oak whose leaf withers, and like a garden without water." Yet in 17:6, the Lord God of Israel declares,

---

[65] Ben C. Ollenburger, *Zion, the City of the Great King: A Theological Symbol of the Jerusalem Cult* (JSOTSup 41; Sheffield: JSOT Press, 1987).

[66] J. J. M. Roberts, "Zion Tradition," *IDBSup* (Nashville: Abingdon, 1976), 985–87.

[67] Kirsten Nielsen, *There Is Hope for a Tree: The Tree as Metaphor in Isaiah* (JSOTSup 65; Sheffield: JSOT Press, 1989 [1985]).

"Gleanings will be left in it, as when an olive tree is beaten—two or three berries in the top of the highest bough, four or five on the branches of a fruit tree."

As with the broader Israelite tradition, the use of symbol is also found within the wisdom corpus of Israel. Leo Perdue's *Wisdom in Revolt: Metaphorical Theology in the Book of Job* provides such a study.[68] Perdue understands Job to represent a response of wisdom to problems with "the domestication of its language and the potential idolatry of its theological formulations."[69] Perdue explains wisdom metaphors which are addressed in the book of Job: *fertility*, *artistry*, *word*, and *battle* (of divine creative activity), and *slave* and *ruler* (of humanity's role).[70] Perdue considers the human imagery to come under critical attack in the book of Job. He describes these as root metaphors and locates them within the broader mythic traditions of the ancient Near East.[71] Several of these may also be considered "symbols" as can other images present in the book of Job. Norman Habel, for example, has noted the "hand" of El as a "major symbol of God's oppressive and arbitrary intervention in Job's life" (cf. Job 10:7; 12:9; 13:21; 19:21; 27:11–12).[72]

The image of a tree, noted above in Nielsen's study of Isaiah, was also taken up within wisdom literature where its use suggests the multivalency of a symbol. It is employed in Prov 3:18, where wisdom is called a "tree of life,"[73] and by the author of Ps 1 who describes the righteous as a "tree planted by streams of water, that yields its fruit in its season," and whose "leaf does not wither."[74] As symbol, the tree can predicate the faithful ones who draw upon the full life God has for them: they meditate upon *tôrâ* (as a tree draws water), accomplish good (as a tree bears fruit), and never know disease, poverty, or failure (as a tree without withered leaf or other blight). The tree in Job, as for the book of Isaiah, is an image of both judgment and hope (14:7; 15:33; 19:10; 24:20).

Norman Habel isolates three symbol polarities within Prov 1–9: the two ways, the two hearts, and the two companions (Lady Wisdom and the Strange

---

[68] Leo Perdue, *Wisdom in Revolt: Metaphorical Theology in the Book of Job* (JSOTSup 112; Sheffield: Almond, 1991).

[69] Ibid., 31.

[70] Ibid., 61.

[71] They may also be described as models or metaphor *systems* (ibid., 27–30).

[72] Norman C. Habel, *Job* (OTL; Philadelphia: Westminster, 1985), 382.

[73] This phrase also occurs in Prov 11:30; 13:12; 15:4.

[74] The statement is made in the form of a simile. For additional tree imagery, see Pss 52:8 [Eng. v. 7]; 92:13–15 [Eng. vv. 12–14]; 105:33; Jer 17:7–8; and Ezek 19:10–14 (vine).

Woman).[75] Each of these involves a symbolic *system* with distinctive entailments. The two ways involve guidance and guidelines, goals and expectations, choices and consequences. The two hearts involve the inner appropriation of truth, emotions, the integration of the whole person, schemes and plans. Finally, the two companions highlight "the transcending worth and compelling goal of the entire endeavor," guardianship and companionship, someone to be cherished and adored, or conversely, one to be feared and abhorred.[76]

Habel considers "the way" to be the primary image, with the other symbols related to it as satellites. Together they "afford vehicles of continuity within the diversity of wisdom literature incorporated into Proverbs 1–9." Thus, Lady Wisdom as subordinate symbol serves as the traveler's divine companion along the way.[77]

However, Claudia Camp argues for Lady Wisdom as the central symbol of Proverbs and views her symbolism as being religious.[78] According to Camp, the sources of Lady Wisdom and its multiple valencies are rooted in several aspects of Israelite life and culture. As Israelite understandings of woman either implicit or explicit in biblical texts, Camp argues that Lady Wisdom must be understood in relation to the following roles: wife and mother, the lover, the harlot and the adulteress, the wise woman, women who use indirect means, and women as authenticators of written tradition.[79] She develops a rationale for such a multivalent wisdom symbol in the culture of Israel's postexilic period and understands Lady Wisdom to be much more than a didactic device.

---

[75] Norman C. Habel, "The Symbolism of Wisdom in Proverbs 1–9," *Int* 26 (1972): 131–57.

[76] Ibid., 135–43.

[77] Ibid., 135, 154–56. Although Habel does not do so, these symbol polarities could be located within the myth-related root metaphors identified by Perdue's study of Job.

[78] Claudia V. Camp, *Wisdom and the Feminine in the Book of Proverbs* (Bible and Literature Series 11; Sheffield: Almond, 1985). She urges that these symbols have a mutual interaction. Her specific response to Habel is found on pp. 57–60. Camp is also critical of Bernhard Lang, whose *Frau Weisheit* (Düsseldorf: Patmos, 1975) relegated Lady Wisdom to the status of didactic aid which "subordinates all other facets of the symbolic range of personified Wisdom to one postulated sociological setting, the academy, and, indeed, to one particular activity within that setting, the instruction of youth" (Camp, 63). In *Wisdom and the Book of Proverbs: An Israelite Goddess Redefined* (New York: Pilgrim, 1986), Lang argues more radically that Lady Wisdom was originally a goddess in polytheistic pre-exilic Israel that was redefined "as a simple personification of the poetic type" and thus could be received into the (monotheistic) Hebrew canon (pp. 132–36). This revision of his earlier work still fails to appreciate the complex symbolism of the imagery as explored by Camp.

[79] Camp, *Wisdom*, 79–147.

These examples illustrate the prominence of symbolic imagery in the Hebrew canon and its particular importance in the wisdom corpus. The tree, the way, the heart, and female companions are wisdom motifs used in a variety of literary settings to predicate a range of meanings. The imagery of female companions is developed with special care and complexity as a symbol of wisdom in the book of Proverbs. It was within this background of symbol-making that Qohelet developed *hebel* as his distinctive contribution.

OTHER PRELIMINARY ISSUES

Genre

Ecclesiastes presents itself as the wisdom of one who had searched and dealt with issues of life and is now instructing his readers on making the best of their days. The book most closely resembles two ancient Near Eastern genres: the instruction and fictional autobiography.[80] Yet Ecclesiastes is distinctive in its relatively sparse use of the imperative, and in its investigative style which weaves together instruction and historical narrative. Ecclesiastes also employs some aspects of dialogue and develops themes associated with existential wisdom.[81] Its concern with human mortality also gives it thematic affinity with the standard version of the *Gilgamesh Epic*.[82]

Qohelet is a creative author—saying things that have never been said in quite this way before—so that he borrows and stretches the literary forms

---

[80] See, for example, the study of Tremper Longman III, *Fictional Akkadian Autobiography: A Generic and Comparative Study* (Winona Lake, Ind.: Eisenbrauns, 1991), and Fox's discussion in *Time to Tear Down*, 153–55.

[81] The term "existential" is employed by Alexander Di Lella to denote texts which challenge the confidence that the workings of the cosmos may be understood and cooperated with to one's benefit, or which lament the enigmas of life. The more optimistic wisdom texts he designates as "recipe" wisdom (Patrick W. Skehan and Alexander A. Di Lella, *The Wisdom of Ben Sira* [AB 39; Garden City, N.Y.: Doubleday, 1987], 32–33).

[82] Among other important parallels between Ecclesiastes and the standard version of *Gilgamesh* are the introduction, which describes Gilgamesh as one who "saw everything," giving a testament of all his toil (which includes buildings, 1.1.1–19), the adaptation of the *narû* form to emphasize the limitations of mortals (1.1.8), the description of humanity living a fleeting life which achieves only "wind" (OB 3.4.3–8), the advice to Gilgamesh to enjoy life (OB 10.3.6–14), the expression "in quest of wind" used of Gilgamesh in pursuit of immortality (10.1.38, 45; [=10.3.7, 14]), and the stark contrast between humans and the gods (particularly their immortality, power, knowledge, and inscrutability, e.g., OB 2.4.35–37; OB 3.4.6–7; OB 10.3.3–5; 11.258–70) (R. Campbell Thompson, *The Epic of Gilgamesh* [Oxford: Clarendon, 1930], 11, 26–27, 54, 55, 23, 27, 53, 66). See esp. C. L. Seow, "Qohelet's Autobiography," in *Fortunate the Eyes That See* (Fs. David Noel Freedman; ed. A. Beck, et al.; Grand Rapids: Eerdmans, 1995), 275–87; and William L. Moran, "Gilgamesh," in *The Encyclopedia of Religion* (ed. in chief Mircea Eliade; vol. 5; New York: Collier Macmillan, 1987), 557–60.

available to him.[83] However, the similarities between his work and that of the instruction and fictional autobiography forms strongly suggest that this is deliberative rhetoric—he writes in order to teach and persuade to action.[84] His attention to themes of existential wisdom also raises expectations associated with that literary corpus. In addition, the narrative elements of his investigative style make it necessary "to uncover the meaning progressively as the text itself presents it."[85] While these familiar patterns provide assistance for interpretation, Qohelet's generic innovations suggest that there will be distinctive aspects to his rhetoric as well. A proposal for the book's rhetoric will be offered in the final chapter of this study.

Structure

Several proposals have been made for a detailed and precise structure in the book of Ecclesiastes, each of which fails to convince completely. However, there are enough indicators in the book to set forth a general structure which mediates between a collection of aphorisms, on the one hand, and extreme detail, on the other. The alertness of Addison Wright to matters of inclusio and repetition is especially helpful and is increasingly noted by commentators.[86] That some structure is evident should not be a surprise considering the epilogue's description of Qohelet as one who was careful in his work (12:9–10).

A narrative voice in the third person begins the work (1:1), briefly reappears at 7:27, and concludes it at 12:9–14, offering a quotation by Qohelet for its motto at the beginning (1:2) and also as inclusio at the end (12:8). The key term of this motto, *hebel*, continues on through the work, which otherwise is in first person. The book divides into two halves between 6:9 and 10. Not only are the halves of approximately equal length, but 6:7–9 appears to

---

[83] Roland E. Murphy calls Ecclesiastes *sui generis* (*The Tree of Life: An Exploration of Biblical Wisdom Literature* [ABRL; New York: Doubleday, 1990], 50). While there are no pure forms, some texts exhibit more variety than others. The *Gilgamesh Epic* is another example of such creativity. It combines narrative with proverbs, lament, and *narû* material in order to comment upon themes of existential wisdom.

[84] While Ecclesiastes is as close to being a philosophical journal as anything of the ancient era (Fox, *Time to Tear Down*, 149–50; Gordis, *Koheleth*, 110; Farmer, *Who Knows?* 149), the author is not writing simply for his own benefit.

[85] Edwin M. Good, "The Unfilled Sea: Style and Meaning in Ecclesiastes 1:2–11," in *Israelite Wisdom* (Fs. S. Terrien; ed. John G. Gammie, et al.; Missoula,Mont. Scholars, 1978), 59. This aspect of his style is similar to other existential wisdom texts. Cf. Gerhard von Rad, *Wisdom in Israel* (trans. James D. Martin; Nashville: Abingdon, 1972 [1970]), 227.

[86] Addison G. Wright, "The Riddle of the Sphinx: The Structure of the Book of Qoheleth," *CBQ* 30 (1968): 313–34. On pp. 315–17, Wright provides a summary of the structural proposals given by fourteen different commentators. Cf. Aarre Lauha, *Kohelet*

summarize and conclude the primary emphasis of the first half (human effort), while 6:10–12 introduces the next primary concern (human knowledge).

The structure of Ecclesiastes is careful, but not mechanical, as reflected in the following outline utilized in this study:

Superscription (1:1)
Statement of Thesis (1:2)
Part I (1:3–6:9)
    A. Preface: Restless Activity (Cosmology and Anthropology, 1:3–11)
      • Focusing Question Part I: What benefit from toil? (1:3)
      • Opening Poem (1:4–11)
    B. Royal Pursuits: Toil, Wisdom, Pleasure (1:12–2:26)
    C. God's Relation to Time and Eternity (3:1–22)
    D. Toil in the Midst of Oppression (4:1–16)
    E. Words Before God (4:17–5:6 [Eng. 5:1–7])
    F. Enjoyment Instead of Greed (5:7 [Eng. v. 8]–6:9)
      • Transition: Toil, Wisdom, Pleasure (6:7–9)
Part II (6:10–12:7)
    A. No one knows what is good (6:10–7:14)
      • Transition: Human Limits (6:10–12)
      • Focusing Question Part II: Who knows what is good? (6:12)
    B. Wisdom and Righteousness (7:15–29)
    C. Even the Wise Do Not Know (8:1–17)
    D. Enjoy Life Now (9:1–10)
    E. Chance (9:11–10:15)
    F. Advice on Living with Risks (10:16–11:6)
    G. Conclusion: Youth and Old Age (Anthropology and Cosmology, 11:7–12:7)
      • Concluding Poem (12:1–7)
Restatement of Thesis (12:8)
Epilogue (12:9–14)

Each half begins with a focusing rhetorical question related to its theme (1:3; 6:12) and contains repeated phrases of assessment along with more questions which reflect that theme. A poem begins the first half and another concludes the second half. Phrases involving "*hebel*" and/or "chasing after the wind" often conclude sections in the book's first half, while the phrases "not find out"/"who can find out" and "do not know" function similarly in the second half.[87]

(BKAT 19; Neukirchen-Vluyn: Neukirchener, 1978), 4–7.

[87] Wright, "Riddle of the Sphinx," 325–26. Wright's observations are valuable even though he overstates his case. His proposal has been accepted on a slightly modified basis by J. S. M. Mulder, "Qoheleth's Division and Also Its Main Point," in *Von Kanaan bis Kerala* (Fs. J. P. M. van der Ploeg; ed. W. C. Delsman, et al.; AOAT 211; Neukirchen-Vluyn:

Although each half of the book has its own distinctive emphasis, themes continue to overlap and are repeated in somewhat of a spiral. Key terms carry through from the first to the second half, such as רָע (evil) and רוּחַ (wind) in addition to *hebel*. Such repetition and development are accounted for by the book's self-presentation as a series of investigations.[88] Throughout there is a unity of tone and focus.

Additional Matters

A few additional matters are worthy of comment, some of which will be discussed further in the final chapter. This study will posit that Ecclesiastes was written by a single sage—with the exception of the superscription (1:1) and epilogue (12:9–14)—sometime between the fifth and third centuries B.C.E. Its implied audience is largely in the "middle" of the socioeconomic strata of its time, and is faced with significant opportunities as well as serious economic risks.

The term "wisdom literature"[89] will refer to a text having the following three characteristics: its purpose is to persuade, its overarching concern is making the best of present human existence, and the data upon which it draws is predominantly that of common and repetitive phenomena.[90]

For the sake of clarity, the term *Ecclesiastes* will refer to the book itself,

---

Neukirchener; Kevelaer: Butzon & Bercker, 1982), 341–65, and by Roland Murphy, *Ecclesiastes*, xxxix–xli.

[88] Michael Fox compares Ecclesiastes favorably to L. Wittgenstein's account of his attempt and failure to systematically structure his *Philosophical Investigations* (Fox, *Time to Tear Down*, 149–50).

[89] Various definitions of "wisdom" have been proposed. Gerhard von Rad offered, "practical knowledge of the laws of life and of the world, based on experience" (*Old Testament Theology* [New York: Harper & Row, 1962 (1957)], 1:418), while in his later work, *Wisdom in Israel* (see pp. 7–8), he hesitated to present a definition. Other proposals include that of James L. Crenshaw: "the quest for self-understanding in terms of relationships with things, people, and the Creator" ("Method in Determining Wisdom Influence Upon 'Historical' Literature," *JBL* 88 [1969]: 133); Henri Cazelles: "La sagesse est l'art de la réussite de la vie humaine, privée ou collective, elle est à base d'humanisme, de réflexion et d'observation sur le cours des choses et le comportement de l'homme" ("Bible, Sagesse, Science," *RSR* 48 [1960]: 42–43); Guy P. Couturier: "la somme des expériences de la vie d'un père transmises à son fils, comme testament spirituel" ("Sagesse Babylonienne et Sagesse Israélite," *ScEccl* 14 [1962]: 309).

[90] Notably missing from this definition are specific philosophic or theological positions such as the so-called "doctrine of retribution" or the "deed-consequence" orientation. Such matters were debated by the sages, as is evident both within the Hebrew canon and among ancient Near Eastern wisdom more generally. Quarrels on these points do not make Ecclesiastes (or Job) any less a part of the wisdom corpus. On the distinction between wisdom as a corpus of doctrine and as a methodology, see Roland Murphy, *Ecclesiastes*, lxii–lxiii.

while the term *Qohelet* will refer to the author of 1:2–12:8.[91] Citations throughout follow the versification of the MT, with English variations in brackets.

In describing the meaning of *hebel* when it refers to actual vapor, the word "literal" has sometimes been used to contrast with "metaphorical." However, this may be confusing. When a word has usages which were perhaps metaphorical at one time but now established in themselves, these may also legitimately be called "literal" meanings.[92] For this reason, the usages of *hebel* which describe actual breath, and so on, will normally be called "material" senses.

CHAPTER CONCLUSION

This chapter introduced the problem in Ecclesiastes studies involving the term *hebel* and outlined three positions taken on this word. It then presented the thesis of this study, that Qohelet employs *hebel* as a symbol in his work. An overview of words and expressions from Ecclesiastes demonstrated Qohelet's rich use of metaphor and his frequent use of terms with multiple senses. It was also shown how symbol plays an important part in literature elsewhere in the Hebrew canon, particularly the wisdom corpus. The chapter concluded with a brief survey of preliminary issues.

In preparation for our study of Qohelet's symbolic use of *hebel*, Chapter 2 will set forth a methodology of symbol and metaphor within the context of rhetorical analysis.

---

[91] The history of the book's composition is a matter worthy of consideration in any study of Ecclesiastes' rhetoric but will be mentioned only briefly in the present work. The term *hebel* does not occur in 1:1 or 12:9–14, sections commonly ascribed to a later editor even by those who discern little or no editorial work in the central portion of the book. The significance of these sections, along with the phrase "says Qohelet" in 1:2, 7:27, and 12:8, will be referred to below. For a defense of the work as the product of essentially a single author employing different voices, see Michael V. Fox, "Frame-Narrative and Composition in the Book of Qohelet," *HUCA* 48 (1977): 83–106.

[92] The "leg" of a table is a good example, and would fit the definition of "literal" offered by G. B. Caird: "Words are used literally when they are meant to be understood in their primary, matter-of-fact sense" (*The Language and Imagery of the Bible* [Philadelphia: Westminster, 1980], 133). That is, the term "literal" indicates a word's established pattern of usage within a given linguistic context, even if that usage began as a metaphor.

Chapter 2

METAPHOR AND SYMBOL

The present chapter gives a brief introduction to rhetorical criticism, the disciplinary context in which this study is conducted. It then introduces and explains the methodology employed with metaphor and symbol in the following chapters. Finally, it distinguishes among several speech types found within Ecclesiastes which enable a more careful appreciation of *hebel*'s role within the work.

RHETORICAL CRITICISM

"Rhetorical criticism" is a relative newcomer to the field of Old Testament studies. Within biblical scholarship, the term itself, if not the actual methodology, was introduced in the presidential address of James Muilenburg at the Society of Biblical Literature convention, 1968.[1] Here he reviewed the contributions of Hermann Gunkel's form critical methodology, particularly the insight that language is genre determined. Muilenburg then called for scholars to move from an emphasis on the typical and representative, to an approach which would identify the devices and unique features of each particular pericope.[2] He was especially concerned to explore the artistry of the biblical

---

[1] Among the number of biblical scholars who were involved in stylistic study at this time, the following are representative: Luis Alonso-Schökel and Umberto Cassuto in Europe, Amos Wilder and Muilenburg himself in the United States. Additional strong appeals to examine the present form of the text were given by Norbert Lohfink in his book, *Das Hauptgebot* (AnBib; Rome: Pontifical Biblical Institute, 1963), and by Edwin M. Good, *Irony in the Old Testament* (Philadelphia: Westminster, 1965).

[2] He seemed to conceive this new direction as a supplement to form criticism, and so too have others.

and ancient Near Eastern texts to better identify the "thought and intention of the writer or speaker." Muilenburg mentions inclusio, chiasmus, repetition, motifs, and key words as examples, while recognizing the need for "literary sensitivity" in making sense of these elements.[3]

It appears that Muilenburg's main concern was to recognize the use of certain phenomena, such as repetition, as purposeful aspects of the text. An awareness of Hebrew literary conventions could alert the critic to points of emphasis and climax in a passage, as well as to its limits and structure.

His charge, to judge by publications in the following years, was received with enthusiasm. The design of this rhetorical-critical effort, however, has been developed in at least two directions. One has been to concentrate on style.[4] While such studies frequently offer some adjudication on matters of the supposed original form of the text or noted shifts of focus within a unit's structure,[5] they essentially explore the artistry of the text as it has been received. However, this approach has frequently ignored form criticism's emphasis on the interaction between text and audience in a specific social location.[6]

A second direction since Muilenburg has been concerned with the persuasive dimension of a text as a socially located event.[7] Aristotle, in fact, defined rhetoric as "the faculty of discovering the possible means of persuasion

---

[3] James Muilenburg, "Form Criticism and Beyond," *JBL* 88 (1969): 1–18. The phrases in quotation marks are from pp. 5 and 9.

[4] Attributed by Martin J. Buss to the "particularist" orientation, "Form Criticism," in *To Each Its Own Meaning: An Introduction to Biblical Criticisms and Their Application* (ed. Stephen R. Haynes and Steven L. McKenzie; Louisville: Westminster/John Knox, 1993), 78.

[5] See, for example, the study of Isa 40 by Kiyoshi Kinoshita Sacon, "Isaiah 40:1–11—A Rhetorical-Critical Study," in *Rhetorical Criticism* (Fs. James Muilenburg; ed. Jared J. Jackson and Martin Kessler; Pittsburgh: Pickwick, 1974), 99–116. In the same collection, J. Kenneth Kuntz, "The Canonical Wisdom Psalms of Ancient Israel—Their Rhetorical, Thematic, and Formal Dimensions," 186–222, surveys the conventions, vocabulary, and structure of the wisdom psalms. His main concern is to clarify the wisdom psalm *Gattung* and then to identify the "sociological contexts which gave birth to and maintained the communication of psalmic wisdom" (p. 216). In his survey of rhetorical elements, he only briefly comments on their persuasive impact.

[6] See Dale Patrick and Allen Scult, *Rhetoric and Biblical Interpretation* (JSOTSup 82; Sheffield: Almond, 1990), 17–19. They note that this approach has strong affinities with New Criticism.

[7] See the helpful introduction by Yehoshua Gitay, "Rhetorical Criticism," in *To Each Its Own Meaning*, 135–49. He describes Muilenburg's program as "stylistic-formalist" and prefers the designation "rhetorical analysis" to indicate a study of "the biblical art of persuasion" (p. 136).

. . . in reference to any given subject."[8] This orientation asks why particular stylistic devices were chosen and in what ways the text was designed to convince its audience. It therefore follows the lead of rhetorical criticism as it has been practiced by classics scholars.[9]

The present study will employ the latter methodology, and it will be referred to simply as "rhetorical criticism" throughout. Rhetorical criticism in classical studies has its origins particularly in the writings of Aristotle, Cicero, and Quintilian.[10] It has developed criteria and vocabulary both for instruction in and analysis of speech, and by extension, written texts. While it has its own "schools" of emphasis and history of development, it has maintained a consistent concern for the persuasive power of the speech it investigates.[11] Ultimately, an analysis of the persuasive element may help to explain the function of texts within their social situation.[12]

Although its potential has yet to be realized, particularly within Old Testament studies,[13] scholarly effort of this type continues to grow. According

---

[8] Aristotle, *The "Art" of Rhetoric* 1355b (Butler, LCL).

[9] Within the current discipline of rhetorical study, at least five major perspectives may be distinguished, each with its own emphasis: the traditional, the experiential, the dramaturgical, the sociological, and the postmodern (see description, analysis, and examples in Bernard L. Brock, Robert L. Scott, and James W. Chesebro, eds., *Methods of Rhetorical Criticism: A Twentieth Century Perspective* [3d rev. ed.; Detroit: Wayne State University Press, 1990], and the summaries by Phyllis Trible, *Rhetorical Criticism* [GBS; Minneapolis: Fortress, 1994], 57–62). The method employed here will draw largely from the traditional while including elements of others, particularly in relation to symbol.

[10] Edward P. J. Corbett, *Classical Rhetoric for the Modern Student* (3d ed.; New York: Oxford University Press, 1990), 540–48. The origins of this form of the discipline in no way imply assumptions of a Greek provenance for Ecclesiastes. Rather, it simply provides categories which may prove helpful to understanding the character and purposes of the book.

[11] See David M. Howard, Jr. ("Rhetorical Criticism in Old Testament Studies," *BBR* 4 [1994]: 13), who concludes that among various types of classical rhetorical criticism, "a common thread . . . is still an attention to various means of persuasion or of influencing thought or action."

[12] Rhetorical criticism thus understood has the same goal as form criticism. In classical studies, the so-called "New Rhetoric" has made this its ultimate objective. See Chaim Perelman and Lucie Olbrechts-Tyteca, *The New Rhetoric: A Treatise On Argumentation* (trans. John Wilkinson and Purcell Weaver; Notre Dame: University of Notre Dame Press, 1969 [1958]). Although Howard ("Rhetorical Criticism," 11) comments that this work has largely been ignored by the mainstream of classical rhetoric, it has been extremely important in biblical studies. George Kennedy refers to it as "perhaps the most influential modern treatise on rhetoric" (*New Testament Interpretation through Rhetorical Criticism* [Studies in Religion; Chapel Hill: University of North Carolina Press, 1984], 29). See also Burton L. Mack, *Rhetoric and the New Testament* (GBS; Minneapolis: Fortress, 1990), 93–102.

[13] See the helpful overview by David M. Howard, Jr., "Rhetorical Criticism," 1–18.

to Wilhelm Wuellner,

> Rhetorical criticism makes us more fully aware of the *whole* range of appeals embraced and provoked by rhetoric: not only the rational and cognitive dimensions, but also the emotive and imaginative ones.[14]

And George Kennedy describes its application to biblical texts as having the potential to "reveal the power of those texts as unitary messages."[15]

Rhetorical criticism is concerned to achieve the following five determinations:

(1)   the limits of the rhetorical unit to be studied;
(2)   the rhetorical situation of the unit, involving persons, events, objects, and relations;
(3)   the particular problem or issue that is addressed;
(4)   the arrangement of the material; and
(5)   the devices of style employed and their function in the process of persuading the unit's audience.[16]

In addition, particularly when addressing more recent rather than ancient material, much concern in modern rhetorical criticism is devoted to evaluation. The critic does research on the context and audience of a given speech or text and then explains the success or failure of the text by his or her analysis of its rhetoric.

The study of an ancient text often requires a modification of this process. The audience and social context of Qohelet's work, for example, must be determined through clues in the text itself. Yet clues to the work's implied audience may suggest a rationale for the rhetoric it exhibits.

In their discussion of rhetorical criticism in the Hebrew Bible, Dale Patrick and Allen Scult urge that one should "interpret a text as the best text (aesthetically, intellectually and affectively) the text can be."[17] Patrick and

---

He urges that the emphasis on stylistics be termed "literary criticism," and only the methodology with a primary concern for persuasion be identified as "rhetorical criticism."

[14] W. Wuellner, "Where Is Rhetorical Criticism Taking Us?" *CBQ* 49 (1987): 461, emphasis his.

[15] *New Testament Interpretation*, 159.

[16] Adapted from Kennedy, *New Testament Interpretation*, 33–38. See also the introduction by Mack, *Rhetoric and the New Testament*, 9–17.

[17] Patrick and Scult, *Rhetoric and Biblical Interpretation*, 84–88; the quotation is from p. 85. They propose that the following criteria be employed in textual interpretation: comprehensiveness, consistency, cogency, plenitude, and profundity. This is their formulation of Robert Dworkin's "Aesthetic Hypothesis," which they offer as a criterion by which interpretations of a given text might be evaluated. According to Dworkin, "An interpretation of a piece of literature attempts to show which way of reading . . . the text

Scult are quite aware of the complications and the tensions which may result from pursuing this dictum, as is clear in their discussion of critical issues in the book of Job.[18] However, their proposal may be a helpful way of describing the recent efforts in Ecclesiastes studies to make sense of the received form of the text, particularly in regard to its apparent contradictions.[19]

The present study is an attempt to continue this effort with another of the critical problems concerning Ecclesiastes: the role of the term *hebel*. It attempts to read the "best text" possible by discerning the place of this term in Qohelet's rhetoric. As with the matter of the apparent contradictions in the book, it gives Qohelet the benefit of the doubt that with *hebel* there is a coherence of purpose and usage.

At the outset of such an examination it is important to consider that Qohelet was both theologian and "artist." It rightly seems implausible that he would have developed an abstract analysis of his work, or deliberated in detail over such matters as "tensive symbols" and "referents." Yet, the process by which a literary piece comes into being may disguise the complexity and consistency of its genius.

A great chef may create a culinary masterpiece using a variety of ingredients, experimenting with spices, adding and subtracting until things are just right. Rhetorical criticism is like the food critic who tastes the entrée and proposes a recipe by which the dish might have been made.[20] Although there is nothing stilted about Qohelet's use of *hebel*, rhetorical criticism may discern the structure and development by which, throughout the book, he has crafted this symbol.

METAPHOR

The following discussion is not intended as a survey of recent scholarship concerning metaphor and symbol. Nor is it a comprehensive review of such investigations in biblical studies. It has two purposes. The first is to explain the way in which certain terms are employed in this study, particularly

---

reveals it as the best work of art" (cited in Patrick and Scult, 84).

[18] Patrick and Scult, ch. 5, "Finding the Best Job." They seek to find this "best text" within the *Sitz im Leben* of the author and audience, while recognizing the complexity of composite texts, and the changing contexts encountered by "classical" texts, both of which (arguably) apply to Job.

[19] The work of Michael V. Fox is an excellent example. See esp. *Time to Tear Down*, a revision of his earlier *Qohelet and His Contradictions*.

[20] Cf. Adele Berlin, *Poetics and Interpretation of Biblical Narrative* (Bible and Literature Series 9; Sheffield: Almond, 1983), 15.

"metaphor" and "symbol."[21] The second purpose is to clarify the method employed in the present investigation.

Definition

As noted in Chapter 1, Qohelet employs metaphor lavishly in his book. He presents images of darkness, light, and wind, among others. As will be demonstrated in this study concerning *hebel*, he employs his metaphors carefully in order to communicate clearly with his audience.

Metaphor is a figure of speech by which a person speaks about one thing using terms which are customarily appropriate of another thing.[22] More technically, this means speaking about the subject (S) in terms of the predicate (P) to communicate the referent or meaning (R).[23] The speaker states, e.g., "She is solid gold" ("S is P")[24] in the context of a work environment, but the message is, "She is valuable" ("S is R").[25] The term "metaphor," then, designates the *linguistic relationship* which obtains among these three components.[26]

----

[21] This study will evaluate the book of Ecclesiastes as a medium of communication, and so a communication model will be adopted involving a "speaker," a "message," and an "audience." Because Ecclesiastes is a written text, the terms "author," "text," and "reader(s)" will frequently be used.

[22] This definition is very similar to that offered by Janet Martin Soskice, *Metaphor and Religious Language* (Oxford: Clarendon, 1985), 49. Her words are, "speaking about one thing in terms which are seen to be suggestive of another." She considers synecdoche, metonomy, and simile as variant types of metaphor (pp. 56–61).

[23] In terms of I. A. Richards' nomenclature, R corresponds to "tenor" and P to "vehicle" (*Philosophy of Rhetoric* [New York: Oxford University Press, 1936], 96, 121–23).

[24] Soskice (19) emphasizes that metaphor need not be grammatically in the form "S is P." For example, the statement, "The old oaf was no match for the young girl," contains the metaphor, "[Subject] is an oaf."

[25] The first may be termed the "word or sentence meaning," while the second is the "speaker's utterance meaning" (John R. Searle, "Metaphor," in *Metaphor and Thought* [2d ed.; Cambridge: Cambridge University Press, 1993], 84, 88–89). In the case of "literal" utterances, the speaker's meaning and the sentence meaning coincide, whereas they do not with metaphor. Or as Richards describes it, "If we cannot distinguish tenor from vehicle then we may provisionally take the word to be literal; if we can distinguish at least two co-operating uses, then we have metaphor" (*Philosophy*, 119). Searle is careful to describe the nature of literal utterances. These are not simply obvious, but require shared background assumptions to determine their truth value. To assert that "The cat is on the mat" as a literal statement makes assumptions regarding the presence or absence of gravity, and various characteristics of cats. The context of such an utterance may clarify the nature of the speaker's assumptions.

[26] Metaphors occur at the level of the sentence or statement. An analogous phenomenon may occur at the level of paragraph or even more. This occurs with some types of parable and even with entire narratives. For example, the reader of a story by Flannery O'Connor or by Ernest Hemingway becomes aware that it is "about" something more than

Metaphors always involve "entailments," associations and implications that structure reality a certain way for those who use them. When argument is described by means of warfare terminology, there must be winners and losers. When it is phrased in terms of a dance, cooperation and aesthetics become important.[27]

Simile, which declares a comparison explicitly ("She is like solid gold"), is understood in this study to differ from metaphor primarily in grammatical form. Janet Soskice acknowledges that there may be a technical point to be made about truth conditions being different in simile than in metaphor, but that this point is of little communicative importance.[28] Both simile and metaphor speak of one thing in terms of another. In each case the audience is dependent upon similar contextual clues to understand what the author means to communicate.

Status of Author and Audience

The author's insight into the subject (S) may be at one of two levels. The *author* may be (a) attempting to communicate something (S is R) by metaphor (S is P) which he or she is also able to conceive in some *other* way. Metaphor is then the preferred way of helping another person understand something, but it is quite clear to the author that this is only *somewhat* satisfactory and does not communicate the whole. It is also possible that (b) the author is using the metaphorical statement as a way of partially expressing something which even the author does not understand. In this case, the author *needs* the metaphor.

The *audience* will receive the metaphorical communication in one of two ways. The S component may be (c) something they know about already,

---

simply a boy going to the big city, or a man fishing in the river. The present discussion will remain primarily at the level of statement, sentence, or paragraph.

[27] George Lakoff and Mark Johnson, *Metaphors We Live By* (Chicago: University of Chicago Press, 1980), 4–5.

[28] She challenges the position taken by Donald Davidson, who contends that, whereas a given metaphor may be false ("Man is a wolf"), its corresponding simile will be clearly true ("Man is like a wolf") because "everything is like everything, and in endless ways" (Davidson, "What Metaphors Mean," in *On Metaphor* [ed. Sheldon Sacks; Chicago: University of Chicago Press, 1979], 36–43, quot. p. 37). Soskice makes her case well by asking whether a reader considers there to be a significant difference between the following metaphor (i) and the original simile (ii) by Flaubert:

(i)   Human language is a cracked kettle on which we beat out tunes for bears to dance to, when all the time we are longing to move the stars to pity.

(ii)   Human language is like a cracked kettle on which we beat out tunes for bears to dance to, when all the time we are longing to move the stars to pity (Soskice, *Metaphor*, 92; see also Wheelwright, *Metaphor and Reality*, 71).

Soskice makes a helpful distinction between an "illustrative" simile and a "modeling" simile.

although perhaps had never thought about in the way the author has verbalized it. In this case, they will now have another way to think about S (S is P), but will not need P in order to do so.

The other situation (d) is one in which the audience knows about S *only* through P. As in (b), the audience is entirely at the mercy of P to understand anything about the S item. C. S. Lewis refers to the metaphor by which one teaches as the "master's metaphor" (a, c) and that by which one learns, the "pupil's metaphor" (b, d).[29] As Lewis summarizes, "Our thought is independent of the metaphors we employ in so far as these metaphors are optional: that is, in so far as we are able to have the same idea without them."[30] The audience is dependent upon the metaphor (P) to understand the subject (S) to the extent that the audience has or has not an independent acquaintance with the subject.

As an example, someone (the master) familiar with locomotives (S) may describe them to another who has never seen one (the pupil) as an "iron horse" (P). The pupil may comprehend some aspects of trains through this metaphor but other aspects will be obscured. For the master, the metaphor is not essential, but the pupil knows about trains *only* as much as can be comprehended through the metaphor and only as long as she or he remains aware that it *is* a metaphor. The master, on the other hand, can appreciate which aspects of locomotives are heightened by the term "iron horse" along with this metaphor's inadequacies.[31]

Metaphors inescapably highlight some things and obscure others. By creating a metaphor, an author seeks to provide coherent structure to some

---

These two may be described as differing in their precision: the former limits the amount of comparison, while the latter is much more open-ended.

[29] Lewis, "Bluspels and Flalansferes: A Semantic Nightmare," in *Selected Literary Essays* (ed. Walter Hooper; Cambridge: Cambridge University Press, 1969), 252–59. Lewis offers these terms as two extremes. Nearly all metaphors fall on a continuum somewhere in between. The essay's main concern is the extent of the metaphorical nature of language.

[30] Ibid., 258.

[31] There are some things, Lewis continues, concerning which the author must also be a pupil: "When we pass beyond pointing to individual sensible objects, when we begin to think of causes, relations, of mental states or acts, we become incurably metaphorical. We apprehend none of these things except through metaphor . . . Our only choice is to use the metaphors and thus to think something, though less than we could wish; or else to be driven by unrecognized metaphors and so think nothing at all. . . . He who would increase the meaning and decrease the meaningless verbiage in his own speech and writing, must do two things. He must become conscious of the fossilized metaphors in his words; and he must freely use new metaphors which he creates for himself" (ibid., 263).

aspect of his or her reality.[32]

Comparison and Interaction Theories

The essence of a metaphor is not a similarity between subject and predicate, as claimed by advocates of the Comparison Theory of metaphor.[33] Such a relationship may appear to be the case because the speaker's intended R values are usually expressible in terms applicable to both S and P, for example, that both elephants and humans have *memories* (He is an elephant at cards), and that both pigs and cars *consume* (My car is a pig). However, the essence of metaphor is better described as an association of the predicate term which can be *applied to* the subject in a given utterance context. This may involve common associations with the term or phrase P, but it is also possible for the author to establish new associations of P.[34]

This explains why there are effective metaphors in which S and P have no apparent similarity.[35] For example, "The argument (S) was heated (P)" (and other connections between emotions and temperature) has been used in contexts which clarify that the speaker means "the argument (S) involved strong emotion/anger (R)."[36] Yet it may not be clear in what sense the

---

[32] Lakoff and Johnson, *Metaphors*, 139.

[33] Some would attempt to resolve the issue at the level of definition, so that, for example, only relationships in which a similarity between the subject and the predicate could be discerned would be called metaphor.

[34] As Max Black comments regarding certain examples of metaphor, "It would be more illuminating in some of these cases to say that the metaphor creates the similarity [between the subject and the predicate] than to say that it formulates some similarity antecedently existing." And yet Black also says that, unlike with simile which often precedes an explicit explanation, we do not expect a metaphor to explain itself (*Models and Metaphors: Studies in Language and Philosophy* [Ithaca, N.Y.: Cornell University Press, 1962], 37). Contextual assistance is typically more subtle in the case of metaphor.

[35] Richards, *Philosophy*, 106. In Wheelwright's terms, metaphors in which subject and predicate have easily recognized commonalities are called "epiphors." Those in which S and P are creatively associated, perhaps on the basis of an emotional congruity, he calls "diaphor" (*Metaphor and Reality*, 72–86). See the critique of Wheelwright by Frank Birch Brown, "Poetry and Reality: A Critique of Philip Wheelwright," chap. in *Transfiguration: Poetic Metaphor and the Languages of Religious Belief* (Chapel Hill and London: University of North Carolina Press, 1983).

[36] This type of situation is common to metaphors predicating something involving one of the senses in terms of another. For example, persons are sometimes described as having a "sweet personality." The *tôrâ* is declared to be "sweeter than honey" in Ps 19:11 [Eng. v. 10]. These are probably examples of Richards' diaphor, in which the R value is accomplished through a *common attitude* toward both the subject and the predicating term, i.e., a feeling of attraction and happiness both toward the person or God's instruction and toward things which are of sweet taste (Richards, *Philosophy*, 117–18).

arguments referred to are "similar to" heat.[37] For the metaphor to be successful, the author must develop a context which clarifies this meaning (R value). Dead or nearly dead metaphors, those with an established history of usage in a given context (e.g., "red tape"), need little contextual help for their sense to be understood.[38]

I. A. Richards proposed that metaphor happens through an "interaction" between the subject and predicate terms:

> In the simplest formulation, when we use a metaphor we have two thoughts of different things active together and supported by a single word, or phrase, whose meaning is a resultant of their interaction.[39]

Max Black, another advocate of this understanding, uses two sets of terms: "frame" and "focus," and "lens" and "filter." The Interaction Theory has been criticized because it is not evident how "interaction" describes what takes place when one interprets a metaphor.

Though Black is not completely clear in his use of these images, it is possible that they are a way of talking about the process of restricting the potential referents under consideration. If a group of people is described as "vermin which run for hiding places when the light is turned on," a number of entailments are suggested: these people are doing something destructive, they want to remain in secret, they and their actions are disgusting, they should be stopped. In one sense, the audience participates in a dialectic involving the predicate, subject, and the utterance context, an "interaction," in quest of the referent. In another sense, the subject and the context "filter" among the possibilities for the referent, thus eliminating some of them. In the present example, whiskers and a tail, a delight in cheese, smallness of size, and an inability to speak would likely be eliminated. In the sense just described, the Interaction Theory of metaphor is a helpful one.[40]

---

[37] It is possible to find connections between the "heat" of an argument and the heat caused by friction when two items rub together, or between an argument and the danger or destruction of a fire. However, it is not necessary to clarify this connection, or even to be sure of such a connection, in order to understand how "heat" is being used metaphorically in the context of arguments.

[38] The image of a "way" or "path" became traditional in ANE wisdom literature. The use of feminine imagery in the wisdom tradition makes evident the creative possibilities of metaphor. Depending upon one's appreciation for Jungian psychology, a theory of archetypes may be used to account for associations which transcend cultures, such as the connection between death and the ocean or light and understanding.

[39] Richards, *Philosophy*, 93.

[40] Black, *Models and Metaphors*, 38–44, and idem, "More About Metaphor," *Dialectica* 31 (1977): 27–28.

The Cognitive Content of Metaphor

There is a cognitive content to metaphor which may be discussed propositionally.[41] The cognitive content can normally be paraphrased, though often the paraphrase will be found to be poor and incomplete.[42]

In its cognitive dimension, metaphor constitutes an argument. It makes a statement which may be true or false. Those in its audience who know S through other means are in a position to evaluate its truth claim. Does the subject "He," in "He is an elephant . . . he never needs a grocery list," possess a memory which is correctly expressed in that way? What did Hitler seek to communicate by his reference to Jews as an "infestation," and how was this accurate or misleading? Those in the audience who are "pupils" will potentially be able to receive the metaphor as instruction, but will have limited ability to assess its truth claim. Those who know the subject through other means may evaluate a metaphor's truthfulness.

On the other hand, a metaphor can never be reduced to simply its cognitive content. Partly this is due to the fact that no statement or complex of statements of any kind can ever *exactly* duplicate the content of another statement or group. There are no true synonyms because each word and phrase has its own connotations and history of use. But in the case of metaphor, the situation is even more complex because the images often raise emotional and valuational aspects that contribute to the persuasive power of the language. This dimension can be talked *about*, but its semantic content cannot be duplicated.[43]

A wonderful illustrative example has been given by Wayne Booth:

> A lawyer friend of mine was hired to defend a large Southern utility against a suit by a small one, and he thought at first that he was doing fine. All of the law seemed to be on his side, and he felt that he had presented his case well. Then the lawyer for the small utility said, speaking to the jury, almost as if incidentally to his legal case, "So now we see what it is. They got us where they want us. They holding us up with one hand, their good sharp fishin' knife

---

[41] Contra Donald Davidson ("What Metaphors Mean," 43) who insists, by his definition of "meaning," that metaphors say nothing except for the literal sense of the words. "He is a pig" means only that the person in question is a four-footed animal with a curly tail.

[42] Searle, "Metaphor," 88–89.

[43] Ian G. Barbour, *Myths, Models, and Paradigms: A Comparative Study in Science and Religion* (New York: Harper and Row, 1974), 14; see also Searle ("Metaphor," 111) who points out the matter of speech acts as an additional important factor. Ted Cohen comments that "often a paraphrase fails to do the job of its metaphor in much the same way that an explanation fails to replace a joke" ("Metaphor and the Cultivation of Intimacy," in *On Metaphor*, 9).

in the other, and they sayin', 'you jes set still, little catfish, we're *jes* going to *gut* ya.'" At that moment, my friend reports, he knew he had lost the case. "I was in the hands of a genius of metaphor."[44]

Authorial Clues

The author provides clues or cues to help the audience understand the relationship between "S is P" and "S is R." Patrick and Scult comment:

> Through the shape into which speakers cast their message they tell the audience how they mean it to be engaged and therefore to be understood. Of course, the auditors are free to interpret the language of the discourse in any way they wish, but the speaker or author attempts to constrain that freedom and direct interpretation by giving the audience cues and indicators as to how he or she means the discourse to function for them. These cues or indicators are communicated through the speaker's management of the conventional forms of discourse prevalent in the community to which speaker and audience belong.[45]

In the present study, the use of such "cues and indicators" will be referred to as "guarding" the referent (R value, "meaning") of the metaphor.[46]

The author may attempt to "guard" against or restrict the entailments of a metaphor by the use of statements in context or even by direct address, e.g., "Now don't push this too far." Restriction addresses the issue of extent of correspondence. This may be quite high in some cases, e.g., God as "father" or "mother," both of which suggest the source of life, parental care, discipline, authority, family unity, and so on. In other cases, such as comparing God to a "dry wadi" (Jer 15:18) or a "festering sore" (Hos 5:12), the degree of correspondence may be low.[47]

The author gives primarily three types of clues which guard a metaphor's intended R value:

Synonyms

These are a term or short phrase roughly equivalent in meaning to the

---

[44] Wayne C. Booth, "Metaphor as Rhetoric: The Problem of Evaluation," in *On Metaphor*, 50. A piece of narrative, as this one, which functions metaphorically is often designated a "parable."

[45] Patrick and Scult, *Rhetoric and Biblical Interpretation*, 15. Thus, they reflect to a great extent the communication model perspective employed in this study. The other extreme is to handle the metaphors (or symbols) of a work as icons concerning which the auditors interpret "in any way they wish."

[46] Monroe C. Beardsley uses the term "guard" to describe an author's attempt to use a metaphor precisely in communication ("Metaphor," in *Encyclopedia of Philosophy* [vol. 5; ed. Paul Edwards; New York/London: Macmillan/Collier, 1967], 286).

[47] Caird, *Language and Imagery*, 153–54.

referent. This is especially prevalent in poetry[48] but may occur with any text, e.g., "That day he was sandpaper, *smoothing out* the difficulties which occurred among such divergent personalities." The term "synonym," as used here, does not require the same grammatical function as the P element (e.g., both do not have to be nouns), but serves to make the same statement, ask the same question, etc., as the P term.[49] As an example, Job 18:3:

> Why are we counted as cattle,
> Deemed stupid in your eyes?[50]

The subject "we" (S) is predicated by "counted as cattle" (P), which is then guarded by "deemed stupid" to clarify the intended R value.

Sometimes an author will guard a metaphor with another metaphor. The reader must then discern among the various possibilities for each metaphor what the author intended in that particular context. For example, in Isa 33:12 the fate of the threatening nations around Israel is presented as follows:

> The peoples will be a burning of lime;
> cut-down thornbushes, they will be set on fire.

As John Oswalt explains:

> The metaphors used here emphasize the completeness of the destruction to come. So when a rock like limestone is burned it is reduced to dust . . . and despite the hazardous nature of thorns when they are alive, once they are cut and dried, fire can consume them almost completely in a very short time.[51]

---

[48] The phenomenon of Hebrew poetic parallelism both assists and complicates the evaluation of metaphor. On the one hand, the study of *hebel* is greatly assisted by parallel terms in the poetic material, which makes up the majority of contexts in which *hebel* is found outside of Ecclesiastes. On the other hand, care must be taken to discern the kind of parallelism involved in such cases (see James Kugel, *The Idea of Biblical Poetry: Parallelism and Its History* [New Haven: Yale University Press, 1981], 1–58; Robert Alter, *The Art of Biblical Poetry* [New York: Basic Books, 1985], 3–26; Adele Berlin, *The Dynamics of Biblical Parallelism* [Bloomington: Indiana University Press, 1985]). Further, the determination of "live" metaphor is less certain in poetry, where it is not easy to distinguish between parallel terms as part of the form and "guarding" terms necessary for clarity. In addition, intentional ambiguity flourishes within poetry.

[49] See the discussion of speech types later in this chapter.

[50] The form נְטְמִינוּ, translated here "deemed stupid," is of some difficulty. See the discussions by Marvin Pope, *Job* (3d ed.; AB 15; Garden City, N.Y.: Doubleday, 1973), 133, and David J. A. Clines, *Job 1–20* (WBC 17; Waco, Tex.: Word, 1989), 404–5.

[51] John N. Oswalt, *The Book of Isaiah Chapters 1–39* (NICOT; Grand Rapids: Eerdmans, 1986), 598. The translation of Isa 33:12 is his, p. 594. See also G. B. Caird's discussion of Eph 4:14 (*Language and Imagery*, 150).

The synonym clarifies that the R value for burning lime in this case means that "the peoples" will be reduced to harmlessness.

Contraries

A contrary is a term or short phrase with a meaning opposite to P. It is usually negated,[52] e.g., "She was a sponge, *never giving* of herself to others." Again, the grammatical function of the term is secondary. Example, Job 14:2:

> They blossom like a flower and wither;
> They flee (ברח) like a shadow (צֵל) and do not remain (עמד).

To guard the simile of the first line (blossom like a flower and wither), the second line provides both a *synonym* (flee like a shadow)[53] and a *contrary* (do not remain). The contrary makes evident that the R value of the first line is shortness of existence despite initial appearance.

Extensions

Sometimes there is an additional statement about S, or that implies something about S, which clarifies the metaphor but does not have the kind of one-to-one correspondence with the metaphor that is true of synonyms and contraries. These are called extensions. For example, "The event became a Jack-in-the-Box in his mind, so that an hour did not go by without him thinking about it." The clause after the comma does not give us a synonym or a contrary for "Jack-in-the-Box," but it describes the situation *so that one might be proposed*, e.g., "recurrence." Job 8:14b–15 provides an example:

> Their trust is but a spider's house.
> They lean on its house, they do not stand;
> They grasp it, they cannot arise.[54]

Here the sense intended by the metaphor "spider's house" (P) is guarded by the following two lines. It is something that cannot support a person leaning on it,

---

[52] Contraries may also occur in antithetic parallelism. When there is a change of subject, they may not be negated even though they still serve to guard the metaphor in question. For example,

> For all the gods of the peoples are useless (אֱלִילִים);
> But Yahweh made the heavens. (Ps 96:5)

If אֱלִילִים was considered to be in metaphorical relation and to predicate the subject, "gods of the peoples," the second half of the verse would serve as contrary to guard the term.

[53] Another example of using a trope (this time a simile) to guard a trope. See the comment above on the relation of simile and metaphor. The R value of shadow (short duration) is clarified by the same contrary ("do not remain") used for flower (first line).

[54] Cf. Job 4:18–20. Job 8:14a contains a *hapax legomenon* for which various proposals have been offered; see the commentaries.

nor is it strong enough for support when one is down and desires to rise. Although these lines develop the metaphor itself into something of a brief parable, they also reinforce that "spider's house" in this setting refers to something fragile, something that is not dependable. Hence, the things in which the wicked place their trust (S) will fail them (R).[55]

Extension, a clarification of the R element, is sometimes intertwined with descriptions which identify the S element. For example, v. 15 above (in an entirely different context) could conceivably be reworded as follows:

> They lean upon a treaty with Egypt, but do not stand;
> They grasp at an alliance with Assyria, but cannot rise.

In that case, the reader would need to separate the identification of Egypt and Assyria from the extension element: a description of failure which makes evident the "spider's house" metaphor.

Stock Metaphors

As Caird points out, certain terms and phrases may be considered "stock metaphors." These are figures of speech which, if not quite "dead metaphors," are common enough that no assistance is needed for the reader to understand them, at least within certain literary forms. The Psalms are especially full of examples, and Caird notes those used of God as father, king, judge, and shepherd. These have a history of usage and really need no guarding at all, though Hebrew poetic parallelism as well as context often reinforces a particular nuance. Caird also notes the extensive use of Exodus, temple, and law-court language in Hebrew literature.[56]

There are clues, then, by which to distinguish live metaphors from those which are stock or even dead. While this is complicated for rare terms, among those of frequency we can notice which are guarded and which are not.[57] The

---

[55] Some commentators argue that v. 15 should be deleted as an explanatory gloss of v. 14b. However, it is one of many similar explanations in the book of Job and there is no reason not to attribute it to the author.

[56] Caird, *Language and Imagery*, 152–58. He notes, "Stock metaphors have an important social function in expressing and reinforcing the accepted system of order or belief. For this reason the metaphors of the Psalter are for the most part stock metaphors, whereas those of the prophets, who are aiming at cognitive and commissive effect, have a greater freshness" (p. 153). Recent attention to theological use of metaphor has drawn attention to the entailments involved with issues such as race and gender. See, for example, the discussion of metaphor in Sallie McFague, *Models of God: Theology for an Ecological, Nuclear Age* (Philadelphia: Fortress, 1987), 31–40.

[57] Such study would require attention to genre, time period, and the phenomenon of poetic parallelism. In the latter case, for instance, a stock or dead metaphor may be

other possibility with such nonguarded terms is that they carry multiple valencies. Symbols commonly employed require no guarding (more below).

Context is determinative for metaphor, as Sonja Foss illustrates:

> The meaning of calling a person a *pig*, for example, would be different when applied to a police officer in the context of the late Sixties than if applied to a teenager in her messy room.[58]

Interpretive Steps

The audience proceeds through three steps to decode a metaphor.[59]

Step A

A determination must first be made whether an utterance actually involves a metaphor, that the literal statement does not work, e.g., "She (S) is solid gold (P)." For a metaphor to be recognized, a speech phenomenon must first be identified as "defective."[60] This may be because a statement is clearly false (the person is not made of gold), or tritely true ("No man is an island").[61] The audience employs the strategy, "Where the utterance is defective if taken literally, look for an utterance meaning that differs from sentence meaning."[62]

Step B

If a metaphorical relation is present, the audience then begins to compute the possible R values of the predicate term, e.g., (of gold) value, purity,

---

complemented by what appears to be a synonym or contrary even though the term was completely understandable on its own.

[58] Sonja K. Foss, *Rhetorical Criticism: Exploration and Practice* (Prospect Heights, Ill.: Waveland, 1989), 191.

[59] Searle, "Metaphor," 103. Sonja Foss (*Rhetorical Criticism*, 191) lists five steps in the process of metaphoric criticism: "(1) examination of the artifact for a general sense of its dimensions and context; (2) isolation of the metaphors in the artifact; (3) sorting of the metaphors into groups according to vehicle if the metaphors deal with the same tenor or subject or according to topic if the metaphors deal with various subjects; (4) analysis of the metaphors to discover how they function for the rhetor and audience; and (5) assessment of the metaphors used."

[60] Searle labels an utterance "defective" when it does not work in its semantic context ("Metaphor," 103).

[61] Even with a true statement, the speaker may give contextual clues to indicate that more than its immediate truth is being intended. For example, if, upon stepping onto the moon, Neil Armstrong would have only said, "That's one small step for a man," and not added, "—one giant leap for mankind," the circumstances would nevertheless have hinted that while the statement about taking a small step was true, a metaphor about a "step" was being employed to say something in addition.

[62] Searle, "Metaphor," 103. In addition to metaphor, speech forms in which utterance

scarcity. Essentially this involves considering any and every possible association the audience might have with the P component.[63] One common way to contemplate R values is to consider those aspects of P which are either a matter of definition, or are most typical. A giant is big by definition, an ant is associated with industriousness, and so on.[64] A second way is to consider ways in which the statement has been used metaphorically in previous encounters with it.[65] For the statement, "He is an elephant," R values for consideration might include large proboscis, good memory, and performance in a circus.

Step C

Finally, a strategy must be used to restrict the range of plausible referents. To accomplish such restriction, an audience will do one or more of the following.[66] First, it will consider which R *associations* considered in Step B are plausible of S. A large nose and good memory would both seem plausible in, "He is an elephant," for these are ways of describing both elephants and human beings. As for circus performance, one could consider whether the association of elephants with a *circus* might be intended as itself metaphorical of some event or situation in which "he" is involved. It is critical that the audience pay close attention to the context of the metaphorical utterance.

Second, the audience will consider "*guarding*" *terms*: synonym, contrary, and extension. If the statement, "He is an elephant" is followed by, "He never needs a grocery list," the possibility of "good memory" increases in likelihood as at least one value of R.

Step C will involve a process of *abstracting*. The phrase, "My car is a pig," may require a recognition of similarity between a car's consumption of fuel and a pig's consumption of food. The term "consumption" is abstract enough to include both activities. The context may also provide the specific basis for the predication. For example, in the process of discovering that "valuableness" is the R value of "She is pure gold," the audience may become

---

and sentence meanings differ include irony, metonomy, and allegory.

[63] This separation of the processes involved in Steps B and C is somewhat artificial but helpful for purposes of discussion.

[64] Searle and others have pointed out that such associations may not be factually accurate, and that they may work metaphorically even though both the speaker and audience know they are not factually accurate. It is possible for a speaker to accuse someone of being mean, nasty, and violent by calling him or her a gorilla, though it has been demonstrated that gorillas are actually shy, timid, and sensitive (Searle, "Metaphor," 92–93).

[65] When a term is used metaphorically within a specific linguistic context for a long enough time, it becomes a "dead" metaphor, another way of saying that the word or phrase has gained a new "literal" meaning, one which has little need for guarding elements.

[66] In this section, I have loosely adapted from Searle, "Metaphor," 104–8.

aware that it is loyalty and/or dependability that has made that person valuable to the speaker.[67]

If none of the associations with P seem to fit the context (resolve the contextual defectiveness), the audience must decide whether the statement is simply nonsense, or whether the speaker has made a new association for P which can somehow be discerned through contextual clues.[68]

SYMBOL

Definition

As described in Chapter 1, Qohelet employs several terms with a diversity of meanings, and some of these with deliberate multivalency. In addition, the term רוּחַ (wind) carries with it such a variety of connotations along with its several uses that it may be described in some sense as a symbol. However, it is the thesis of the present work that Qohelet's primary symbol, as evidenced by its use in the book's thematic statements, is the term *hebel*.

The term *symbol*, as used in this study, indicates a literary device which, like metaphor, communicates on a level beyond the most simple usage of a word or phrase. Philip Wheelwright gives the following broad definition:

> A symbol, in general, is a relatively stable and repeatable element of perceptual experience, standing for some larger meaning or set of meanings which cannot be given, or not fully given, in perceptual experience itself.[69]

Thus, a symbol is representative, referring beyond itself to something else.

Wheelwright uses the term *tensive symbol* for an image which holds together a *set* of meanings that can neither be exhausted nor adequately expressed by any one referent.[70] Whereas a metaphor has a single valency (R value), a tensive symbol is multivalent; it embraces several meanings at the same time.

Tensive symbols may be (1) *universal or archetypal*, the way ocean, light, and voyage function across time and civilizations, (2) *cultural*, such as a

---

[67] I am considering here primarily a linguistic process of testing. It is possible for the audience to have a context larger than the one offered by the text. It may know S by other means, or be able to accomplish such means (e.g., measure a car's miles per gallon). It will be able to use this knowledge both in coming to a conclusion concerning the referent and in judging the adequacy of the author's predicating term. But if the audience is a "Pupil," in Lewis's terms, it will have only the author's text as a source of information about the subject.

[68] Cf. Philip Wheelwright, *Metaphor and Reality*, 76.

[69] Ibid., 92.

[70] Ibid., 92–110. Wheelwright describes two types of symbols. A *steno-symbol* is a matter of convenience. It has a one-to-one relationship to that which it represents. Common

country's flag or the cross within Christianity,[71] and/or (3) *artistic or literary*, the presiding image within a work of art, such as the way the white whale functions in *Moby Dick*, or the Brooklyn Bridge in Hart Crane's poem, "The Bridge."[72] Symbols within literature may also be cultural or archetypal symbols. However, it is possible for them to have no life as multivalent *symbol* outside of the work itself (although they might function as metaphor elsewhere).

For a tensive symbol, there is never a simple correspondence with its R-value complex. This kind of symbol, e.g., a flag, often functions as one of the most powerful images in a given culture.[73] It picks up multiple and usually emotion-laden connotations through its use over time in a variety of contexts. It is not possible for Christians to give a simple explanation for what the cross represents, nor does such an explanation ever adequately substitute for the cross itself.

Literary Symbols

Although a literary tensive symbol may or may not function on the literal level (e.g., a national flag), it will always function metaphorically. Thus it may be described as the predicate term (P) communicating an R-value "system," or multiple R values, about a subject or subjects (S). Such a symbol provides, for example, that daylight (P) in a story is both actual light, with all that its material sense normally means, and also a message that, say, the hero has suddenly realized (S) the truth (R). But to say that daylight in the story represented "truth" would not be a complete explanation of its function, for light has further connotations (R values), such as warmth, purity, and epiphany. Because of this multivalency, the message of the story is conveyed more adequately by the story itself than by any attempt to summarize it.

An author may employ a tensive symbol for its ability to gather up these

---

steno-symbols are those used in mathematics (e.g., π, $+$, $-$, $\neq$), or in traffic regulation (e.g., a stop sign). The explanation for a steno-symbol is usually brief and nothing is lost through it.

[71] The term "cultural" is used broadly here to include, among others, religious symbols. Cf. Peter L. Berger and Thomas Luckmann, *The Social Construction of Reality: A Treatise in the Sociology of Knowledge* (Garden City, N.Y.: Anchor, 1967), 40, 95–104. Also, Clifford Geertz, *The Interpretation of Cultures: Selected Essays* (New York: Basic, 1973), 126–41.

[72] The categories "universal," "cultural," and "artistic" may overlap in any given case. They differ in the range and social extent of their expressive ability. Wheelwright describes two additional types of literary symbol: (4) an image developed by a poet as having special personal significance, and (5) an image passed from poet to poet and given new life in continually fresh contexts (Wheelwright, *Metaphor and Reality*, 98–110).

[73] Although, as Wheelwright notes (*Metaphor and Reality*, 96), a flag may also

multiple connotations within one image. Such a symbol differs from a simple image, say Wellek and Warren, primarily in its recurrence and persistence:

> An "image" may be invoked once as a metaphor, but if it persistently recurs, both as presentation and representation, it becomes a symbol, may even become part of a symbolic (or mythic) system.[74]

Indeed, symbols often partake of a symbol "system," involving satellite symbols and terms.[75]

Certain images have the ability to embody a diversity of meanings (R values) according to the diversity of their contexts. Water may alternatively symbolize chaos, death, regeneration, and purification. Likewise, according to its location, fire may be devouring, purifying, or life-giving.[76] In addition, used as a tensive symbol, fire or water might also assume multiple R values within a *given* context.

Within a story, the term "pig" might begin to approach a tensive symbol if it was used in reference *both* to a Sixties police officer (R^1) *and* to a messy roommate (R^2).[77] This hypothetical story could either implicitly or explicitly (perhaps through the narrator) convey that, "In those days, pigs were everywhere." In such a statement, more than one R value for "pig" would be involved. Likewise, after establishing several R values for "pig," the narrator might call someone a pig and effectively refer to several R values of the term at once.

Process of Interpretation

The process of interpreting a symbol builds upon the steps described above for interpreting metaphor. First, the audience must recognize the inadequacy of the literal use of the P term within its context, e.g., "Truth (S) is a fire (P)." Next, associations of P ("fire") must be calculated. Third, clues within the context must be employed for restricting possible R values. Finally, the unity of the symbol must be determined, its ability to incorporate all metaphorical and nonmetaphorical occurrences in the work. As mentioned above, this unity may be stated by the author, or the audience may recognize it by implication.

"harden" (become essentially a steno-symbol) or "evaporate" (become essentially ignored).

[74] René Wellek and Austin Warren, *Theory of Literature* (3d ed.; San Diego: Harcourt, 1977), 189.

[75] Clifford Geertz, *Interpretation of Cultures*, 17–18, 215–20.

[76] Barbour, *Myths*, 15. Barbour notes that religious symbols, in contrast to poetic metaphors, become part of the ongoing life of a religious community.

[77] There could even be scenes involving the animals (R=P).

SPEECH-TYPES IN ECCLESIASTES

Simply put, Qohelet's overall program is to give reports about what he has observed and experienced, to assess and evaluate these matters, and then to give advice concerning them to his readers. To communicate this, he employs the four primary speech-types: report, inference, judgment, and injunction. Because commentators have variously determined Qohelet's *hebel*-statements to be matters of inference or judgment, an overview of Qohelet's speech-types is important to understanding *hebel*'s function in the book.[78]

Statements of Report

Some of Qohelet's statements are reports, assertions which are (in principle) verifiable. For example, he says, "I am Qohelet. I have been king over Israel in Jerusalem" (1:12) and "I determined to know wisdom and knowledge" (1:17).[79] Eccl 2 reports on his building projects: "I made great works; I built houses and planted vineyards for myself; I made myself gardens and parks, and planted in them all kinds of fruit trees" (2:4–5, etc.). He also tells the reader "I hated life" (2:17) and that "I saw under the sun that in the place of justice, there was wickedness, and in the place of righteousness, there was wickedness" (3:16).

These are all statements of report, which in principle can be confirmed. Those who lived in Qohelet's day, if they investigated, should have been able to learn whether he actually was king over Israel in Jerusalem, whether indeed he made the investigations he described, whether he accomplished great building projects, etc., whether he was at some point discouraged and "hated life,"[80] and whether he actually observed wickedness in a place where righteousness was to be expected.

These samples of reports make us immediately aware of the complexity of Ecclesiastes since, as most scholars today believe, Qohelet never was a king, and thus may not have "built houses and planted vineyards" or made "gardens and parks" (Eccl 2:4–5). In addition, the determination of a person's emotional state at some period of his or her life is difficult, requiring evidence such as the testimony of witnesses for corroboration. On the other hand, statements such that wickedness was found in places of ostensible righteousness (3:16), seem to anticipate that the reader will assent because of similar observations.

---

[78] For a popular overview of these semantic distinctions, see S. I. Hayakawa, *Language in Thought and Action* (3d ed.; New York: Harcourt, Brace, Jovanovich, 1972), ch. 3.

[79] This verse involves textual difficulties.

[80] Self-reporting can only be directly verified by the person making the statement.

Statements of Inference

Many more of Qohelet's statements may be considered inferences, statements which are conclusions based upon his experiences and other premises, such as beliefs he accepts from his tradition. To categorize a statement as an inference requires a determination of the basis upon which the speaker has made the statement. A person may *report* that today is hotter than yesterday because he or she has compared thermometer readings (which report temperature), or may *infer* that it is hotter on the grounds that more people are at the local swimming pool today than yesterday.

Inferential statements involve a two-part process. First, there is an inductive gathering of information, and second there is a generalization, or labeling, on the basis of the data. Qohelet says in 1:9: "What has been is what will be, and what has been done is what will be done; there is nothing new under the sun." He finds nothing to put in the category of "new things," and then infers that all must fit into the category of "not new."

In 1:17 (referred to above), Qohelet first makes a report about his investigations ("I determined to know wisdom and knowledge"), and follows it with an inference: "I discovered that this also is chasing wind." That is, based upon his attempts to achieve wisdom, he has placed such efforts within the category of things which are "a chase after wind," a phrase which most likely means "pursuit of the impossible."

To assess the truth of such a statement, one is not primarily concerned with verifying factual data (the results of Qohelet's investigations). Rather, the issue is whether one accepts the categories (some things are not as they seem), and whether those matters included in a category are appropriate to it (wisdom does not deliver what it seems to promise).[81]

Qohelet expresses a number of his inferences through rhetorical questions, that is, sentences which take the form of questions but actually make statements.[82] Through this means, Qohelet makes absolute declarations regarding "no one," "everyone," "always," or "never," e.g., 3:21, "(no one) knows whether the רוּחַ of human and animal differ."[83] Some of these inferential

---

[81] It is a long-standing philosophical question whether God-statements are verifiable. Qohelet accepts a number of truths from his cultural and religious tradition as givens.

[82] With few exceptions, the questions in the book of Ecclesiastes are rhetorical, that is, a form of speech which gives the appearance of a question but actually makes a statement. Possible exceptions occur at 7:10 and 8:4. See Raymond Johnson's discussion and examples from the HB, "The Rhetorical Question as a Literary Device in Ecclesiastes" (Ph.D. diss., Southern Baptist Theological Seminary, 1986), 198–200.

[83] This is true of the fourteen questions introduced by the interrogative particle מִי (who?) which make statements that "No one" knows certain things or can do certain things.

question-statements also involve an implicit evaluation or judgment. For example, when Qohelet exclaims in 2:15, "The fate of the fool will happen to me also; why then have I been so wise in excess?" he implies his negative evaluation of wisdom's shortcomings.

Statements of Judgment

Judgments are statements which express approval or disapproval of the events, persons, objects, or activities they describe. Such statements may be direct, as when Qohelet says, "There is nothing better for the human than to eat and drink and see itself good in its toil" (2:24) or "There is an evil, an illness that I have seen under the sun: wealth was kept by its owner to its harm" (5:12 [Eng. v. 13]).[84]

However, often statements of judgment are made by using words that involve implicit evaluation. To say that someone is a *thief* involves an inference (he or she has stolen *and will steal again*) and, commonly, a judgment (*stealing is wrong*). Discerning implicit judgments can be a complex matter. When the epilogist calls Qohelet a sage in 12:9, we expect that this includes a positive value judgment. Yet this statement must be examined carefully, since both the strengths and limits of wisdom have been discussed previously in the book.

Another form of implicit judgment in Ecclesiastes arises from its particular rhetoric. Because ethos (establishing the speaker's credibility) is so dominant in the book, when Qohelet says, "I hated life" (2:17), we must take this as more than simply a statement of Qohelet's emotions or his personal evaluation. It becomes a claim that "life is hate-worthy," there is something wrong about it.[85]

Judgment may also be communicated by the structuring of words. For example, in 4:1 Qohelet says:

Similar absolute declarations are made beginning with מָה. However, not all commentators agree with Johnson's assessment that all of these questions make statements. For example, Fredericks understands the question in 1:3, "What surplus (יִתְרוֹן) is there for toil?" as the controlling question of the book, to which Qohelet finally gives a specific answer (*Coping*, 48–49, 63).

[84] See the summary of Ogden's work on the *ṭôb*-sayings in Chapter 1.

[85] Fox notes the pattern repeated in 1:12–18, 2:1–11, and here in 2:12–17: "Qohelet tells how he undertook an investigation, reports the finding, tells how he pondered the finding, and reports his reaction" (*Time to Tear Down*, 182). The statement in 2:17 is complicated by the fact that Qohelet reports it as an evaluation he made at a particular point in his past, as a conclusion to his royal investigations. It is not immediately clear that it is meant as his ongoing conviction or stance toward life (ibid., 312).

> Again I saw all the oppressions that are worked under the sun. Look (הִנֵּה), the
> tears of the oppressed—with no one to comfort them. On the side of their
> oppressors there was power—with no one to comfort them.[86]

The use of הִנֵּה to arrest attention, and the repetition of the phrase "with no one
to comfort them" communicates an evaluation that, for Qohelet, oppression is a
terrible thing.

This interpretation of Qohelet's statement is reinforced by the following
verse (4:2), another example of implicit judgment:

> And I praised the dead, who have already died,
> more than the living, who are still alive.

By making a statement of report on what he did ("I praised," i.e., congratulated, "the dead"), he communicates a judgment: Being dead is praise-worthy;
it is better than being alive.

Rhetorical questions also express judgments, e.g., 2:15, "One should not
be excessively wise"; 5:5 [Eng. v. 6], "One should keep free of God's anger";
and 7:16–17, "One should not have to destroy oneself through excessive effort
or die before one's time."[87] Very often rhetorical questions supply motivations
for doing or thinking what Qohelet is urging his readers to do or think.

Injunctions

Classifying Ecclesiastes as deliberative rhetoric means that the book as a
whole is devoted to motivating its readers to certain specific courses of action.
Certain speech types in the book, called injunctions, are specifically devoted to
that end. The most obvious of these are imperatives or negative imperatives,
such as the following:

- Guard your steps when you go to the house of God (4:17 [Eng. 5:1])
- Never be rash with your mouth (5:1 [Eng. v. 2])
- Do not give your heart to all that people say (7:21)
- Go, eat your bread with enjoyment, and drink your wine with a good
  heart (9:7)

In addition, as with other wisdom writings, we must recognize that
certain statements, such as "*ṭôb*-sayings" and other "wisdom sentences,"
though in the form of an inference, are also a means of exhortation:

- Two are better than one, for they have a good reward for their toil (4:9)

---

[86] The repetition of the phrase "with no one to comfort them" is taken by some
commentators to be the result of dittography.

[87] These questions are introduced by למה.

- The heart of the wise is in the house of mourning;
  but the heart of fools is in the house of mirth (7:4)

In the case of traditional sayings, Qohelet's use must be carefully discerned. Sometimes he wishes to parody them or qualify them with his own considerations, e.g., 4:13–16. On other occasions Qohelet will combine an imperative or negative imperative with a *ṭôb*-saying or rhetorical question to emphasize his point, e.g., 4:17–5:6 [Eng. 5:1–7].

To summarize these four speech types, Qohelet presents himself as an investigator who makes *reports* and *inferences* concerning his experiences. This involves a process of categorization, which has the effect of organizing his disparate experience: it is much simpler to deal with a few categories than with many. He also makes evaluative *judgments* of his results, some positive and some negative. Rhetorical questions are an important means by which Qohelet makes statements of inference and of judgment. Finally, he makes *injunctions*, recommending certain orientations and courses of actions based upon what he has presented.

The distinction between report and inference, though rightly defined in terms of verifiability, is difficult to accomplish in practice. For this study, however, it will be more important to distinguish both these kinds of descriptive statements from those of judgment, Qohelet's declaration that something is good or bad. Fox, for example, has argued that the *hebel*-statements in Ecclesiastes are evaluative: *hebel* means "absurd."[88] Others, such as Fredericks, view the *hebel*-statements as primarily descriptive: *hebel* means "transient."[89]

Three aspects of *hebel*'s material sense—transience, insubstantiality, foulness—are the basis for the metaphorical referents of the term in Ecclesiastes. By use of the first two of these, Qohelet expresses inferences that are not in themselves a negative judgment. Yet, as stated above, the expression of inference and judgment often overlaps. Certainly Qohelet thinks that some of the things which are transient or insubstantial are undesirable, e.g., youth should not be so brief, pleasure should not be so empty, toil should accomplish more than it does. However, the evaluative dimension of *hebel* is developed much more significantly by the third referent group for *hebel*—foulness —which is accomplished by association with the term רַע (bad) and a few others. Just as a flag may be both a descriptive symbol (e.g., indicating the country in which a product was made) and express value (products from country A are better than products from country B), so Qohelet's *hebel*-symbol involves both description and evaluation.

---

[88] *Time to Tear Down*, 30.
[89] *Coping*, 32.

CHAPTER CONCLUSION

This chapter has given an introduction to the purposes and practice of rhetorical criticism. It also presented the understanding of metaphor and symbol employed in this study. Finally, it outlined four important speech-types in Ecclesiastes: statements of report, inference, and judgment, and also injunctions.

In its presentation of metaphor and symbol, this chapter outlined a three-step method of R-value discernment which will be employed in the exegetical investigations which follow. This is not an attempt to be overly rigid, for an author may use a symbol with great fluidity.

However, to a large extent studies of *hebel* in Ecclesiastes have been characterized by proposals of the "possible" and the "plausible." While interpretation must always proceed in a dialectic between the specific context and a determination of the whole, this study will seek to carefully follow the indicators of the text itself in conformity with the proposed method. There is reason to believe that Qohelet has proceeded by a careful and deliberate process to construct his symbol, and is consistently precise about the meaning of *hebel* in each context.

From the thematic statement of 1:2, "All is *hebel*," it is evident that Qohelet does not use the term in its material sense of "vapor" or "breath." The investigation of its meaning will have to carefully discern which of various possibilities is being employed in each context.[90] To consider the potential range of that usage, it will be valuable to investigate, in Chapter 3, the contexts in which *hebel* is used outside the book of Ecclesiastes.

---

[90] As Geoffrey Leech has stated it, "learning meaning through context is . . . a process of inductive approximation to the semantic categories that the linguistic community operates with" (*Semantics* [Harmondsworth, England: Penguin, 1974], 80). Cf. Hayakawa, *Language*, 51.

Chapter 3

MATERIAL AND METAPHORICAL USES OF *HEBEL*

This chapter identifies and evaluates occurrences of the term *hebel* in texts other than Ecclesiastes. For each text, discussion includes a short description of the literary context and brief comments as necessary regarding textual and other critical issues. These are kept in footnotes as much as possible to streamline the presentation. The following steps, explained in the previous chapter, are employed:

> Step A: A determination whether a material or metaphorical sense of the term suits the context.
> Step B: In the case of metaphor, a consideration of possible referents (R values), based on what is presented in this chapter about the material senses of *hebel*.[1]
> Step C: A narrowing of the metaphor's possible referents, determined by its guarding elements: synonym, contrary, and extension.

In each case of metaphor, the subject (S) will be specified, *hebel* constitutes the predicating element (P), and the goal is to discern the referent (R). When *hebel* is not used with its material sense, and when guarding elements are present (which is nearly always), this investigation will assume the metaphor is a "live" one.[2] There is probably no way to confirm that such is

---

[1] That is, although one should always be open to the possibility of a new R value with *hebel*, or one concerning which we have no awareness, we will look first for known referents of *hebel* or plausible connections with what can be established about the word's material sense.

[2] A "live" metaphor is a metaphorical relation which requires the reader to engage the linguistic relationship for a way to resolve its defectiveness. A "dead" metaphor (e.g., "red tape") does not require this engagement because it has only one possible meaning.

true in every case, although the way the term is used overall justifies the assumption.

THE MATERIAL SENSE OF *HEBEL*

There is a consensus among scholars that the material meaning of *hebel* during the classical period of Hebrew is something like "breath" or "vapor."[3] This judgment is based upon several considerations: postbiblical use of *hebel* and its Aramaic cognate *hablā'* (הַבְלָא), the use of *hebel* in the Hebrew Bible, and some additional factors of less significance. These considerations are presented below. Because the material use of *hebel* is so rare in the HB, the discussion will begin with a survey of postbiblical texts.

Postbiblical Texts

In the rabbinic writings, the nouns *hebel* (הֶבֶל, Hebrew) and *hablā'* (הַבְלָא, Aramaic) are found in similar contexts.[4] Their range of usage is discussed below.[5]

Heat/Steam

This category involves vapor with the associated meanings of "heat" and "steam." Examples with *hebel* are found in *Ḥul.* 8a, a discussion of burns caused by the "heat" of a hot spit, and at *B. Bat.* 73a, a reference to the "heat" of a star. An example of the second meaning is found in *Giṭ.* 69b which describes a remedy for fever blisters involving "steam" which one allows to rise upon oneself.

---

[3] So e.g., Rainer Albertz "הֶבֶל *hæbel* Hauch," *THAT* 1:467–69. A significant exception to this consensus is the position of W. E. Staples ("Vanity," 95–104). He makes a case that *hebel* means "unknowable, incomprehensible," beginning with a supposed connection with the Meccan chief God Hubal, along with the assumption of a cultic connection in Israel evidenced by its use in Dtr and Jeremiah (where it is usually translated "idols"; see discussion below). The etymological connection along with much else of Staples' reasoning has not been accepted. For responses to Staples' thesis on several points, see Klaus Seybold, "הֶבֶל," 314–15, 317–18, and Bob Becking, "Hubal," *DDD*, 814–15.

[4] Together, the nouns occur over one hundred times in the Babylonian Talmud. The verb הבל occurs only a few times there, mostly in quotations from the HB. Talmudic sources cited are from the Babylonian Talmud unless otherwise indicated, and translations are adapted from Isadore Epstein, ed., *The Babylonian Talmud*. London: Soncino, 1935–52.

[5] For an overview of the distinctives which mark the Hebrew language in the postexilic and rabbinic periods, see Angel Sáenz-Badillos, *A History of the Hebrew Language* (trans. John Elwolde; Cambridge: Cambridge University Press, 1993), 112–201; also, Eduard Yecheskel Kutscher, "Hebrew Language: The Dead Sea Scrolls, Mishnaic," *EncJud* 16:1583–1607.

For other instances of this type it is not as easy to distinguish between heat and steam.[6] Plausibly the meaning "heat" developed later, arising by association with hot steam, e.g., the steamy heat of the baths (*Šabb.* 40b), and the radiant heat of cooking stoves (*Šabb.* 38b, et al.).[7]

Texts in this category sometimes describe the positive effects of such vapor, e.g., the medicinal use of hot springs (*Šabb.* 47b; cf. the previous reference to *Giṭ.* 69b). At other times heat/steam is destructive, e.g., an oven's heat may harm a wall (*B. Bat.* 18a; cf. 19a), human lives may be taken through intense heat (*Zebaḥ.* 113b), and the vapor of the bath room is said to be injurious to the teeth (*y. ʿAbod. Zar.* III, 42[d] bot.).[8]

Breath

Both *hebel* and *hablāʾ* may refer to vapor in the sense of breath, either that of humans or of animals. The breath of Leviathan is said to cause waters to boil (*B. Bat.* 75a), and even human breath may be threatening due to its heat (*Šabb.* 88b).[9] Another possible example occurs in *Šabb.* 41a, where a reference is made to opening the mouth and expelling heat.[10]

Vapor within a Living Being

Sometimes these terms refer to vapor within the body, a sense possibly related to the previous. *Bek.* 7a–b, in a discussion concerning the urine of an ass (apparently used medicinally), makes reference to its thickness being caused by the "exudations" (*hablāʾ*) of the body. Also, certain rabbis interpreted the syntax of Ps 62:10 [Eng. v. 9] such that הֵמָּה מֵהֶבֶל יָחַד read, "they are together from *hebel*," and applied it to the foreordination of marriage, i.e., that it was decreed from before the partners were born that they should be

---

[6] In *Eccl. Rab.* a connection is made between Eccl 1:2 הֲבֵל הֲבָלִים (vapor of vapors) and Ps 144:4 which declares that mortals are *hebel*. The referent of the metaphor is understood to be insubstantiality. Rabbi Samuel b. Naḥman explains the superlative in terms of seven pots placed on a fire, one on top of the other (*hebel* occurs seven times in the verse if the plural is counted as two). In such a case, the "steam" (*hebel*) from the topmost pot would have "no substance in it" (Abraham Cohen, *Midrash Rabbah: Ecclesiastes* [3d ed.; London: Soncino, 1983], 4–5).

[7] Of course, it is also possible that "heat" was the earlier sense and that "steam" developed as a meaning by connection with hot steam. However, other material senses of these words have more in common with air than with temperature.

[8] Cited in Jastrow 1:329.

[9] The reference to injury in the latter example is probably intended figuratively.

[10] Rabbi Samuel concludes that "הַבְלָא expels הַבְלָא." This could mean that breath expels heat from the body. However, Rashi interprets this to mean that opening the mouth in a steam bath was to *take in* the warm air for the purpose of expelling perspiration (*Babylonian Talmud*, ad loc. n. 15; see below).

married (*Lev. Rab.* 29:8).[11] In this connection, Rabbi Ḥiyya explains that while they are yet a vapor (*hebel*) in the womb of their mother they are united.[12] It is not clear from the context whether *hebel* in Rabbi Ḥiyya's comment is to be understood metaphorically (e.g., "nothingness") or as a material vapor, either as a phenomenon in the womb, or as the breath of life within the emerging child.

Vaporous Perspiration

Both *hebel* and *hablāʾ* are used of vapor which is given off by the body, particularly in connection with bathing (*Yebam.* 80b). Some contexts indicate something visible rising from a person's body after a warm bath in winter. That is, body vapors are involved rather than liquid perspiration.[13] In addition, the verb הבל, in the Hiphil stem, is used to describe wet flax giving off vapor (*Šabb.* 17b).

Noxious Vapor

In a variety of contexts, both *hebel* and *hablāʾ* designate a kind of vapor which has life-threatening properties within itself.[14] For example, one who becomes asphyxiated in a sealed environment is said to be killed by its vapor (*Sanh.* 77a–b). It is even pondered whether inanimate objects might also be "killed" by such air (*B. Qam.* 54a). More common are references to animal deaths due to the "unhealthy air" of a pit into which the animal has fallen (e.g., *B. Qam.* 50b, 51a,b). The talmudic debates concern the size of such a pit that would qualify as life-threatening to the animal. In addition, a case of negligence is discussed in which an animal is allowed to stray onto marsh land (אגמא) and is killed by the toxic vapor there (*B. Meṣiʿa* 36b).[15] In the latter cases, marsh gas and the stench and decay of pits with stagnant water are credited with these threats to life and health. Thus, *hebel* and *hablāʾ* may refer to vapor which is noxious.

---

[11] The explanation is from Judah Slotki and Jacob Israelstam, eds., *Midrash Rabbah: Leviticus* (3d ed.; London: Soncino, 1983), 375 n. 4. More likely this is the pregnant use of מן, allowing "they are together (lighter than) *hebel*" (see discussion of Ps 62:10 [Eng. v. 9] below).

[12] Ibid.; Jastrow 1:329. Cf. also Isa 26:18; 33:11 (see commentaries).

[13] "His body gives off vapor," בשרו מעלה הבל. Cf. also *B. Meṣiʿa* 107b and *Šabb.* 41a.

[14] That is, in contrast to instances in which steam causes harm through accident or neglect.

[15] "The air of the meadowland killed it," הבלא דאגמא קטלה.

The Hebrew Bible

Although the term *hebel* occurs thirty-five times in the Hebrew Bible outside of Ecclesiastes,[16] there appear to be no examples of the term used in a strictly material sense.[17] However, there are two texts in which the material sense of *hebel* is evident within a parable.

Ps 62:10 [Eng. v. 9]

אַךְ הֶבֶל בְּנֵי־אָדָם
כָּזָב בְּנֵי אִישׁ
בְּמֹאזְנַיִם לַעֲלוֹת
הֵמָּה מֵהֶבֶל יָחַד:

The children of mortals (בְּנֵי־אָדָם) are only *hebel*,
Human offspring (בְּנֵי אִישׁ) are a lie (כָּזָב);
In the balances going up,
They are (lighter) than *hebel* together.[18]

Psalm 62 is a psalm of trust which enjoins confidence in Elohim. Only brief and nonspecific mention is made of the psalmist's enemies. They are addressed in v. 4 [Eng. v. 3] and their activity described in v. 5 [Eng. v. 4] to the effect that they are violent and deceitful. Then the enemies are evaluated in v. 10 [Eng. v. 9].[19]

Ps 62:10 must be understood in two parts, two cola of text each. The first two cola constitute synonymous parallelism. Each colon uses an expression meaning "humanity"; then these enemies are described first as *hebel* and then as כָּזָב (lie, falsehood). The reader is expected to seek out the commonalities between the latter two terms. As will be discussed below, terms meaning deception (e.g., כָּזָב) are used on several occasions as synonymous guarding terms for *hebel*.

----

[16] Excluded from this count are eight occurrences of the name "Abel," also spelled *hebel*.

[17] Ecclesiastes may contain the sole exception (see Chapter 4 on Eccl 6:4). As mentioned previously, this study will employ the term "material" to refer to *hebel*'s presumably earlier meaning, a referent which was able to be encountered by the physical senses and involved air.

[18] This exhibits the pregnant use of מִן; cf. Job 11:17; Isa 10:10; GKC §133e; NJPS: "they weigh even less than a breath."

[19] Some commentators and versions (e.g., RSV, NRSV) make a distinction in status between the בְּנֵי־אָדָם and the בְּנֵי אִישׁ. This inference has some justification in comparative literature. So Marvin Tate, who acknowledges that both Hebrew expressions are commonly used of humanity generally (*Psalms 51–100* [WBC 20; Waco, Tex.: Word, 1990], 119).

The final two cola of the verse, however, represent a slightly different tropical use of *hebel*, one which may be considered a "parable" in its most terse form. The psalmist pictures human beings on one side of a (large) two-pan balance where they are compared in weight to *hebel*—and *hebel* turns out to be heavier.

The reference to elements of this passage as "parable" means that there is a narrative, however brief or implied, that has two levels of meaning. Madeleine Boucher emphasizes that "the whole meaning [of a text] can be tropical even when the constituent meanings are not," and that is what is proposed here. These passages give us a very brief narrative, almost as small as possible, within which the elements function on a single, material level. But as a whole, this unit functions metaphorically and thus may be called a parable.[20]

Nathan's parable of the wealthy man who seized a pet lamb from his poor neighbor (2 Sam 12:1–4) provides a good analogy. The employment of characters within the story is a material one. The lamb is an animal with wool which may also be consumed as food. However, in its tropical sense, the lamb represents Bathsheba whom the rich man (David) took from his poor neighbor (Uriah). Likewise in Ps 62:10b, *hebel* functions within the parable in its material sense, while tropically it refers to the psalmist's enemies.

The sense of the last two cola of v. 10 is ironic. It is unexpected and remarkable that these mortals are so light. This requires that *hebel* be something extremely light in order for the contrast to be striking. The literary imagery is a parable because the psalmist wants the reader to use the narrative itself, in which *hebel* is weighed against a group of people in a two-pan balance, as the predicating element of the metaphor. The enemies of the psalmist, indicated in the first two cola of v. 10, are the subject term.

We will discuss this text further below. For now, we may recognize that it suggests that *hebel* in the material sense is very light in weight. Although this is not much information, it is consistent with the properties of vapor evident in the postbiblical material.

Isa 57:13

בְּזַעֲקֵךְ יַצִּילֵךְ קִבּוּצַיִךְ
וְאֶת־כֻּלָּם יִשָּׂא־רוּחַ
יִקַּח־הָבֶל
וְהַחוֹסֶה בִי יִנְחַל־אֶרֶץ
וְיִירַשׁ הַר־קָדְשִׁי:

---

[20] Madeleine Boucher, *The Mysterious Parable* (CBQMS 6; Washington, D.C.: Catholic Biblical Association of America, 1977), 17–25; the quotation is from p. 23.

When you cry out, let your collection (of idols)[21] deliver you!
The wind (רוּחַ) will carry all of them,
Hebel will take (them).
But whoever takes refuge in me shall possess the land
And inherit my holy mountain.

Within a prophetic oracle of judgment (Isa 57:7–13), Israel is being charged with apostasy. Isaiah 57:13 contains part of the (extremely brief) pronouncement of sentence, along with a word of hope and promise. The picture here, again a parable, is of idols being of such light weight that the wind (רוּחַ) or *hebel* might carry them away.

The text is not concerned with the actual weight of these images. Rather, Yahweh tells a story about objects light enough to be blown away in order to comment concerning the quality of these deities in comparison to the true God.

However, within the parable itself, the use of *hebel* in parallel with רוּחַ (wind) suggests the semantic domain of air, and more specifically of air that moves. Since, like Ps 62:10 [Eng. v. 9], the tone is ironic, we realize that something surprisingly weak, as opposed to a violent wind, is being indicated. This could be a "breeze," though in view of *hebel*'s material sense elsewhere, a vapor such as "breath" is more warranted for the context.[22]

Other Considerations

There are less important considerations for the determination of *hebel*'s material sense which nevertheless deserve brief comment. The translators of the Hebrew Scriptures into Greek, when they used terms indicating a material (rather than abstract) sense to translate *hebel*, chose those meaning "vapor," particularly ἀτμός "steam, vapor."[23] It may also be noted that semitic terms in addition to הֲבְלָא which are cognate to *hebel* likewise share the semantic domain

---

[21] MT קִבּוּצַיִךְ is a puzzle to commentators and appears nowhere else. The form as given comes from the root קבץ, meaning "to collect, gather." Thus the translation "collection (of idols)" since it fits the context. Many emend to שִׁקּוּצַיִךְ "abominations" (so John McKenzie, *Second Isaiah* [AB 20; Garden City, N.Y.: Doubleday, 1968], 157, and Claus Westermann, *Isaiah 40–66* [trans. David M. G. Stalker; OTL; Philadelphia: Westminster, 1969 (1966)], 323). This emendation retains the understanding that false objects of worship are described here.

[22] Another parabolic use of *hebel* is found at Prov 21:6 (discussion below).

[23] The LXX translates *hebel* in Ecclesiastes almost exclusively as ματαιότης "vanity"; the exception is LXX[B] and LXX[P] at 9:9b, ἀτμός. Aq., Sym., and Theod. also used ἀτμός there, as well as elsewhere sporadically. At other *hebel* passages in the HB, the other textual witnesses are also more inclined than LXX to use the material rather than the abstract sense (Seybold, "הֶבֶל," 315; Georg Bertram, "Hebräischer und griechischer Qohelet," *ZAW* 64 (1952): 30–31; HRCS, s.v. "ἀτμός," "ματαιότης").

of air, including (visible) vapor and moving air (wind, breeze).[24]

Summary of *Hebel*'s Material Sense

In postbiblical texts, the term *hebel* is used in contexts which indicate heat/steam, breath, vapor within a living being, vaporous perspiration, and noxious vapor. The use of *hebel* in Ps 62:10 [Eng. v. 9] suggests something light in weight, and in Isa 57:13, *hebel* involves a mild movement of air. Overall, cognate terms, the Greek translations of the Hebrew canon, and metaphorical uses of the term support rather than contradict this range of usage. Thus, although the best evidence for *hebel*'s material sense comes from the postbiblical era, all indicators suggest a continuity in the meaning of the term across the periods of its use.

The word *vapor* is the most satisfactory single term in English to express the breadth of *hebel*'s material sense: "a quantity of visible matter diffused through or suspended in the air."[25] *Vapor* allows for a slight movement of air as well as for a visible quality.[26] Further, the term is general enough to embrace such rabbinic usages as steam, marsh air, gaseous perspiration, breath, and radiant heat. For these reasons, and to allow for metaphorical uses of *hebel*, the term *vapor* will be employed to translate *hebel* throughout this study.

As for the range of the term's usage, perhaps the English word *fumes* provides a good comparison. Its essential meaning is "any smokelike or vaporous exhalation from matter or substances, esp. of an odorous or harmful nature."[27] While it is often used of fumes which are harmful, this is not a part of the word's fundamental sense as it is with words such as *poison* or *toxin*. The specific qualities and attributes of the fumes in question must be determined from context. Thus it is possible to speak of "noxious fumes of carbon monoxide," but also of "pleasant fumes from the bakery oven." In both cases, there is a "vaporous exhalation from matter or substances," but one is pleasant and the other harmful.

Likewise with *hebel*, its use always involves "a quantity of visible matter diffused through or suspended in the air," but this may at times be warm steam

---

[24] See Seybold, "הֶבֶל," 313–14; *HALOT*, s.v. "הֶבֶל."

[25] *The Random House Dictionary of the English Language: Second Edition—Unabridged*, s.v. "vapor."

[26] Scott states that the term "connotes what is visible or recognizable, but unsubstantial, momentary, and profitless" (*Proverbs, Ecclesiastes*, 202). The limited number of contexts in which the material sense is found makes it difficult to determine whether *both* the aspect of "slight movement" and that of "a visible quality" are always present as the term is used. In each case, various qualities of vapor are highlighted according to the specific emphasis in that context.

[27] *Random House Dictionary*, s.v. "fume."

from a bath, at other times toxic marsh air, and so on. To anticipate the investigation of *hebel*'s metaphorical uses in the remainder of this chapter and in Chapter 4, the following qualities of *hebel* may be noted: (1) it is insubstantial; (2) as a mist, it dissipates quickly and so is transient; (3) since it is visible, it may give the illusion of being more than it is; and (4) it is possible for it to bear substances which are harmful just as it is possible for it to be hot. Authors provide clues in context to indicate which aspect(s) of *hebel* is/are in focus.

The discussion which follows will demonstrate that the metaphorical uses of *hebel* arise from the range of its material sense. It is important to clarify that the terms "transient," "insubstantial," and "foul" are used in this study primarily to express qualities of *hebel*'s material sense. *Referents* of *hebel* which are related to these qualities will most often be expressed in different terms. For example, a referent of *hebel*'s quality of transience may be labeled "fleeting," while a referent of the term's quality of insubstantiality may be called "futile" (of labor) or "frail" (of human life).

THE METAPHORIC SENSES OF *HEBEL*

Metaphor has been defined and described in Chapter 2. The following discussion will explore, first, the use of *hebel* as metaphor in the Hebrew Bible and, second, its metaphorical use in the postbiblical writings. The discussion will consider the range of material sense for *hebel* outlined above.

The noun *hebel* occurs thirty-five times in the HB (apart from Ecclesiastes and apart from eight occurrences of the name "Abel"), and the denominative verb הבל occurs five times: four times in the Qal, and once in the Hiphil. Except in the latter case, it is always accompanied by the noun *hebel*. The verb, as with the noun, is consistently involved in metaphoric expressions.

The biblical passages discussed below are organized by qualities of *hebel* as vapor. For each context, the subject and *hebel*'s guarding elements are indicated. Referents for *hebel* are related to its qualities of insubstantiality and transience, and the term is also used as a stock metaphor. Postbiblical writings are organized by text group: Ben Sira, rabbinic writings, and Qumran.

Hebrew Bible Metaphor Texts

The Name "Abel"

A brief word may be said about *hebel*'s use as the proper name "Abel" in Gen 4 (8*x*). Scholars have speculated over the designation of this character whose life ends so abruptly. Because the name Abel occurs nowhere else and its meaning is not explained (cf. Cain 4:1; Seth 4:25), some claim that Abel's name was really an appellative (breath, nothingness) rather than a proper name.[28] While this is plausible, and *hebel* is used elsewhere of human life in the way reflected by Abel's story, it is a thesis which is difficult to substantiate. These texts will not be discussed further in this study.

Insubstantiality (11x + 1 verb)

A number of texts employ *hebel* in terms of vapor's lack of substance, insubstantiality. The following subjects are included:

wealth	acquired without effort (Prov 13:11)
human life	which is spoiled (Job 7:16; Prov 21:6)
thought or speech	which is in error (Ps 94:11; Job 35:16; 27:12)
labor	which is futile (Isa 49:4; Job 9:29)
sources of help	which are unreliable (Isa 57:13; Lam 4:17; Ps 39:7 [6]).

Prov 13:11. Proverbs 13:11 is an example of how difficult it is to interpret a proverb without a situational context:[29]

הוֹן מֵהֶבֶל יִמְעָט
וְקֹבֵץ עַל־יָד יַרְבֶּה:

Wealth from *vapor* (*hebel*) will dwindle,
but the one gathering little by little (עַל־יָד) will increase (it).

The idiom "upon hand" (עַל־יָד) almost certainly indicates progression a little at a time[30] and serves as a contrary for *hebel*. The verse therefore is concerned with the obtaining of wealth (S): a contrast between those who achieve riches by acquiring them gradually, and those who lose it for the reason indicated by the term מהבל. The LXX and the Vulg. translate this term with words which mean "hastily," so the contrast is between those who gain wealth quickly and those who do so slowly.[31] The LXX employs ἐπισπουδάζω (to make haste) which, in its only other use in the OT, translates מְבֹהֶלֶת (Qere) at Prov 20:21, the root בהל "to be in haste."

Thus one possibility is that the *Vorlage* of the LXX translators contained

---

[28] Claus Westermann understands this character as a comment upon human contingency in general (*Genesis 1–11: A Commentary* [trans. John J. Scullion; CC; Minneapolis: Augsburg, 1984 (1974)], 292). Cf. Seybold, "הֶבֶל," 315–16.

[29] See Carol R. Fontaine, *Traditional Sayings in the Old Testament: A Contextual Study* (Bible and Literature Series 5; Sheffield: Almond, 1982), 43–53.

[30] So B. Gemser (*Sprüche Salomos* [Tübingen: Mohr/Siebeck, 1963], 62), LXX, Vulg., and modern versions.

[31] LXX ἐπισπουδάζω, "to urge on, to further; (mid/pass) gotten hastily" (Johan Lust, Erik Eynikel, and K. Hauspie, eds. *A Greek-English Lexicon of the Septuagint*, Part 1 [Stuttgart: Deutsche Bibelgesellschaft, 1992], 174) and Vulg. *festinata* (adv.), "hastily."

the Pual participle מְבֹהָל.[32] However, the LXX of Proverbs is known for its free translations, and the MT is the *lectio difficilior*. G. R. Driver would retain the MT consonants and repoint to מְהֻבָּל, also a Pual participle. Thus he translates "got by scheming" based on the way the verb הבל is used in Ps 62:11 [Eng. v. 10].[33] As discussed below, it is more likely that *hebel* in Ps 62 indicates a mistaken placing of confidence (in robbery), and does not itself have to do with "scheming." In addition, the resulting syntax seems strained. It is better to retain the MT.

Yet the possibility of a moral element for *hebel* here should not be discounted.[34] Just as the false threat of enemies could be compared to God in terms of the lightness of air (Ps 62:10 [Eng. v. 9]), so it would be plausible to compare the כָּבוֹד (glory, weight) of Yahweh to human depravity in a metaphor which would make use of *hebel*'s lightness of weight.[35] In this case, *hebel* could indicate a moral insubstantiality, with affinities to that used of false deities. Alternatively, immoral actions could be compared to harmful vapor, repugnant and disgusting. In either case, the contrary "upon hand" would be taken as honest, diligent work that is "sweet-smelling" to God (cf. Gen 8:21; Exod 29:18).

Though *hebel* may be used of something which happens quickly (transience), it is otherwise applied to things which *vanish* rapidly, like the dissipation of a mist, not of things which suddenly appear. Thus, it seems an unlikely predication for gathering wealth.

Yet the latter meaning could be achieved through a referent involving insubstantiality more generally, and is probably the best solution to the present text. By this reasoning, wealth which is achieved "from nothing" indicates a windfall, such as from an inheritance.[36] First there was nothing, now there is a large amount. The contrary "upon hand," then, represents a long duration of time, and the sense of 13:11a is "easy come, easy go."[37] Such a quick

---

[32] Some would so emend the text, e.g., Richard J. Clifford, *Proverbs: A Commentary* (OTL; Louisville: Westminster/John Knox, 1999), 135–36.

[33] G. R. Driver, "Problems in 'Proverbs,'" *ZAW* 50 (1932): 144.

[34] Such in fact appears in the postbiblical material, e.g., *Lev. Rab.* sec. 29, 1QS 5:18–19.

[35] Similarly, Ps 39:5–6 [Eng. vv. 4–5] declares the length of the human lifespan to be short in comparison with that of the deity.

[36] William McKane translates the MT, "Wealth made out of nothing . . . will dwindle." He understands this as a reference to wealth obtained other than by honest and/or diligent effort. He further notes comments by the Egyptian sage Ptahhotep who considers the obtaining of wealth to be the "gift of God" and who counsels against greed (*Proverbs, a New Approach* [OTL; Philadelphia: Westminster, 1970], 64, 458–59).

[37] According to the Talmud, in an interpretation attributed to Rabbi Huna, Raba stated

acquisition of wealth could also suggest unethical behavior, but such would need to be indicated by the utterance context, which here is ambiguous.[38]

Job 7:16; Prov 21:6. In Job chapters 6 and 7, the suffering Job complains of his anguish and pleads that God would let him die (6:8–9). His days and nights are tests of endurance, full of misery (7:1–6). In 7:7–10, he claims that he is heading for Sheol, that he will be gone and not return.[39] Therefore he complains about the unrelenting pain of his nights (7:13–15). It is in this context that he makes the statements found in 7:16:

מָאַסְתִּי לֹא־לְעֹלָם אֶחְיֶה
חֲדַל מִמֶּנִּי כִּי־הֶבֶל יָמָי:

I reject (life);[40] I would not live forever.
Leave me alone! For my days are *vapor* (*hebel*).

He then alludes to the attention God gives to human beings (7:17), a seeming parody of the concern which is praised in Pss 8 and 144. Job experiences this attention only as "testing" every morning (7:18).

The broader context, Job 6–7, presents a complex picture of a man whose days go by in agony, yet who sees his end coming. In these chapters, Job does not refer to his life going by quickly and thus *hebel* does not indicate transience in 7:16.[41] The common translation of 7:6a, to the effect that Job's days are rushing by, makes no sense in this section and is surely in error.[42]

---

about Prov 13:11, "If one takes his studies by heaps at a time, he will benefit but little, but if one gathers [knowledge] little by little he will gain much." Raba went on: "The Rabbis know this thing, and yet they disregard it." However, Rabbi Naḥman b. Isaac apparently saw himself as an exception: "I have acted up to it and it stood me in good stead" (*'Abod. Zar.* 19a; cf. *'Erub.* 54b).

[38] The LXX, not untypically, makes additions. Note the words emphasized below:
Wealth gotten hastily *with transgression* (μετὰ ἀνομίας) is diminished,
but he that gathers for himself *with piety* (μετ᾽ εὐσεβείας) shall be increased.
The righteous one has pity and lends (δίκαιος οἰκτίρει καὶ κιχρᾷ).

[39] It is not the swiftness of his going that is in focus but the quality of his life. Job 7:7 states, "Remember that my life is רוּחַ (wind), my eye will never again see good." His life is insubstantial, diminishing.

[40] Marvin Pope calls מָאַסְתִּי "troublesome" due to the missing object here, and suggests it may have been a gloss (*Job*, 62).

[41] Contra David Clines, *Job 1–20*, 165–66, 191–92, who takes each colon of the verse to be a choice against God, followed by a statement predicting that the end will, as result, come soon; also contra Daniel Fredericks, *Coping*, 21. Job does speak in terms of his transience elsewhere; cf. 8:9; 9:25–26; 14:1–2.

[42] Job 7:6a is traditionally translated (RSV), "My days are swifter (קלל) than a weaver's shuttle (אֶרֶג)." The term אֶרֶג (loom) occurs only here and in Judg 16:14. Because of the verb קלל, which can mean "to be swift," אֶרֶג is assumed here to mean some part of the loom, viz., the shuttle which moves swiftly as the weaver works. The context, however, makes it

The surrounding text is a mixture of images involving pain on the one hand (7:1–5, 11–15) and insignificance on the other (7:6–10). Several terms in the context function as synonyms for *hebel* and indicate a referent of insubstantiality: שָׁוְא (falsehood v. 3), קְלָל (trifling v. 6), and רוּחַ (wind v. 7). There is also the extensional phrase involving a cloud that fades and vanishes (v. 9).[43] Therefore, Job demands, why should God bother with one of so little importance (7:16–19)? In 7:16b it is the quality of the days of his life (S) which are in view: they have been spoiled and are insignificant (*hebel*); therefore he does not wish to live forever (7:16). He welcomes the end he sees coming, and wishes it would come sooner (7:15).[44]

Prov 21:6, a wisdom sentence, has a related focus. The MT reads:

פֹּעַל אוֹצָרוֹת בִּלְשׁוֹן שָׁקֶר
הֶבֶל נִדָּף מְבַקְשֵׁי־מָוֶת׃

The obtaining of riches by a lying (שֶׁקֶר) tongue
is a *vapor* (*hebel*) scattered[45] unto the seekers of death.

However, the LXX, reflecting a different Hebrew *Vorlage*, has the following:

ὁ ἐνεργῶν θησαυρίσματα γλώσσῃ ψευδεῖ
μάταια διώκει ἐπὶ παγίδας θανάτου.

The Hebrew underlying LXX may be reconstructed as follows:

פֹּעַל אוֹצָרוֹת בִּלְשׁוֹן שָׁקֶר
הַבָלִים רֹדֵף בַּמְקַשֵׁי־מָוֶת׃

---

virtually impossible that Job can be saying his days go by quickly. He is lamenting just the opposite: they go agonizingly slowly. He would be happy if they *did* go quickly. A plausible solution to this difficulty has been offered by Heidi M. Szpek, "The Peshitta on Job 7:6: 'My Days are Swifter Than an ארג,'" *JBL* 113 (1994): 287–90. Based upon the Peshitta version of this text and suggestive ancient commentary, she argues that אֶרֶג here does not refer to the loom's shuttle, but is a synecdoche for the *thrums*, the small ends of thread left over in the loom. The verb קלל has here another of its senses, "to be trifling, or insignificant." Szpek thus translates Job 7:6, "My days are more trifling than the thrums of a loom, and they end without hope/thread" (the double entendre with תקוה continues to work well within this understanding).

[43] Thus, an element of time is *part* of this scenario; Job's life is doing a fade, though a slow one.

[44] Norman Habel suggests that 7:15–16 is an allusion to the Ugaritic myth of Aqhat, in which Aqhat unknowingly rejected the offer of eternal life. In contrast, Job knowingly rejects it and chooses death in the hope that the deity will leave him alone (*Job*, 163–64).

[45] נִדָּף (vapor scattered) is often rendered "fleeting vapor" (so NRSV, NIV). A vapor blown away has quickly ceased to exist.

The one who obtains (פֹּעַל) riches by a lying tongue
pursues (רֹדֵף) *vapors* (pl.) unto the snares (בְּמֹקְשֵׁי) of death.[46]

However, if the text reflected by the LXX was original, most differences
between it and the MT are not easily explained as transmission errors. First we
may note that the distinction between פֹּעַל and פָּעַל does not require a change in
the consonantal text (more on this below). Also, the plural μάταια can probably
be discounted as a free translation of an original singular *hebel* (cf. Ps 62:10
[Eng. v. 9]; 94:11).

The required change from רדף to נדף is not easily explained on the basis
of graphic confusion without postulating several steps in between. It appears
more likely that the phrase מבקשי מות ("seekers of death," unique to this verse)
was read, either inadvertently or deliberately, to conform with the more
common מקשי מות ("snares of death," cf. 2 Sam 22:6; Ps 18:6; Prov 13:14;
14:27). The snares of death are precisely that from which wisdom saves one.
Then, not appreciating the metaphor of "scattering" vapor or breath,[47] the
translators opted for a verb with a sense parallel to פעל. The verb רדף is
attractive because it has two consonants in common with נדף. The resulting
sense for the LXX is that the one who obtains riches falsely is pursuing the
snares of death. While this makes sense, the MT is to be preferred as the *lectio
difficilior*.[48]

There remains the matter of how to read פעל (to obtain) in the first colon.
The participle was likely read by the LXX translators to conform to the changes
made in the second colon. However, either the noun or the participle is possible
for the MT, taken here to be original. Either (1) the *obtaining* of wealth falsely,
or (2) the *person* doing the obtaining is the subject (S) declared to be *hebel* (P).
Either of these is possible, depending upon the larger utterance context in
which the proverb is put to use. However, the act of deception in either case
reflects upon the quality of the person, so that the lying person must be

---

[46] So Gemser reads with the LXX as indicated (*Sprüche Salomos*, 81): "Wer erwirbt
Schätze mit falscher Zunge, Hauch jagt er nach in Schlingen des Todes." So also *HALOT*
2:674. Alternatively, Gemser (113) suggests *hebel* to be adverbial, "wird zwecklos
forgetrieben in Stricken des Todes." The Vulg. follows the LXX with the major exception that
the one who obtains riches "vanus est" (is vain), reflecting a singular *hebel*.

[47] נדף is used frequently with wind associations, cf. Ps 68:3, of smoke; Lev 26:36 and
Job 13:25, a driven leaf; Isa 19:7, of crops; 41:2, driven stubble.

[48] William McKane adopts the metathesis of ב and מ reflected in LXX and Vulg., and
understands the referent in terms of insubstantiality. The message is "that ill-gotten wealth is
insubstantial and unreal, and he who has it is not a man of weight . . . but one who is being
borne at speed, without the ability to resist, towards the snares of death" (*Proverbs*, 552).
There is a tension reflected in this verse between wealth as a badge of a truly fulfilled life,
and wealth separated from true character. According to McKane, those who would achieve

considered the concern of the imagery.[49]

The text, possibly a parable, appears to be structured chiastically with two oral images at the center, opposite to images of those seeking something:

The one obtaining riches	by a lying tongue,
Is *breath* (*hebel*) scattered	unto seekers of death.

To obtain wealth through false speech is to have one's life become insubstantial: spoiled and in danger of death. The prospect of death suggests that transience too must be considered part of the referent of *hebel* here.[50]

Ps 94:11; Job 35:16; 27:12. In three texts, *hebel* is used of speech or thoughts which are in error. Psalm 94, a psalm of lament, begins by urging Yahweh to arise and bring vengeance upon the "proud" and the "wicked," those who behave as follows (vv. 4–6):

speak arrogantly . . . do wickedness . . . crush your people . . . afflict
your heritage . . . slay the widow and the stranger, and murder the orphans.

The psalmist describes these violent ones as expecting impunity. But the arrogant will not escape from Yahweh, who sees and hears all (94:10b–11):

$$\text{הַֽמְלַמֵּ֖ד אָדָ֣ם דָּֽעַת:}$$
$$\text{יְֽהוָ֗ה יֹ֭דֵעַ מַחְשְׁב֣וֹת אָדָ֑ם}$$
$$\text{כִּי־הֵ֥מָּה הָֽבֶל:}$$

The one who teaches humans knowledge,
Yahweh, knows human thoughts,
That they are *vapor* (*hebel*).

In ironic contrast, the arrogant ones who expect God not to know about themselves thereby demonstrate their own ignorance. These are (v. 8) "fools" (כְּסִילִים), "stupid" (בֹּעֲרִים) and not "wise" (שׂכל). These synonyms and contrary, along with the extension concerning God's pervasive knowledge as a contrast, prepare the reader for the use of *hebel* in v. 11. Here it is often translated as "vanity" or "breath."[51] The thinking (S) of these arrogant ones is in error. Their mind lacks substance, is nothing.

---

wealth unethically show evidence of a flaw that will drag them along to death.

[49] It is not impossible that the wealth itself is the subject of *hebel*, perhaps in the sense of transience. However, the element of death at the conclusion of the proverb makes the above proposal more likely.

[50] The element of death in both Job 7:16 and here in Prov 21:6 also recalls the noxious vapor sometimes indicated for the material sense of *hebel*.

[51] So, e.g., H.-J. Kraus (*Psalms 60–150* [trans. Hilton C. Oswald; CC; Minneapolis: Augsburg, 1989 (1978)], 241), Tate (*Psalms 51–100*, 482, 484), and Artur Weiser (*The Psalms* [trans. Herbert Hartwell; OTL; Philadelphia: Westminster, 1962], 624).

In Job 35:16, Elihu claims,

וְאִיּוֹב הֶבֶל יִפְצֶה־פִּיהוּ

בִּבְלִי־דַעַת מִלִּין יַכְבִּר׃

Job (in) *vapor* (*hebel*) opens his mouth,
Without knowledge (בִּבְלִי־דַעַת) he multiplies words.

The parallel phrasing suggests a correspondence between "opens his mouth" and "multiplies words" on the one hand, and "without knowledge" and *hebel* on the other. Words (S) should supply knowledge, but Elihu claims that Job's do not. This is an example of guarding with a contrary so the reader understands that the R value of *hebel* relates to insubstantiality. Knowledge which is insubstantial is "nonsense."

Job 27:12 is in the section of the book thought by many scholars to be misarranged. Some attribute these words to Job and others to Zophar.[52] Again, the topic is the issue of understanding:

הֵן־אַתֶּם כֻּלְּכֶם חֲזִיתֶם

וְלָמָּה־זֶּה הֶבֶל תֶּהְבָּלוּ

Now all of you have seen (חזה) (this),
So why do you *make vapor* of *vapor* (or vaporize vapor)?[53]

Those addressed have encountered the substantive matters (S) to which the speaker refers, but by denying them, they have portrayed them as being insubstantial. The verb חזה serves as a contrary to the verbal expression *hebel* + *hbl* (Qal stem).

Isa 49:4; Job 9:29. On two occasions, *hebel* is used of human effort which is futile. In Isa 49:4, רִיק (empty) and תֹהוּ (nothingness) are synonyms used to clarify *hebel*:

וַאֲנִי אָמַרְתִּי לְרִיק יָגַעְתִּי

לְתֹהוּ וְהֶבֶל כֹּחִי כִלֵּיתִי

אָכֵן מִשְׁפָּטִי אֶת־יְהוָה

וּפְעֻלָּתִי אֶת־אֱלֹהָי׃

But I said, "For emptiness (רִיק) I have labored,
For nothing (תֹהוּ) and *vapor* (*hebel*) I used up my strength;
Yet surely my cause (מִשְׁפָּט) is with Yahweh,
And my reward with my God."

This text is about labor (S) and its results. The speaker states that this has

---

[52] See, e.g., Pope, *Job*, and Habel, *Job*, ad. loc.

[53] Similar to Habel's translation. He concludes with, "So why talk nonsense?" (*Job*, 376). The combination of *hebel* and the verb *hbl* of the same stem intensifies the expression.

resulted only in emptiness and nothing, an indication that *hebel*'s referent here concerns insubstantiality, the futility of wasted effort.

In regard to the second text, Job 9:27–35 states in various ways the futility of seeking to be justified before God. In 9:29, Job's speech employs *hebel* with the verb יגע (to exert oneself) in a rhetorical question,

אָנֹכִי אֶרְשָׁע
לָמָּה־זֶּה הֶבֶל אִיגָע׃

I will be (considered) wicked.
Why do I exert myself (יגע) for *vapor* (*hebel*)?

Job's effort is futile, a labor with no result.

Isa 57:13; Lam 4:17; Ps 39:7 [Eng. v. 6]. Finally, three texts refer to sources of help which prove unreliable.[54] Isaiah 57:13, discussed earlier in this chapter, contains a parable which exhibits the material sense of *hebel*. The parable represents a placing of trust in a collection of false deities whose images are blown away into the breeze. רוּחַ (wind) serves as synonym to *hebel* *within* the parable. Then, placing trust in Yahweh, which results in "possessing the land" and "inheriting my holy mountain," serves as contrary *to* the *parable*. These inappropriate objects of worship are unable to accomplish what the worshipers require.

Likewise, the speaker in Lam 4:17 mourns concerning a nation which was unable to rescue:

עוֹדֵינָה תִּכְלֶינָה עֵינֵינוּ אֶל־עֶזְרָתֵנוּ הָבֶל
בְּצִפִּיָּתֵנוּ צִפִּינוּ אֶל־גּוֹי לֹא יוֹשִׁעַ׃

Still our eyes failed, our help was *vapor* (*hebel*).
From our watch points we watched for a nation that could not save (ישׁע).

The verb ישׁע serves as a contrary here guarding the "unreliability" referent.[55]

The last text to consider in this regard is found in Psalm 39, an individual lament in which the psalmist three times employs the word *hebel*.[56] Psalm 39:7b–8 [Eng. vv. 6b–7] reads:

---

[54] It is possible that these should be included in the following section on deception. However, their contexts do not suggest a particular emphasis on being misguided or victimized.

[55] The textual difficulty in the first part of the verse does not affect the role of *hebel*. For discussion, see Delbert Hillers, *Lamentations* (rev. ed.; AB 7A; New York: Doubleday, 1992), 144.

[56] While the psalm has elements of the lament, it is meditative and does not follow common lament structure. See comments by Weiser, *Psalms*, 328. H.-J. Kraus classifies it as a "prayer song" (*Psalms 1–59* [trans. Hilton C. Oswald; CC; Minneapolis: Augsburg, 1988 (1978)], 416–17).

אַךְ־הֶבֶל <הָמוֹן> יִצְבֹּר
וְלֹא־יֵדַע מִי־אֹסְפָם:
וְעַתָּה מַה־קִּוִּיתִי אֲדֹנָי
תּוֹחַלְתִּי לְךָ הִיא:

Indeed *vapor* (*hebel*) is <wealth>[57] one heaps up (צבר),
And does not know who will gather it.
And now, for what do I wait (קוה), O Adonai?
My hope (תּוֹחֶלֶת) is in you!

Since no guarding terms suggesting time are used here, the issue appears
not to be the transience of wealth.[58] It is not the fleeting nature of wealth during
one's lifetime, but its failure to help; it just sits there in heaps, long after its
owner is gone. Rather, the emphasis is upon Adonai as the appropriate source
of one's hope (תּוֹחֶלֶת), the one worthy of anticipation (קוה). Thus, v. 8 provides
clarification by extension. Wealth (S) is *hebel*[59] in the sense of being an
insubstantial, unreliable basis for help, to be gathered by someone else after the
death of the one who heaped it up.

Insubstantiality, Emphasizing Deception (6x + 2 verbs)

Each of the *hebel* texts with a referent of insubstantiality involves the
phenomenon of expectation versus reality. Yet the metaphorical use of *hebel*
may sometimes be used in contexts which particularly emphasize deception:
the difficulty which occurs when something appears to be substantial though it
actually is not.[60] Notice that intentionality is not necessarily implied. The
deception element likely draws upon the fact that *hebel*, as a mist, appears to be
more substantive than it is. Examples of this particular aspect of
insubstantiality occur with the following subjects:

beauty	which misrepresents (Prov 31:30)
human help	which is deficient (Isa 30:7; Ps 62:10 [Eng. v. 9; bis])
words	which fail to console (Job 21:34; Zech 10:2)

In addition, the verb הבל is used of:

---

[57] Emending יהמיון to המון (wealth), so Peter C. Craigie (*Psalms 1–50* [WBC 19;
Waco, Tex.: Word, 1983], 307). This fits well with צבר which is used elsewhere of silver
(כֶּסֶף, Job 27:16; Zech 9:3). Other commentators understand the verse similarly without the
emendation, e.g., Weiser, *Psalms*, 327–29.

[58] Contra Fredericks (*Coping*, 19–21) who argues that *hebel* indicates transience in
each of its three occurrences in Ps 39. Cf. discussion of Ps 39:6, 12 below.

[59] It is also possible to take *hebel* as an adverb here, yielding a similar sense.

[60] There may be an element of deception in all *hebel*-texts that concern insubstantiality, but for those discussed here, this element is in the foreground.

wealth   which is a false trust (Ps 62:11)
words   which are ignorant (Jer 23:16)

Prov 31:30. The poem devoted to praise of the virtuous woman in Proverbs presents *hebel* with a referent involving deception. Verse 31:30 reads,

שֶׁקֶר הַחֵן וְהֶבֶל הַיֹּפִי
אִשָּׁה יִרְאַת־יְהוָה הִיא תִתְהַלָּל:

Charm is deceitful (שֶׁקֶר), and beauty is *vapor* (*hebel*),
A woman who fears Yahweh will be praised.

This is another excellent example of the use of a synonym to make the sense of *hebel* plain. The term שֶׁקֶר is unambiguous and corresponds to *hebel*, as does "charm" with "beauty" (S). The impact of this parallel phrasing is to claim that charm and beauty are unreliable; they represent themselves one way but the reality may be quite another.[61] In contrast, the woman who fears the Lord is the truly desirable woman, worthy of praise.

Isa 30:7; Ps 62:10 [Eng. v. 9]. Two texts involving three occurrences of *hebel* emphasize the deception of relying upon people for help. Isaiah 30:6–7 initiates an "oracle of the beasts of the Negev." Here Egypt, whom the audience has sought for assistance, is described as a "people that cannot profit (them)" (עַם לֹא יוֹעִילוּ; cf. 30:5). According to v. 7, Egypt's help (S) "is *vapor* (*hebel*) and empty (רִיק), therefore I have called her, 'Rahab who sits.'" The verb יעל (profit) and the term רִיק (empty) serve as contrary and synonym respectively to clarify that *hebel* means here something lacking substance. But in addition, the context makes clear that this help is something they sought with sincere expectation of aid. What appeared dependable was deceptive.

For the second example, we return to Ps 62:10 [Eng. v. 9], the psalm of trust discussed earlier in connection with *hebel*'s material sense:

אַךְ הֶבֶל בְּנֵי־אָדָם
כָּזָב בְּנֵי אִישׁ
בְּמֹאזְנַיִם לַעֲלוֹת
הֵמָּה מֵהֶבֶל יָחַד:

The children of mortals (בְּנֵי־אָדָם) are only *vapor* (*hebel*),
Human offspring (בְּנֵי אִישׁ) are a lie (כָּזָב);
In the balances going up,
They are (lighter) than *vapor* (*hebel*) together.[62]

---

[61] Interestingly, the Akkadian term *šāru* (wind), used in other ways similar to *hebel* and רוּחַ, is also used of deception, e.g., "The lies (*šāru*) that this false brother of mine spoke to you, I heard them; it is all lies (*šāru*)" (*ABL* 301:3, 6, cited in *CAD*, Š part 2, 140).

[62] As mentioned in the previous discussion of this passage, this exhibits the pregnant

Previously we noted the parabolic nature of the verse as a whole, accomplished by the reference to the two-pan balance in the final phrases. The first two cola, however, are parallel statements making assessments of certain human beings. Here we also have a synonymous indicator of *hebel*'s R value, the term כָּזָב (lie, falsehood).

The poet, in parallel metaphorical statements, declares these persons to be a false source of hope in contrast to the true God who alone has power and is a legitimate source of refuge. The psalmist works masterfully here, first conveying deception with the help of כָּזָב as synonym, and then powerfully emphasizing the impotence at the heart of the deception by means of the scale imagery.

The following verse, Psalm 62:11 [Eng. v. 10], concerns wealth, using the verb הבל in parallel with בטח "to trust":

אַל־תִּבְטְחוּ בְעֹשֶׁק וּבְגָזֵל אַל־תֶּהְבָּלוּ
חַיִל כִּי־יָנוּב אַל־תָּשִׁיתוּ לֵב:

Do not trust (בטח) in extortion, do not הבל in robbery.
If riches increase, set not your heart on them.

Extension indicates that trust in robbery (S) is only a deception because strength (עֹז) and faithfulness (חֶסֶד) are with God alone (vv. 12–13 [Eng. vv. 11–12]). As v. 10 [Eng. v. 9] declares that human beings are of little substance (i.e., ability), likewise the effort to achieve wealth by unrighteous means is only a deception. Finally, the synonym בטח (trust) suggests that the verb הבל here indicates an unwarranted placing of confidence.

As in all cases of metaphor, the determination of *hebel*'s meaning is dependent upon the sense of its context as a whole. Weiser, for example, emphasizes the psalm's concern for trust in God and considers the statements of v. 10 [Eng. v. 9] to place human beings in contrast to the deity in three aspects. In comparison to God, human glory is nothing, human beings are not reliable, and mortals are intentionally deceptive. There are elements of all three in the immediate context. He translates, "Set not vain hopes on robbery!"[63]

H.-J. Kraus, while categorizing Ps 62 as a "prayer song" with didactic elements, chooses to emphasize its call for assistance and judgment against enemies when interpreting the word *hebel*. The image of the pan-balance by his understanding is an allusion to the Egyptian scales of divine judgment (cf. Dan 5:27; Job 31:6; Sir. 21:25; 26:15). The issue is that God's judgment demonstrates the enemies to be ineffectual and frail even in all their power;

---

use of מִן, GKC §133e.

[63] Weiser, *Psalms*, 446, 451.

their imposing appearance is all lie and deception. He translates exactly as Weiser.[64]

Although elements of judgment are present in the poem, and such cannot be denied as part of the entailment of the scale image (Kraus), Weiser is correct to discern that the primary and controlling emphasis is upon God, to which human beings are placed in contrast.[65] The verb הבל thus indicates that placing one's confidence in something less than God only deceptively appears adequate.

Job 21:34; Zech 10:2. Sometimes, *hebel* is used of deceptive speech. Job, in Job 21:34, says:

וְאֵיךְ תְּנַחֲמוּנִי הָבֶל
וּתְשׁוּבֹתֵיכֶם נִשְׁאַר־מָעַל:

How then will you console (נחם) me with *vapor* (*hebel*)?
There is nothing left of your answers but falsehood (מָעַל).

This statement comes as a conclusion to Job's lengthy description of his friends' erroneous assertions. They have been saying that the wicked, or at least their offspring, receive justice. But Job insists that the wicked are spared such treatment. The term מָעַל suggests not only factual falsehood but, in addition, a falsehood of friendship. They have been disloyal, only appearing to be true friends. Instead of true comfort, Job received *hebel*, deception.[66]

The verb הבל is used in Jer 23:16 in a similar reference to the deception of words:

כֹּה־אָמַר יְהוָה צְבָאוֹת
אַל־תִּשְׁמְעוּ עַל־דִּבְרֵי הַנְּבִאִים הַנִּבְּאִים לָכֶם
מַהְבִּלִים הֵמָּה אֶתְכֶם
חֲזוֹן לִבָּם יְדַבֵּרוּ לֹא מִפִּי יְהוָה:

Thus says Yahweh Sabbaoth:
"Do not listen to the words of the prophets who prophesy to you;
they are *making vapor of* (הבל) you.
They speak visions of their own minds, not from the mouth of Yahweh."

The Hiphil stem of הבל, used here, is found in Mid. Heb. to mean "give

---

[64] Kraus, *Psalms 60–150*, 12, 15.

[65] So also Tate, *Psalms 51–100*, 121–22.

[66] Job elsewhere accuses the friends of speaking lies (e.g., 13:4). Habel translates מָעַל here as "perfidy" (*Job*, 330; cf. Robert Gordis, *The Book of God and Man: A Study of Job* [Chicago: University of Chicago Press, 1965], 236). Gerald Janzen agrees and further speculates whether the use of *hebel* here suggests an idolatry or false religion on the part of the friends (*Job* [IBC; Atlanta: John Knox, 1985], 155, 157).

off steam" (e.g., *Šabb.* 17b). The direct object marker here supports an image of the false prophets making their audience to give off *hebel* or to become *hebel*. In either case, the idea is probably that these false diviners create an illusion with regard to knowledge, that they deceive the minds of their audience.[67] This is indicated by the extensions "visions of their own minds," and "not from the mouth of Yahweh" which describe the speech of these prophets.

A final example of deceiving words occurs in Zech 10:1–2:

שַׁאֲלוּ מֵיְהוָה מָטָר בְּעֵת מַלְקוֹשׁ

יְהוָה עֹשֶׂה חֲזִיזִים וּמְטַר־גֶּשֶׁם

יִתֵּן לָהֶם לְאִישׁ עֵשֶׂב בַּשָּׂדֶה:

כִּי הַתְּרָפִים דִּבְּרוּ־אָוֶן

וְהַקּוֹסְמִים חָזוּ שֶׁקֶר

וַחֲלֹמוֹת הַשָּׁוְא יְדַבֵּרוּ

הֶבֶל יְנַחֵמוּן

עַל־כֵּן נָסְעוּ כְמוֹ־צֹאן

יַעֲנוּ כִּי־אֵין רֹעֶה:

Ask from Yahweh rain in the season of the spring rain,
Yahweh maker of the storm clouds and showers of rain,
Who gives to every one the vegetation in the field.
For the teraphim speak deceit (אָוֶן),
And the diviners prophesy[68] lies (שֶׁקֶר);
False dreams (חֲלֹמוֹת הַשָּׁוְא) they tell,
Vapor (*hebel*) they console (נחם).
Therefore they wander like sheep;
They suffer for lack of a shepherd.

Here terms indicating falsehood and deceit (אָוֶן, שֶׁקֶר) and one hendiadys (false dreams) are used as synonyms of *hebel*. They describe the failure the oracle's audience is experiencing from the sources of help they thought would assist them. As with Job's friends (Job 21:34, above), these diviners console (נחם) through messages (S) which are of no help or comfort (cf. Isa 40:1–2).[69]

---

[67] *HALOT*, s.v. הבל. Cf. Arab. *habla*, "to make a fool of." In contrast to Jer 2:5, where it is described how the people "went after" *hebel* and became the same (הבל Qal), here the activity of the prophets is said to cause this to happen. William L. Holladay translates, "filling you as they do with nothingness" (*Jeremiah 1* [ed. Paul Hanson; Hermeneia; Philadelphia: Fortress, 1986], 634–35). For לֵב (heart) in the sense of "mind," cf. Jer 5:21; 7:31.

[68] In prophetic material, חזה is often equivalent to נבא, "to prophesy"; cf. Isa 2:1; 13:1; Amos 1:1; Mic 1:1; Hab 1:1.

[69] Meyers and Meyers are correct that here and in Job 21:34 *hebel* is used adverbially. That is, *hebel* does not represent the content of consolation but indicates its effectiveness

Transience (4x)

In four texts, *hebel* is used with a referent of "short duration." The nuance here is not that of pretense. Rather, it indicates something which is unquestionably present but only for a brief time: in three cases the duration of human life, in the fourth, the swiftness of God's judgment.

Ps 39:6, 12 [Eng. vv. 5, 11]. In Psalm 39:5–7a [Eng. vv. 4–6a], the psalmist guards *hebel* with synonyms which make this clear:

הוֹדִיעֵנִי יְהוָה קִצִּי וּמִדַּת יָמַי מַה־הִיא

אֵדְעָה מֶה־חָדֵל אָנִי׃

הִנֵּה טְפָחוֹת נָתַתָּה יָמַי

וְחֶלְדִּי כְאַיִן נֶגְדֶּךָ

אַךְ כָּ<>הֶבֶל[70] כָּל־אָדָם נִצָּב סֶלָה׃

אַךְ־בְּצֶלֶם יִתְהַלֶּךְ־אִישׁ

Make known to me, O Yahweh, my end, what is the measure of my days.
Let me know how fleeting (חָדֵל) I am.
Behold, you have made my days handbreadths (טְפָחוֹת),
And my lifetime is as nothing (אַיִן) before you.
Surely <as> a *vapor* (*hebel*) every human stands.[71] Selah.
Surely as an image (צֶלֶם) every person walks about.[72]

The focus of interest is introduced by the request to "make known my end . . . the measure of my days" (v. 5). The quality of human existence is the subject for *hebel*, and its referent is guarded by three terms/phrases: חָדֵל (fleeting), טְפָחוֹת (handbreadths of days),[73] and "lifetime (חֶלֶד) as nothing

---

(Carol L. Meyers and Eric M. Meyers, *Zechariah 9–14* [AB 25C; New York: Doubleday, 1993], 191–92). It is consolation done in a fruitless and deceptive way.

[70] Emending, to read with the Syriac, from כל־הבל to כהבל. Several MT MSS omit both כ and ל here (Craigie, *Psalms 1–50*, 307, cites de Rossi, IV, 27). In such texts, the initial כ of original כהבל may have been elided through haplography.

[71] This is similar to the translation of Craigie, *Psalms 1–50*, 306.

[72] Kraus translates (6c–7a), "Only like a breath [reading כהבל with Syr.] does every person stand upright, only like the specter of a dream does one walk along" (*Psalms 1–59*, 415). As with the above translation, he understands סלה (omitted by many Syr. MSS) to be misplaced. The dream allusion is similar to imagery in Ps 73:20 and in an Egyptian text: "The time a person spends on earth is only a vision in a dream" (Adolf Erman, *Die Religion der Ägypter* [Berlin: Walter de Gruyter, 1934], 238–39, cited by Kraus, ibid., 418). The use of צֶלֶם in Ps 73:20, in terms of dream phantoms that disappear upon waking, has motivated proposals for a צֶלֶם II, meaning "shadow." In any case, vv. 5–6 suggest that transience is indicated.

[73] Although the term is a *hapax legomenon*, the sense of טְפָחוֹת is suggested by the terms טֶפַח and טֹפַח, both of which mean "handbreadth."

(כָּאַיִן)."[74] Human life is transient, and yet the element of insubstantiality is also involved, as guarded by צֶלֶם "image" in v. 7a [Eng. v. 6a].

Later in Ps 39 we find (v. 12 [Eng. v. 11]):

בְּתוֹכָחוֹת עַל־עָוֹן יִסַּרְתָּ אִישׁ
וַתֶּמֶס כָּעָשׁ חֲמוּדוֹ
אַךְ הֶבֶל כָּל־אָדָם סֶלָה:

> In punishment for sin you chastise mortals
> And consume what is dear to them like a moth.
> Surely every human is *vapor* (*hebel*). Selah.

Most centrally, v. 12 [Eng. v. 11] concerns chastisement and punishment. However, the broader scope of this portion of the psalm (vv. 8–14 [Eng. vv. 7–13]) emphasizes both the insubstantiality and the transience of human beings. Verse 8 [Eng. v. 7] expresses the psalmist's needful trust (בטח) in Yahweh, and v. 11 [Eng. v. 10] describes the speaker as being "spent" (כלה) by the afflictions Yahweh has brought. Yahweh's consumption of that which is dear to mortals (v. 12 [Eng. v. 11]) also suggests the frail nature of humanity.

It is possible that *hebel* in v. 12 [Eng. v. 11] may serve as "Janus parallelism." It looks back to the emphasis on human *frailty* (insubstantiality) in vv. 8–11 [Eng. vv. 7–10], but looks forward to the comment on human *brevity* (transience) in vv. 13–14 [Eng. vv. 12–13], a renewal of the theme in vv. 5–7a [Eng. vv. 4–6a] where *hebel* indicates shortness of time. Two related but distinguishable qualities of *hebel* enable it to play such a role.[75]

Ps 144:4; 78:33. In Ps 144:4, *hebel* likewise has a referent of transience. Verse 3 of this lament psalm uses a rhetorical question to exclaim concerning human insignificance,

יְהוָה מָה־אָדָם וַתֵּדָעֵהוּ
בֶּן־אֱנוֹשׁ וַתְּחַשְּׁבֵהוּ:

> O Yahweh, what are humans that you take notice of them,
> Or human offspring that you think of them?

Then v. 4 more specifically emphasizes human transience:

אָדָם לַהֶבֶל דָּמָה
יָמָיו כְּצֵל עוֹבֵר:

---

[74] For other proposed examples of חֶלֶד meaning "lifetime" (which require emendations), see Ps 89:48; Job 10:12, 20; 11:17.

[75] In the psalm's final two verses, the speaker's self-description is as a stranger (גֵּר) and a "sojourner (תּוֹשָׁב) like all my ancestors," terms which indicate somewhat tenuous residency. God is then urged in v. 14 [Eng. v. 13] to turn away from chastisement, "before I go and am no more" (אֵינֶנּוּ).

Humans are like a *vapor* (*hebel*);
Their days are as a passing shadow (צֵל).

The psalmist continues to appeal that Yahweh come to the rescue, and emphasizes the duress of a precarious situation, before making promises to praise God. The "passing shadow" simile suggests brevity of time; the days of mortals pass quickly. However, the parallelism in v. 4 is not quite synonymous. It is mortals themselves who are like (דָּמָה) *vapor* (*hebel*), not their days. The rhetorical questions of v. 3 reflect the emphasis of the context more generally, which belittles human strength in comparison to God's ability to give strength in battle. Thus, once again the referent for *hebel* combines both transience and insubstantiality.[76]

Psalm 78 recounts both the faithfulness of God and the waywardness of Israel throughout its history. Although God was faithful, "they still sinned, despite his wonders they did not believe" (Ps 78:32). The text then continues (v. 33):

וַיְכַל־בַּהֶבֶל יְמֵיהֶם
וּשְׁנוֹתָם בַּבֶּהָלָה:

So he made their days vanish in a *vapor* (בַּהֶבֶל),
And their years in sudden terror (בַּבֶּהָלָה).

The subject here is God's judgment on human lives (their days). Translators have taken various approaches to the metaphoric intention of the first of these cola. The NRSV offers, "He made their days vanish like a vapor,"[77] although elsewhere *hebel*'s use in a simile does not employ the preposition בְּ, and the referent for *hebel* remains unexplained.[78] Other translations have reflected a meaning of futility (so NIV) or emptiness (REB).

However, there is reason for understanding *hebel* here as communicating something which rapidly transpired.[79] While the biblical texts are somewhat

---

[76] The term צֵל itself may be used with either of these referents. Cf. 1 Chr 29:15, where the simile "our days on earth are like a shadow" is clarified by the statement "we are sojourners" (גֵּרִים). In Job 17:7, Job complains, "My eye has also grown dim because of grief, and all my members are as a shadow" (or "have wasted like a shadow"; see commentaries on textual issues).

[77] So also Weiser, *Psalms*, 535.

[78] Psalm 144:4 employs the verb דָּמָה ("be like, resemble"), Ps 39:6 [Eng. v. 5] (emended) has בְּ.

[79] NAB: "he quickly ended their days." H.-J. Kraus reads for 78:33, "Then he let their days vanish into nothing, their years into terrors" (*Psalms 60–150*, 120). Tate translates, "And so he ended their days in a breath, and their years in sudden calamity" (*Psalms 51–100*, 279).

inconclusive,[80] it is evident from use of בֶּהָלָה elsewhere that it indicates a terror which happens suddenly.[81] Because *hebel* may also refer to a short duration of time, and there is a similarity of sound between בַּהֶבֶל and בֶּבֶּהָלָה, this pair was a good choice for the poet in Ps 78:33.[82] It seems that *hebel* is adverbial in v. 33a, indicating shortness of time, and v. 33b builds upon it by adding the element of destruction. The potential for *hebel* to refer to noxious, life-threatening vapor makes the combination of these two terms even more apt.[83]

Stock Metaphor (14x + 2 verbs)

In texts previously discussed (Job 21:34; Zech 10:2; and Jer 23:16 with the verb), the words of certain diviners were declared to be *hebel* in the sense of being deceptive. We turn now to a group of texts which also concern deception. However, it is evident that, essentially, in these contexts *hebel* is being used idiomatically, that is, as a "stock metaphor."

The subject is "foreign gods," that is, divinities other than Israel's Yahweh. Most often in these texts, *hebel* is used in the plural, the only biblical texts except for Ecclesiastes in which the plural is used.[84] Though in poetic texts the equivalent of guarding terms are present, it is clear from other texts that no guarding terms are needed. Yet in nearly every context there are sufficient clues that deities are being indicated. Out of fourteen examples, four are found in the Deuteronomistic writings and eight in the prophet Jeremiah.

In some cases, then, there is no referent because there is no metaphor. Using the term *hebel* is simply equivalent to saying "foreign deities." However, as I. A. Richards points out, even "stone dead" metaphors can be easily awoken.[85] When guarding elements are used in the contexts now to be considered, they involve matters of unreliability and falsehood, making this section a fitting corollary to the previous discussions of *hebel*'s insubstantiality and deception dimensions.

1 Kgs 16:13, 26; Jer 14:22. Three texts represent the clearest examples of *hebel* as stock metaphor. In 1 Kgs 16:26, the narrator comments on the

---

[80] Lev 26:16, Jer 15:8, and Isa 65:23.

[81] See Jastrow 1:142.

[82] So notes Tate, *Psalms 51–100*, 282. Though the similarity of ב and כ make an emendation to כהבל (like a vapor) plausible, LXX and Vulg. support MT. This is an unusual use of בְּ and may have been chosen for euphony.

[83] The context in Ps 78 is one of destructive judgment. Note the first phrase of v. 34, "When [God] slew them."

[84] Although in six cases the word *hebel* is used in the singular for this stock metaphor, every context is concerned with multiple deities.

[85] He cites as examples the phrase "strong light" to indicate intensity, and "cloud" to indicate confusion (Richards, *Philosophy*, 101–2).

extent of Omri's wickedness:

וַיֵּלֶךְ בְּכָל־דֶּרֶךְ יָרָבְעָם בֶּן־נְבָט
וּבְחַטֹּאתָיו אֲשֶׁר הֶחֱטִיא אֶת־יִשְׂרָאֵל
לְהַכְעִיס אֶת־יְהוָה אֱלֹהֵי יִשְׂרָאֵל בְּהַבְלֵיהֶם׃

He walked in all the way of Jeroboam son of Nebat,
and in his sins that he caused Israel to commit,
provoking (כעס) Yahweh, the God of Israel, by their *vapors* (הַבְלֵיהֶם).

This "provoking" (כעס) of Yahweh to irritation by worship of these gods is a frequent part of the idiom, as also in 1 Kgs 16:13. Another example of this pattern with *hebel* is found at Jer 14:22:

הֲיֵשׁ בְּהַבְלֵי הַגּוֹיִם מַגְשִׁמִים
וְאִם־הַשָּׁמַיִם יִתְּנוּ רְבִבִים
הֲלֹא אַתָּה־הוּא יְהוָה אֱלֹהֵינוּ
וּנְקַוֶּה־לָּךְ כִּי־אַתָּה עָשִׂיתָ אֶת־כָּל־אֵלֶּה׃

Are there among the *vapors* (הַבְלֵי) of the nations rain-givers?
Or can the heavens (הַשָּׁמַיִם) give showers? (רְבִבִים)
Is it not you, O Yahweh our God?
We set our hope on you, for it is you who did all these.[86]

In this text, the "*hebel*'s of the nations" (הַבְלֵי הַגּוֹיִם) are contrasted with Yahweh who is the true rain-giver. Although the nations seek out their various gods for rain, only Yahweh who made the heavens is a legitimate source of hope.[87]

Deut 32:21; Jer 8:19; 10:3, 8, 15; 51:18. In several texts, poetic parallelism demonstrates that deities are indicated, and guarding terms begin to revive the *hebel*-metaphor. For example, in Deut 32:21, Moses' poetic testament, Moses quotes Yahweh as follows:

הֵם קִנְאוּנִי בְלֹא־אֵל
כִּעֲסוּנִי בְּהַבְלֵיהֶם
וַאֲנִי אַקְנִיאֵם בְּלֹא־עָם
בְּגוֹי נָבָל אַכְעִיסֵם׃

---

[86] William Holladay would change the pointing of אֵלֶּה (these) to אָלָה (curse, i.e., the drought) in light of the apparent confusion between these two reflected in MT and the versions at Jer 2:34; 4:12; and 5:25. He acknowledges that the MT of 14:22 makes sense, with "these" as a reference to the rain (*Jeremiah 1*, 439). However, it could also refer to the various indications of judgment all around (14:17–21).

[87] For example, in the Ugaritic legend of Aqhat, Baal withholds the rain so that the crops fail, 19.39–49 (J. C. L. Gibson, *Canaanite Myths and Legends* [2d ed.; Edinburgh: T & T Clark, 1977], 114–15).

They made me jealous with what is no god,
Provoked (כעס) me with their *vapors* (הַבְלֵיהֶם).
So I will make them jealous with what is no people,
Provoke (כעס) them with a foolish nation (גּוֹי נָבָל).

Just as the people worshiped "no god," so Yahweh will get their attention with "no people"; just as they provoked him with their false deities, so Yahweh will provoke them with a "foolish" nation. The parallelism of the first two cola indicates that הַבְלֵיהֶם designates false gods, while the parallelism between the first pair of cola and the second pair emphasizes the deceptive character of these objects of worship by comparing them to a nation which is of no substance.[88]

In Jer 10:1–16 (10:15=51:18; cf. 8:19), a passage mocking idols which is similar to passages in Second Isaiah (e.g., Isa 44:9–20), *hebel* occurs three times.[89] From the term פֶּסֶל (v. 14) it is evident that *hebel* makes reference to improper objects of worship. Jeremiah goes on to use a variety of terms to ridicule these gods, calling them stupid (בער) and foolish (כסל), saying their instruction is wood, and calling them a work of delusion (תעתע).[90] These terms recall the insubstantiality of vapor. Jeremiah 10:15 (=51:18) particularly emphasizes the deceptive nature of these deities, using שֶׁקֶר as a synonym, and (the lack of) רוּחַ as a contrary.[91]

Jer 16:19; Jonah 2:9 [Eng. v. 8]; Ps 31:7 [Eng. v. 6]. Some additional texts use terms which emphasize the deception as well as the unreliability of these deities. For example, Jer 16:19 reads:

יְהוָה עֻזִּי וּמָעֻזִּי וּמְנוּסִי בְּיוֹם צָרָה
אֵלֶיךָ גּוֹיִם יָבֹאוּ מֵאַפְסֵי־אָרֶץ וְיֹאמְרוּ
אַךְ־שֶׁקֶר נָחֲלוּ אֲבוֹתֵינוּ
הֶבֶל וְאֵין־בָּם מוֹעִיל:

O Yahweh, my strength and my stronghold,
　　my refuge in the day of trouble,
to you shall the nations come from the ends of the earth and say:
Nothing but falsehood (שֶׁקֶר) have our ancestors inherited,
vapor (הֶבֶל) in which there is no profit (מוֹעִיל)."

---

[88] The adj. נָבָל suggests religious and moral insensibility and not simply a deficiency of the intellect.

[89] Jer 51:15–19 duplicates 10:12–16.

[90] The order of the material in Jer 10:1–16 varies among the MT, LXX, 4QJer[a], and 4QJer[b]. On the basis of its style and content, it appears to be a secondary addition to the material in chs. 8–10. Scholars are divided whether or not to ascribe it to Jeremiah. See discussion in Holladay, *Jeremiah 1*, 322–37.

[91] In an interesting play on words, the images are said to have "no breath (רוּחַ)" in

The unreliability of these gods is established through the contrary מֹועִיל (no profit), while the deception element is communicated by the synonym שֶׁקֶר (falsehood). That deities are being discussed here is established by the description in v. 19a of the nations coming "to you (Yahweh)," and by the following verse (v. 20) which flatly declares, "They are not gods!"[92]

In both Jonah 2:9 [Eng. v. 8] and Ps 31:7 [Eng. v. 6], prayers of thanksgiving and lament respectively, *hebel* occurs in construct with שָׁוְא (falsehood; cf. Zech 10:2). The context in each case declares that a choice for Yahweh is a choice against "vapors of falsehood" (הַבְלֵי־שָׁוְא), so that *hebel*'s reference to other deities is unmistakable. Also in both texts, key words of religious loyalty are used, such as שׁמר (to revere) and בטח (to trust).

According to H. W. Wolff, "The construct chain הבלי־שׁוא intensifies the meaning of the individual, almost synonymous nouns into a powerful superlative." He translates as "unfounded Nothingness."[93] J. M. Sasson, however, treats it not as a superlative, nor as a hendiadys (so some of the ancient versions).[94] Rather he suggests it is analogous to an adjective in plural construct state before the noun it modifies. Therefore, he translates the phrase in Jonah 2:9 with the expression "empty faiths": "They who hold to empty faiths, give up their hope for mercy."[95]

Craigie notes that Ps 31 has significant formulaic similarity with Jonah 2 and Jeremiah.[96] In this prayer of thanksgiving, the psalmist declares, "I have hated those who worship (שׁמר) *vapors* of falsehood (הַבְלֵי־שָׁוְא), but I have trusted (בטח) in Yahweh." Thus, through this construction, the deceptive, illusory dimension of *hebel* is drawn upon.

2 Kgs 17:15; Jer 2:5. Two texts demonstrate even more clearly that, even when used in an idiom, the metaphorical dimension of *hebel* can be easily revived.[97] In 2 Kgs 17:15 the narrator states,

---

them; they are *hebel* (vapor, breath)!

[92] Cf. Page Kelley, in Peter C. Craigie, Page H. Kelley, and Joel F. Drinkard, Jr., *Jeremiah 1–25* [WBC 26; Dallas, Tex.: Word, 1991), 218.

[93] Hans Walter Wolff, *Obadiah and Jonah* (trans. Margaret Kohl; CC; Minneapolis: Augsburg, 1986 [1977]), 126, 137–38. So James Limburg, "worthless idols" (*Jonah: A Commentary* [OTL; Louisville: Westminster/John Knox, 1993], 64, 69). Likewise Paul Joüon and Takamitsu Muraoka, *A Grammar of Biblical Hebrew* (2d ed., SubBi 14; Rome: Pontifical Institute, 1991), §141m. For a discussion of שָׁוְא, see *HALOT* 4:1425 and the literature cited there.

[94] J. M. Sasson, *Jonah* (AB 24B; New York: Doubleday, 1990), 196–98.

[95] Ibid., 160. He defends the word "faith" as a better modern equivalent than "worship of idols."

[96] *Psalms 1–50*, 259–60.

[97] See Richards, *Philosophy*, 101–2, and n. 85 above.

וַיִּמְאֲסוּ אֶת־חֻקָּיו
וְאֶת־בְּרִיתוֹ אֲשֶׁר כָּרַת אֶת־אֲבוֹתָם
וְאֵת עֵדְוֹתָיו אֲשֶׁר הֵעִיד בָּם
וַיֵּלְכוּ אַחֲרֵי הַהֶבֶל וַיֶּהְבָּלוּ
וְאַחֲרֵי הַגּוֹיִם אֲשֶׁר סְבִיבֹתָם
אֲשֶׁר צִוָּה יְהוָה אֹתָם לְבִלְתִּי עֲשׂוֹת כָּהֶם:

They despised [Yahweh's] statutes,
and his covenant that he made with their ancestors,
and the testimonies that he testified against them.
They went after *vapor* (הֶבֶל) and *became vapor* (הבל),
and (went) after the nations that were around them,
concerning whom Yahweh had commanded them not to do as they (did).

The context demonstrates that illicit worship is being described. The following verse (2 Kgs 17:16) refers specifically to molten images, an Asherah pole, and the worship of Baal. The play on words in v. 15 between the term *hebel* (singular) and the corresponding verbal use of the same root (הבל) requires that the reader be alert to additional connotations of *hebel*.[98]

The *hebel*-phrase in 2 Kgs 17:15 is similar to that found in Jer 2:5 and may have been borrowed from Jeremiah.[99] It is not being claimed here that the people pursued other gods and became gods. Rather, they "went after" (gave allegiance to[100]) false gods and became false themselves. That is, they either became deceived or perhaps became empty with regard to the truth of Yahweh's instructions.[101]

In sum, the use of *hebel* as an appellative for false gods is found in Dtr and Jeremiah, writings whose kindred vocabulary has long been recognized.[102] It is also found in Jonah 2 and Ps 31, writings which exhibit formulaic language in common with each other and also with Jeremiah. The way the term

---

[98] Cogan and Tadmor translate, "they went after emptiness and became empty themselves" (Mordechai Cogan and Hayim Tadmor, *II Kings* [AB 11; New York: Doubleday, 1988], 203).

[99] Holladay, *Jeremiah 1*, 86. Bright suggests that הַהֶבֶל is chosen as a pun on הַבַּעַל "Baal" (John Bright, *Jeremiah* [AB 21; Garden City, N.Y.: Doubleday, 1965], 15).

[100] The phrase "to go after" (הלך + אחרי) may also used of allegiance to humans, e.g., in 1 Sam 17:13 (Saul) and Judg 9:49 (Abimelech).

[101] Note that earlier in this context (17:12), הַגִּלֻּלִים is used for idols and Israel is said to have "served" them. A number of Israel's problems are described here, and it is possible that going after *vapors* may refer quite broadly to the other nations they copied, the ways of living they adopted, in addition to service of foreign gods. So John Gray (*I & II Kings* [OTL; Philadelphia: Westminster, 1963], 589). This "going after *hebel*" is associated with Israel's rejection of Yahweh, but also of the covenant, the statutes, the prophetic warnings, and so on.

[102] Cf. William Holladay's proposed explanation for this, *Jeremiah 1*, 1–2.

is used suggests it had become a "stock metaphor" in these contexts, yet the metaphoric dimension of *hebel* is sometimes developed, particularly in regard to unreliability and deception.

Summary of Hebrew Bible Metaphors

This overview of *hebel* as metaphor in the HB, which includes all its occurrences there apart from Ecclesiastes and the name "Abel," has demonstrated referents of *hebel* which are related to its qualities of insubstantiality and transience. This includes particular meanings such as futility, error, unreliability, frailty, deception, brevity, and swiftness. In addition, several contexts gave indications of a negative moral evaluation associated with the word. The live metaphorical use of the term, then, has strong connections with its material sense. Finally, the term was found over a dozen times as a stock metaphor meaning "false gods." Yet even in these texts, the tropical use of the term was frequently revived.

Postbiblical Metaphor Texts

Ben Sira

Hebel occurs twice in the extant Hebrew texts of Ben Sira, both times as metaphor. The first occurrence has a referent of transience, while the second uses *hebel* to refer to false gods.

Sir 41:11. The Hebrew of this verse reads:

הבל אדם בגויתו
אך שם חסד לא יכרת[103]

The human body is a *vapor* (הבל),
but a faithful name will never be cut off.[104]

The interpretation of this verse is complicated by the homonyms חֶסֶד, "faithful," and חֶסֶד, "shame, disgrace." The LXX reads with the second of the two ("shame") and apparently takes the first word as אֵבֶל (πένθος "mourning") instead of *hebel*:

Πένθος ἀνθρώπων ἐν σώμασιν αὐτῶν,
ὄνομα δὲ ἁμαρτωλῶν οὐκ ἀγαθὸν ἐξαλειφθήσεται

---

[103] Following Geniza MS B which presents an unbroken text (Zeev Ben-Ḥayyim, ed., *The Book of Ben Sira: Text, Concordance and an Analysis of the Vocabulary* [The Historical Dictionary of the Hebrew Language; Jerusalem: The Academy of the Hebrew Language/The Shrine of the Book, 1973], 45).

[104] Cf. Skehan and Di Lella, *Ben Sira*, 465. Ben-Ḥayyim's *Book of Ben Sira* similarly interprets this use of חֶסֶד.

People grieve about their bodies,
but the bad name of sinners will be blotted out.

The context would seem to allow for this interpretation of the second colon.[105] However, the use of חָסֶד, meaning "shame," requires that the Hebrew text of the second colon must be read as a question: "Surely/However will not the shameful name be cut off?" Yet elsewhere, אַךְ is not used to begin a question.[106]

Thus, the text of Geniza MS B is to be preferred over LXX. As indicated by the contrary כרת (to cut off), *hebel* has an R value of transience. It provides a satisfying contrastive relationship between the two cola, and fits extremely well in its context, which is concerned with time and annihilation.[107] The human body (S) may be fleeting, but a trustworthy name will last forever.[108] Similar use of *hebel* for the human lifespan is found, e.g., in Pss 39:6 [Eng. v. 5] and 144:4.

Sir 49:2.

כי נחל על משובתינו
וישבת תועבות הבל[109]

For he [Josiah] sickened over our betrayals,
And caused the abominations of *vapor* (הבל) to cease.[110]

The LXX reads:

αὐτὸς κατευθύνθη ἐν ἐπιστροφῇ λαοῦ
καὶ ἐξῆρεν βδελύγματα ἀνομίας·

He was led aright in converting the people,
and took away the abominations of iniquity (RSV).

---

[105] The preceding verse (41:10) states that whatever comes from nothing returns to the same, likewise the ungodly (see commentaries on textual issues). 41:12 urges the reader to have respect for their name more than precious treasure.

[106] Skehan/Di Lella read the אַךְ as antithetic (*Ben Sira*, 465).

[107] Sir 41:12–13 reads:
Take care of your name, for it will remain for you
more than thousands of precious treasures;
The good things of life last but for a few days,
but a good name, for days without number.
Cf. Skehan/Di Lella, *Ben Sira*, 465.

[108] Cf. Sir 41:9–10; Prov 10:7.

[109] Found in Geniza MS B only (Ben-Ḥayyim, *Book of Ben Sira*, 61).

[110] A translation similar to that of Skehan/Di Lella, *Ben Sira*, 540.

Skehan/Di Lella consider נחל to be a by-form of נֶחֱלָה ("infirmity"; cf. Amos 6:6), and comment that LXX and Syr. appear to have been confused by it in their rendering of the colon.[111] Josiah's "sickening," or grieving, is a reference to his tearing his garments upon hearing the Law read (2 Kgs 22:10–13, 19). Second Kings 23:1–19 recounts Josiah's iconoclasm. It appears that Ben Sira has employed the Deuteronomistic usage of *hebel* to refer to false gods (cf. 1 Kgs 16:13, 26), though it is not employed in relation to Josiah in the biblical text. Ben Sira praises Josiah for removing these from the worship life of his kingdom.

Rabbinic Writings

The metaphoric use of *hebel* is also evident in the rabbinic writings. A few examples will suffice to illustrate this. In *B. Bat.* 16b and *Ketub.* 10b, *hebel* is used metaphorically in the phrase "console (נחם) *hebel*" to mean the giving of unreliable or ineffective consolation, a referent related to insubstantiality.[112] This is likely an allusion to Zech 10:2 and/or Job 21:34 which contain the same phrase.[113]

In *Lev. Rab.* sec. 29, Rabbi Naḥman's explanation concerning "all the *hebel*'s and falsehoods (כזבים) which the children of Abraham our father commit," suggests not so much deception as moral emptiness (insubstantiality), falling short of God's standards.[114] Similarly, in a commentary on Eccl 11:10, "youth and the prime of life are *hebel*" is understood to refer to the shameful and immoral deeds of youth (*Šabb.* 152a).

In summary, the rabbinic writings evidence a metaphorical usage similar to that found in the biblical materials, with heightening of the moral dimension.

Qumran

In the nonbiblical material from Qumran, *hebel* is found ten times, all of which are metaphorical.

1QS 5:18–19. This text from the *Rule of the Community* urges that no holy persons should obtain gain for themselves from any "deed of *vapor*" (מעשי הבל) by a person who is not part of the covenant. The end of line 19 explains that "all his deeds are uncleanness (נדה)." Thus, the referent for *hebel* here appears to involve unrighteousness (moral insubstantiality). Line 19 also

---

[111] Ibid., 540–41. Perhaps LXX and Syr. were reading נהל "to guide."

[112] *Ketub.* 10b, "Consolations of vapor he consoled him," תנחומים של הבל ניחמו.

[113] On these texts, see discussion above. "Console *hebel*" is used in *B. Bat.* 16b to rebuke the comment that a baby daughter is as wonderful as a son (cf. *Ketub.* 10b).

[114] Rabbi Naḥman claims that Abraham is nevertheless sufficiently worthy to atone for all these indiscretions (Slotki, *Midrash Rabbah: Leviticus*, 375).

declares, as a reason for the above exhortation, that *"vapor* are all those who do not know his covenant" (כיא הבל כול אשר לוא ידעו את בריתו).[115] This "not knowing" the covenant suggests a referent of ignorance (insubstantiality of mind), undoubtedly involving a moral dimension.

1QM 4:12; 6:6; 9:9; 11:9; 14:12. The phrase גוי הבל ("nation of *vapor"*) is used five times in the *War Scroll* of enemy nations.[116] It appears, since no explanation or contextual clues are given, that it is used as a stock metaphor in this work, analogous to the biblical use of *hebel* to refer to false gods. As with several of those examples, these employ *hebel* in construct relation; however here, as with Sir 49:2, *hebel* is the term in the absolute state.

An additional, broken text, 1QM 14:12, has the following:

וכול יקום[117] הבלי[]   יין[
ואנו עם קודשכה במעשי אמתכה נהללה שמכה

The second half of the line is clear and may be translated as follows:

And/But we, your holy people, for the deeds of your truth
will praise your name. . . .

Unfortunately, the first half of the line is broken and difficult at one place. Yadin fills the lacuna as follows, הבלי[הם יהיו כא]יין, and translates: "All their creatures[118] of vanity [shall be as] nothing." If Yadin is correct in filling the lacuna, the author appears to be making a pun. God will take their *hebel*

---

[115] James H. Charlesworth, ed., *Rule of the Community and Related Documents* (The Dead Sea Scrolls, vol. 1; Tübingen: Mohr/Siebeck; Louisville: Westminster/John Knox, 1994), 22–23; Millar Burrows, ed., *The Dead Sea Scrolls of St. Mark's Monastery*, vol. 2 (New Haven: American Schools of Oriental Research, 1951), pl. v; Florentino García Martínez, *The Dead Sea Scrolls Translated* (trans. Wilfred G. E. Watson; Leiden: Brill, 1994), 9.

[116] These are as follows: 1QM 4:12, on one of the banners is written: "God's destruction of all *futile* nations"; 1QM 6:6, in reference to God's judgment, "to pay the reward of their badness towards all the nations of *futility"*; 1QM 9:9, "the blood of *futile* nations," a warning to the priests not to be defiled by foreign dead soldiers from battle; and 1QM 11:9, "the seven nations of *futility*," Israel's enemies, also called the "hordes of Belial" (the translations are those of Martínez, *Dead Sea Scrolls Translated*, 98–104, emph. added).

[117] The space between יקום and הבלי] is due to a fault in the leather (Yigael Yadin, ed., *The Scroll of the War of the Sons of Light Against the Sons of Darkness* [trans. Batya Rabin and Chaim Rabin; Oxford: Oxford University Press, 1962], 328).

[118] The term יקום "creatures" is a rare one. It occurs elsewhere at Gen 7:4, 23; Deut 11:6; 1QM 15:11. In the biblical examples (not in construct, but with כל in each case), it refers first to the living creatures destroyed in the flood, and second to the lost livestock of Dathan and Abiram. In 1QM 15:11, it is in construct, again accompanied by "all" (כול).

livestock and make them disappear, a referent of insubstantiality and/or transience for *hebel*. However, it is doubtful there is enough space in the MS to allow for all the letters Yadin proposes.[119] Other conjectures are possible.[120] The broken text leaves the role of *hebel* here uncertain.

4Q184 1:1–2. In 4QWiles 1:1–2 (4Q184, *Wiles of the Wicked Woman*) is an allegorical text possibly inspired by Prov 7. Seductive speech is a very important part of the harlot's character. The first two lines are as follows:

הזונ]ה תוציא הבל ובן   ]א תועות
תשחר תמידן ל]שנן דברי]ה
וקלס תחל]י]ק והליץ יחד בש]וא]
עול לבה יכין פחוז וכליותיה מקן

[The harl]ot utters *vapor* (הבל), and [. . .] errors.
She seeks continually [to] sharpen [her] words, [. . .]
she mockingly flatters and with emp[tiness]
    to bring altogether into derision.
Her heart's perversion prepares wantonness, and her emotions [. . .][121]

The words of her mouth (S) are associated with the following: *hebel*, "mock flattery" (קלס + חלק), and "falsehood" (שׁוא). These synonyms suggest that *hebel* is used here of speech which is insubstantial and worthless, but that it also has a negative moral aspect, especially since she is characterized with perversion of heart and wantonness.

1QH 7:32. In the *Hymn Scroll* of praise and thanksgiving is a line which recalls Ps 94:11. In the midst of celebrating Adonai's willingness to discipline and forgive, the author contrasts the eternal God with mortals:

ומה הוא איש תהו ובעל הבל
להתבונן במעשי פלאך [גדו]ל]י]ם

---

[119] Yadin, *Scroll of the War*, 328–29.

[120] The plural הבלים or a plural construct might be considered. The reconstruction of the 3d person pl. suffix is suggested by the pattern of statements which precede this one ("their mighty ones," "their swift ones," "their nobles"). In addition, the other occurrence of יקום in the DSS, 1QM 15:11, has, יקום הוותם "their creatures of calamity." Jean Duhaime proposes הבליהם and כאין at 14:12, but makes no conjecture for any letters between these (James H. Charlesworth, ed., *Damascus Document, War Scroll, and Related Documents* (The Dead Sea Scrolls; vol. 2; Tübingen: Mohr/Siebeck; Louisville: Westminster/John Knox, 1995), 126–27. Martínez translates, "All their useless existence [you have turned into] nothing" (*Dead Sea Scrolls Translated*, 109). Perhaps the unrighteous activities of the "nations of *vapor* (*hebel*)" being discussed here are placed in contrast to God's "deeds of truth," to guard a referent for *hebel* of either insubstantiality or transience.

[121] Reconstruction and translation according to John M. Allegro, *Qumrân Cave 4* (vol. 1; DJD 5; Oxford: Clarendon, 1968), 82–84; idem, "'The Wiles of the Wicked Woman': A

And what is an empty (תהו) mortal, and a master of *vapor* (הבל),
to understand your [great] wondrous deeds?[122]

As in Isa 49:4, the term תהו (emptiness) is used as a synonym for *hebel*. The context includes a reference to comprehension (בין), to indicate that the referent in this case is insubstantiality applied to the mind.

4Q511 15:5. One additional Qumran text may be mentioned briefly. 4Q511 (4QShir^b) 15:5 is a fragment which includes the phrase רוחי הבלים, "spirits/winds of *vapors*."[123] Unfortunately there is not enough context to confirm the possibility that this is a hendiadys, or determine what its referent might be.

Summary of Postbiblical Metaphors

The occurrences of *hebel* in the postbiblical texts are relatively few, yet reflect a range of metaphoric use similar to that in the HB. The referents of *hebel* in the postbiblical texts may be summarized as follows:

Ben Sira: transient (human body); stock metaphor (false deities)
Rabbinic: unreliable (consolation); immorality (human deeds)
Qumran: immorality (human deeds); immoral and worthless (speech); uncomprehending (pagans, human condition); stock metaphor (pagan nations)

It is notable that *hebel* occurs with a negative moral dimension, just as there are hints of this in several biblical texts (Prov 13:11; 21:6; Ps 94:11; Zech 10:2). Also, a new stock metaphoric use was identified in the Qumran material: pagan nation.

CHAPTER SUMMARY AND CONCLUSIONS

The Material Sense of *Hebel*

This chapter has argued that the material sense of *hebel* is best designated by the term *vapor*: a quantity of visible matter diffused through or suspended in the air. Postbiblical texts evidence a range of contexts in which *hebel* may represent the following types of vapor: heat/steam, breath, vapor within a living being, vaporous perspiration, and noxious vapor. In two biblical texts, Isa 57:13 and Ps 62:10 [Eng. v. 9], *hebel*'s use in a parable is consistent with vapor, as is its tropical use throughout the Hebrew Bible.[124]

Sapiential Work from Qumran's Fourth Cave," *PEQ* 96 (1964): 53–55, pl. xiii.

[122] Text in Eleazar L. Sukenik, ed., *The Dead Sea Scrolls of the Hebrew University* (Jerusalem: Magnes, 1955), pl. 41; cf. Martínez, *Dead Sea Scrolls Translated*, 345.

[123] Maurice Baillet, *Qumrân Grotte 4* (vol. 3; DJD 7; Oxford: Clarendon, 1982), 229.

[124] For further summary of the information discussed in this chapter, see Appendix II.

The Metaphoric Senses of *Hebel*

Postbiblical texts—Ben Sira, Qumran, rabbinic—followed by texts in the Hebrew Bible apart from Ecclesiastes are listed according to *hebel*'s subjects.

Postbiblical Metaphor Texts[125]

Subjects of *hebel*	Insubstantial	Deception	Transient	Stock Metaphor	M-V	Texts
Consolation	unreliable					*B. Bat.* 16b; *Ketub.* 10b
Human Deeds	immoral					*Lev. Rab.* 29; *Šabb.* 152a; 1QS 5:18
Human Condition	uncompre-hending					1QH 7:32
Human Body			does not last			Sir 4:11
Words	worthless & immoral					4Q184 1:1–2
Pagans	uncompre-hending					1QS 5:19
Pagan Nations				stock met.		1QM 4:12; 6:6; 9:9; 11:9
Foreign Deities				stock met.		Sir 49:2

Hebrew Bible Metaphor Texts (5 verbs + 35 nouns)

Subject of *hbl* vb.	Insubstantial	Deception	Transient	Stock Metaphor	M-V	Texts
Words	error					Job 27:12
Trust in Wealth	misplaced					Ps 62:11[10]
Words of Prophets	ignorant					Jer 23:16
People (paranomasia with הֶבֶל noun)	become false like false gods					2 Kgs 17:15; Jer 2:5

---

[125] Texts from Ben Sira (2x) and Qumran (10x – 2 broken texts) are complete, but rabbinic texts are only representative.

Subjects of *hebel*	Insubstantial	Deception	Transient	Stock Metaphor	M-V	Texts
Labor	futile					Isa 49:4; Job 9:29
Obtaining Wealth	without effort					Prov 13:11
Wealth	unreliable					Ps 39:7[6]
Life of one getting wealth by deceit	spoiled		brief		x	Prov 21:6
Human Condition	spoiled					Job 7:16
Human Condition	frail		brief		x	Pss 144:4; 39:6,12[5,11]
Beauty		misrepresents				Prov 31:30
Thought or Speech	error					Ps 94:11; Job 35:16; 27:12
Words		fail to console				Job 21:34
Sources of Help	unreliable					Isa 57:13; Lam 4:17
Sources of Help		deficient				Isa 30:7; Ps 62:10a[9a]; 62:10b[9b]
Divination		fail to console				Zech 10:2
God's Judgment			swift			Ps 78:33
False Deities				strictly stock		1 Kgs 16:13, 26; Jer 14:22
False Deities				clues deities are involved		Deut 32:21; Jer 8:19
False Deities: paranomasia with הבל vb.				clues deities are involved		2 Kgs 17:15; Jer 2:5
False Deities				deception emphasis		Jer 10:15; 16:19; 51:18; Ps 31:7[6]; Jonah 2:9
False Deities				weakness emphasis		Jer 10:3, 8

Chapter 4

HEBEL AS SYMBOL IN ECCLESIASTES

The use of *hebel* in Ecclesiastes is consistently metaphoric. Employing the methodology introduced and demonstrated previously, this chapter explores the use of *hebel* in the MT of the book. After an introduction to *hebel*'s metaphorical uses in Ecclesiastes, the study begins with the first verses and proceeds subunit by subunit, giving attention to textual, grammatical, and vocabulary issues as necessary.[1] Qohelet provides guarding terms in nearly every context so that the subject (S) being discussed is predicated by *hebel* (the P term) with one or more referents (R values).[2] It is demonstrated that Qohelet draws primarily upon the following three qualities of *hebel*'s material sense which were identified in the previous chapter: insubstantiality, transience, and foulness.

The thesis defended here is that Qohelet incorporates the rich range of *hebel*'s metaphoric expressions into a tensive symbol to communicate that all of human experience is *hebel* in one way or another. Because of the care with

---

[1] The arrangement of the book's units and subunits presented here is, of course, not the only defensible one. The thesis argued for *hebel* in this study could be adapted to other understandings of the book's structure as well.

[2] The method of interpreting *hebel*'s metaphorical meaning employed in this study has similarities to the one offered by Graham Ogden (*Qoheleth*, 18). He lists three factors by which to ascertain the meaning of *hebel* in Ecclesiastes: (1) the painful scenarios [subjects] to which the *hebel*-phrase is added as a response; (2) the meaning of parallel and complementary phrases such as "striving after wind," a "sore affliction," and "an unhappy business" [guarding elements]; and (3) the positive exhortations to enjoyment, etc., which punctuate the book at key points. To these should be added the importance of (4) the framing statements in 1:2 and 12:8, as well as (5) the relationship between Qohelet's use of *hebel* and its uses in other literature.

which Qohelet guards *hebel* and constructs this symbol, it is likely that in the few sections where guarding terms are lacking, Qohelet is being intentionally ambiguous. This deliberate reference to all that *hebel* symbolizes, designated "omnivalency," is manifest in the opening and concluding announcements by Qohelet that "All is *hebel*." It occurs a few times elsewhere in the book as well. In several other cases, "multivalency" occurs, that is, when two or even three specific referents for *hebel* are guarded in the same context. For each pericope or larger unit, the number of times *hebel* occurs is given in parentheses. We begin with an overview of Qohelet's use of *hebel*.

THREE QUALITIES OF *HEBEL* IN ECCLESIASTES

Determining the Subject of *Hebel*

A method for working with metaphor depends upon the interpreter's ability to identify the primary metaphorical elements: subject, predicate, and guarding terms. Commentators of the book of Ecclesiastes have long recognized the difficulty of determining the subject of *hebel* in every case.[3] Sometimes Qohelet declares what is *hebel*, e.g., 11:10 youth and black hair. At other times there is consensus among interpreters as to the term's subject, e.g., 4:7–8 obsessive toil.

But other times there is uncertainty. Qohelet may say, "This is *hebel*," but the antecedent of the pronoun is unclear. Often guarding terms can be a great help, but we have already seen in Chapter 3 with texts outside of Ecclesiastes that there can nevertheless be doubt regarding *hebel*'s subject. As in that discussion, options and proposals will be summarized in this chapter whenever there is controversy.

Insubstantiality Referents

When Qohelet wants to highlight the insubstantiality aspect of *hebel*, he complements it with negated contrary terms such as יִתְרוֹן (advantage, benefit, 1:3), מוֹתָר (advantage, 3:19), יוֹתֵר (excess, 6:8, 11), כִּשְׁרוֹן (gain, 5:10 [Eng. 5:11]), and שׂבע (satisfaction, 1:8; 5:9 [Eng. 5:10]). In other cases, he associates it with such synonym terms as עָפָר (dust, 3:20) and חֲלֹמוֹת (dreams, 5:6 [Eng. 5:7]).

Especially important synonym phrases in this regard are רְעוּת רוּחַ and its variant רַעְיוֹן רוּחַ. These phrases occur eight times with *hebel* (1:14; 2:11, 17, 26; 4:4, 6; 6:9 and, for the latter, 4:16), once more without *hebel* (for the latter, 1:17), and once in the similar form שֶׁיַּעֲמֹל לָרוּחַ, "(one who) toils for wind" (5:15 [Eng. 5:16]).

---

[3] For example, Fox, *Time to Tear Down*, 36.

When Qohelet uses metaphors such as this to guard his metaphoric use of *hebel*, which he does on occasion, we should anticipate additional complexities. The term רוּחַ, when used metaphorically in the HB, has referents of both insubstantiality and transience (e.g., Isa 41:29; Hos 12:2 [Eng. v. 1]; Job 7:7; Ps 78:39). The terms רְעוּת and רַעְיוֹן, which appear in construct relation with רוּחַ only in Ecclesiastes, are less clear and have elicited several proposals.

The Vulgate reads, *universa vanitas et adflictio spiritus*, "all is vanity and distress of spirit," apparently assuming the root רעע (Heb. and Aram.) "to do harm."[4] For LXX it is τὰ πάντα ματαιότης καὶ προαίρεσις πνεύματος, "all is vanity and a choice of wind/spirit," a translation which does not require, but is suggestive of, a subjective genitive: the wind/spirit does the choosing. In this case, the phrase would imply whim or chance. This may be plausible for certain texts (e.g., 2:26), but for others it is unclear how they would be any more a matter of whim than others for which Qohelet does not use the phrase.

Some commentators have traced the terms רְעוּת and רַעְיוֹן to the Aramaic root רעא I (cf. Heb. רעה I), meaning "to feed, to graze, to shepherd" (so Aq. and Theod. in Ecclesiastes). This may be compared to Hos 12:2 [Eng. v. 1] where רֹעֶה רוּחַ (shepherding wind) is parallel to רֹדֵף קָדִים (chasing the east wind). In that passage, both these activities are attributed to Ephraim as the fool who desires things that are ephemeral and unreliable, a meaning which would also fit in Ecclesiastes.[5]

Many commentators relate these phrases to Aramaic רְעוּתָא ("pleasure, will"; "good will"; "ambition") and רַעְיוֹנָא ("desire, thought"), from the Aramaic root רעא II (cf. Heb. רעה III), meaning "to desire, take delight in." Just as shepherding wind would be a vain pursuit, the same could be true of desiring, i.e., pursuing, the wind.

Michael Fox, however, notes that רַעְיוֹנָא also refers to thoughts, and cites the use of that word in Aramaic portions of Daniel (2:29–30; 4:16 [Eng. 4:19]; 5:6, 10; 7:28). He questions whether the sense of a vain pursuit works with every occurrence of these phrases, pointing especially to Eccl 2:17, 26; 4:16, and the phrase רַעְיוֹן לִבּוֹ in Eccl 2:22: some concern that which has already been attained (not a pursuit), and others he considers evaluative descriptions of a situation. He argues that the phrases are better translated "windy thoughts," with a referent of chaotic thinking or absurdity which alludes to the restlessness of the wind cited by Qohelet in 1:6.[6]

Fox, however, unduly downplays the concern of these passages with

---

[4] Bertram, "Hebräischer und griechischer Qohelet," 48.

[5] C. L. Seow, "Hosea 14:10 and the Foolish People Motif," *CBQ* 44 (1982): 221–22.

[6] Fox, *Time to Tear Down*, 42–48. Fox says that this chaotic thinking may be internal to the one referred to in the passage or from the perspective of an outside observer (ibid., 48).

human effort and toil. In fact, all occurrences of רְעוּת רוּחַ and רַעְיוֹן רוּחַ are found in the first half of the book where this is the primary focus. Qohelet's first employment of them in 1:14 and 2:11 particularly highlights the futility of human toil, and the others also fit with this understanding. Fox's complaint that many of these contexts involve matters which have already been attained overlooks Qohelet's point that humans are *not* finding what they are *really* looking for: יִתְרוֹן (surplus). Finally, יִתְרוֹן serves as a contrary in both 2:11 and 5:15 [Eng. v. 16], while מלא, and יוֹתֵר do likewise in 6:7–9 to indicate that something pursued has not been accomplished.

Qohelet's use of רַעְיוֹן, rare compared to רְעוּת, may reflect his penchant for word play similar to the examples of antanaclasis (use of words with similar roots) and intentional multivalency cited in Chapter 1. While human effort is important to each of the contexts in which רַעְיוֹן is used—and when combined with רוּחַ in 4:16 it is rightly considered a variant of רְעוּת רוּחַ—these contexts also involve human wisdom in each case (Eccl 1:17; 2:22; 4:16, only the latter includes *hebel*). Thus Qohelet can suggest futility (desiring of wind) while he also alludes to human thought.[7]

The use of wind as a metaphor for that which is insubstantial (including futile effort) is a common one in the wisdom literature of Israel: inheriting wind (Prov 11:29), restraining wind (Prov 27:16), gathering wind (Prov 30:4), windy knowledge (Job 15:2), windy words (Job 16:3).[8] A similar idiom is found in an Old Babylonian wisdom text where the expression *sākil šārim*, "one who acquires wind," designates one who does something foolish.[9] Likewise, in the *Gilgamesh Epic* (OB version, 3.4.8), all that humans achieve is mere wind (*šāru*), and Gilgamesh's futile pursuit of immortality is designated a "quest of wind" (10.1.38, 45 [=10.3.7, 14]).[10]

Thus, whether the terms רְעוּת רוּחַ and רַעְיוֹן רוּחַ suggest shepherding wind or desiring (seeking) it, the contexts in which Qohelet uses them as well as similar metaphorical uses of wind indicate the attempt to achieve the impossible. Though toil, wisdom, goodness, and popularity have been achieved, the quest for "surplus" is not attained.

When Qohelet uses *hebel* with these guarding terms as well as the ones listed previously, he does not say that one cannot achieve pleasure, wisdom, or wealth, nor does he say that these things once achieved are necessarily gone quickly. Nor is it that wisdom and pleasure are wrong or bad (foul), although

---

[7] Note the use of the same root in Prov 15:14, where יְבַקֶּשׁ־דָּעַת (seeks knowledge) is contrasted with יִרְעֶה אִוֶּלֶת (pursues folly).

[8] Seow, *Ecclesiastes*, 122. Cf. also Sir 34:1–2 (LXX).

[9] Moshe Held, "A Faithful Lover in an Old Babylonian Dialogue," *JCS* 15 (1961): 6.

[10] E. A. Speiser, "The Epic of Gilgamesh," in *ANET*, 91, n. 170.

he may give negative evaluation to the circumstances around them. Rather, *hebel* in these cases describes things with little substance: wealth and pleasure do not satisfy, words are empty, wisdom cannot be relied upon, toil presents a deceptive hope for security, and the human condition is fragile.

Transience Referents

Qohelet uses *hebel* in a second metaphoric way to assess things which *are* transient and pass along quickly. This metaphoric sense is employed least by Ecclesiastes but is nevertheless clearly distinguishable. Elsewhere in the HB, *hebel* is used in this way to describe the quick destruction of humans before God's judgment (Ps 78:33), and the short span of human life (Ps 39:5–6, 12 [Eng. 4–5, 11]; Ps 144:4; cf. Sir 4:11).

Similarly, Qohelet employs the synonym צֵל (shadow) and the phrase "few days" when *hebel* refers to the brevity of human life (Eccl 6:12). In Eccl 11:7–10, Qohelet particularly laments that the period of youth is fleeting. He establishes *hebel*'s meaning of transience through the context as a whole (extension): the high praise of youth ("rejoice, O youth, while you are young," 11:9), and the urgency to enjoy such life while one may ("before the evil days come," 12:1). In 11:7–10, an attribution of *hebel* does not mean that youthfulness is something negative (it is celebrated), nor is the *frailty* of human life in focus as in 3:18–22 (the period of youth is characterized by vigor). Rather, Qohelet is drawing attention to youth's *brevity*.

Foulness Referents

The previous metaphoric uses of *hebel* were primarily descriptive. We now consider a third use: as an evaluative term for things in his experience which he finds to be fundamentally foul. This use of *hebel* is frequent and important, describing realities which, for example, are an affront to Qohelet's sense of justice. In this case, vapor has become "bad air," something repulsive and even life-threatening.

While there is general agreement that *hebel*'s metaphoric uses include transience and insubstantiality, a metaphoric sense of foulness has not been considered previously. However, there are two considerations which make this the capstone component to the present thesis. The first is a consistent application of method. Attention to the terms in these texts which "guard" the *hebel* metaphor demonstrates that Qohelet is describing something "foul." Second, we have noted evidence from *hebel*'s use in extrabiblical sources that the term would lend itself to this kind of metaphor.

The most important guarding term for this sense is רָע,[11] usually

---

[11] The two forms of the masculine noun, the feminine noun רעה, and the similarly

translated elsewhere as "evil," "adversity," "disaster," and similar terms.[12] In short, רַע is a term of negative evaluation concerning matters which are unacceptable and/or harmful, either from a divine or a human perspective.

The synonymity between הֶבֶל and רַע in Ecclesiastes has been recognized previously.[13] That the term רַע functions in a clarifying role similar to that of the synonym phrase "chasing wind" is apparent from syntactically similar *hebel* passages:

> "This indeed is/was *hebel* and . . ."
>   (a) chasing wind (2:26; 4:4, 16; 6:9)
>   (b) רָע (great evil, 2:21; evil business, 4:8; evil sickness, 6:2)
> "All is/was *hebel* and . . ."
>   (a) chasing wind (1:14; 2:11, 17)[14]
>   (b) רָע (9:2 txt. em.)[15]

Just as the "chasing wind" phrase is found with *hebel* in texts where Qohelet is concerned about the insubstantial nature of toil, so רַע is found with *hebel* in contexts where Qohelet focuses on things which are foul. In addition, other terms likewise serve to clarify the foulness referent though with lesser frequency than רַע, e.g., the synonyms כַּעַס (vexation) and חֳלִי (sickness), and the contraries טוֹב (good) and שׂבע (satisfy).

We turn now to the question of the *rationale* for a metaphoric connection between vapor and foulness. First, it is important to remember regarding metaphor that authors sometimes simply develop their own associations for a given term. They may, in effect, *create* a similarity.[16]

---

spelled adjectives will be discussed together since they appear to have effectively the same semantic range. They occur a combined thirty-one times in Ecclesiastes, seven with *hebel*.

[12] In the Hebrew canon, רַע is used to indicate that which is destructive (Exod 32:14) or dangerous (Ps 144:10), such as famine (Ezek 5:16) and disease (Deut 7:15). It may also be used of things which are of inferior quality (Gen 41:3–4, 19–20), and sorrowful (Neh 2:1–2). It may describe inner attitudes or conditions (Ps 7:10) as well as activities (Gen 6:5). In its more abstract sense, it is set in contrast to טוֹב (good) and שָׁלוֹם (well-being). It is used most often of moral deficiencies (Prov 15:3), both those which are unacceptable from a human perspective (1 Kgs 22:8), and those which are unacceptable "in God's sight" (Jer 52:2; Mal 2:17). It is doubtful whether it is ever used in a cosmic or metaphysical sense. God is opposed to those who are רַע or who do רַע (Isa 31:2), yet God also is an agent of רַע (Judg 9:23; 1 Sam 18:10; Amos 9:4). See Walter Grundmann, "κακός," *TDNT* 3:476–79; Günther Harder, "πονηρός," *TDNT* 6:549–54.

[13] Polk ("Wisdom of Irony," 9) understands them to be essentially synonyms in these contexts, and Fox grants at least a partial synonymity between the terms (*Contradictions*, 33).

[14] Cf. also the use of עָפָר—"all are from/to dust"—as synonym at 3:19–20.

[15] Many interpreters emend the text at 9:1–2. See discussion to follow.

[16] See the comments of Max Black on this point cited in Chapter 2.

However, though such novelty is possible, the ways *hebel* is employed in the rabbinic writings provide ample substantiation for Qohelet's foulness referent. In addition to uses of *hebel* which indicate breath and steam, rabbinic texts show how both *hebel* and its Aramaic cognate הַבְלָא designate a kind of vapor which contains life-threatening properties within itself. For example, in Chapter 3 we saw that one who becomes asphyxiated in a sealed environment is said to be killed by its vapor (*Sanh.* 77a–b). It is even pondered whether inanimate objects might also be "killed" by such air (*B. Qam.* 54a). More common are references to animal deaths due to the "unhealthy air" (*hebel*) of a pit into which the animal has fallen (e.g., *B. Qam.* 50b, 51a,b). These texts demonstrate how *hebel* may refer to vapor which is poisonous.

Thus, Qohelet uses רַע as a guarding term for *hebel* because *hebel* can refer to bad air, air which is putrid and brings illness. We have a rationale, then, for the way *hebel*, when associated with רַע, can be used metaphorically to give a negative evaluation of situations Qohelet finds revolting.

Two additional points should be noted. First, רַע in Ecclesiastes does not have a scope equal to that of *hebel*. Qohelet states emphatically that "all is vapor" (e.g., 1:2; 2:17; 3:19), but he will not say that "all is evil." Second, since Qohelet's theme statements (1:2; 12:8) declare everything to be *hebel*, the scope of the term רַע is subsumed within the "all" that is *hebel*. Thus, certain things that are *hebel* are also רַע, but there are other *hebel* things that are not רַע.

Qohelet uses רַע when he talks about issues that are an affront to his sense of propriety or justice, such as the unbearable suffering of the oppressed (4:1–3).[17] Similarly, he combines it with *hebel* when he talks about such matters as one's wealth being passed along to a fool (2:18–23). Likewise the combination of *hebel* and רַע describe compulsive toil which brings no satisfaction (4:7–12), wealth which cannot be enjoyed (6:1–6), and the fact that the same fate comes to all persons (9:1–3).

Just as vapor can be repugnant and even life-threatening, Qohelet uses *hebel* in certain texts to evaluate things which he finds abhorrent and unacceptable. I will use the word *disgusting* for this referent. He is not saying that things such as compulsive toil or oppression of the poor are transient, nor that they are insubstantial. Rather, he is describing things which are a corruption of the way they should be. These things are wrong, even absurd.[18]

---

[17] Of the various terms used to "guard" *hebel*, רַע is used most often in contexts apart from *hebel*. Such passages include 4:1–3 (oppressive deeds); 7:13–14 (God's activity); 8:1–9 (people with power over others); 9:11–12 (animal and human experience); 10:5–7 (reversal of social position); 10:12–15 (result of fools' talk); 11:1–6 (trouble which effects economics); and 12:1 (old age).

[18] I use "absurd" here in Michael Fox's sense of the term, for in several contexts his

QOHELET'S USE OF *HEBEL*

The remainder of this chapter discusses the pericopae in Ecclesiastes which involve *hebel.*

1:2–11 (5*x*) Preface: Restless Activity

After the superscription in 1:1, Qohelet states his thesis in v. 2 and proceeds with a meditation on ceaseless activity. The role of people in 1:3–11 prepares the reader for Qohelet's emphasis on human effort, the primary focus of the book's first half. In a similar way for the second half, the collection of sayings in 7:1–14 prepares for a focus on the limits of human understanding.[19]

1:2 Statement of Thesis (5x)

Qohelet begins his work with the cry (v. 2):

הֲבֵל הֲבָלִים אָמַר קֹהֶלֶת הֲבֵל הֲבָלִים הַכֹּל הָבֶל

"Completely *vapor!*" says Qohelet, "Completely *vapor!*[20] All is *vapor.*"

---

thesis for *hebel* is apt. Certain things for Qohelet exhibit a "disjunction between two phenomena that are thought to be linked by a bond of harmony or causality, or that *should* be so linked," Fox's definition of the absurd (*Time to Tear Down*, 31). Qohelet grieves these things as bewildering and frustrating. But contra Fox, this is not Qohelet's sole use of the term *hebel.*

[19] Seow, *Ecclesiastes*, 111, 240–41. This general distinction is demonstrated by the focus of the book's rhetorical questions and its *hebel* statements in each half respectively. Yet, there is not a rigid division: the first half anticipates the later treatment of human knowing (e.g., 3:21; 6:8), and the second half also comments upon human effort (e.g., 7:16).

[20] The form of expression in which a substantive in the construct state stands before the plural of the same word normally indicates the superlative, e.g., קֹדֶשׁ הַקֳּדָשִׁים = most holy place (Exod 26:33), מֶלֶךְ מְלָכִים = greatest king (Ezek 26:7); GKC §133i. But Ellermeier questions whether there can be degrees of nothingness (i.e., *hebel*) and argues that the concluding statement "All is vapor" would seem to weaken the force of a preceding statement that something was superlative in that regard (cf. hypothetically, "The most holy place. The most holy place. All places are holy!"). Ellermeier suggests an iterative sense for the *hebel* phrase ("immer wieder 'hebel'"), so that the point of 1:2 is that Qohelet repeatedly said "*hebel*" through the course of his investigations (*Qohelet*, 99). Fox counters that a meaning of "absurd" for *hebel* addresses both of Ellermeier's concerns: there can be degrees of absurdity (Qohelet is saying life is absurd to the highest degree), and the concluding "all" follows the initial intense expression about absurdity by designating and emphasizing its subject (i.e., *everything* is absurd). Similarly, the midrash suggests that, unlike other vapors, the one in Eccl 1:2 and 12:8 is the vapor given off by vapor itself, i.e., truly slight! (Cohen, *Midrash Rabbah: Ecclesiastes*, 4–5; Robert Gordis, *Koheleth*, 205; also cf. Collins, *Proverbs, Ecclesiastes*, 72, who translates as "vapor of vapors"). On the other hand, there is indication that such a grammatical construction may sometimes indicate extent or

This statement is at once Qohelet's thesis and his presentation of a challenge to his audience.[21] He takes the familiar term *hebel* and makes an unprecedented two-fold claim: Vapor is all-pervasive, and all is vapor. To determine what this means will require patience and careful attention on the part of the reader.

Because there are difficulties reconciling the statement that "all" is *hebel* with the ways Qohelet uses *hebel* term throughout his book, some interpreters have assigned 1:2 and 12:8 to a later editor who, they say, framed the work with these statements either appropriately, inappropriately, or inadequately.[22]

Part of the difficulty involves the referent for the "all" (הַכֹּל) that is *hebel*. Except for the prefix particles ב, ה, ל, and ו, כֹּל is the most common word in Ecclesiastes, evenly distributed ninety-one times through the book. As N. Lohfink and M. Fox have rightly noted, the term כֹּל in discourse throughout the

---

completeness. In Gen 9:25, Noah curses Canaan by calling him עֶבֶד עֲבָדִים to his brothers, which may suggest complete servitude in the relationship rather than the lowest of all slaves. Likewise in 1 Kgs 8:27, שְׁמֵי הַשָּׁמַיִם, though complicated by issues of cosmology, probably expresses that the farthest reaches of heaven cannot contain Yahweh, rather than the "greatest" heaven (so Gray, *I & II Kings*, 205). Expressing the completeness or pervasiveness of *hebel* would be a fitting way to introduce an investigation which repeatedly identified examples of *hebel* (cf. "Completely holy. Completely holy. All places are holy!").

[21] Gordis (*Koheleth*, 204) says v. 2 presents the "dominant theme" of the work; so Crenshaw, *Ecclesiastes*, 58; Barton, *Ecclesiastes*, 69; and Ogden (*Qoheleth*, 28) who goes on to designate 1:3 the "programmatic" question of the book. Michael V. Fox says: "The book's motto is a thesis that we can expect to see validated in the following monologue" (*Time to Tear Down*, 163). According to Scott, "[Qohelet] begins by stating a thesis [1:2] . . . He then proceeds to describe and analyze the various kinds of experience which have led him to this result" (*Proverbs, Ecclesiastes*, 196). Murphy (*Ecclesiastes*, 3) cites the inclusio (12:8) and frequency of *hebel* as indicative that 1:2 is the work's motto.

[22] Examples include (respectively) Rashbam, Ellermeier (*Qohelet*, 94–96, 100), and Gerald T. Sheppard (*Wisdom as a Hermeneutical Construct* [BZAW 151; Berlin: de Gruyter, 1980], 122–26). However, Franz Backhaus (*Denn Zeit*, 326, 330) concludes that 1:2 is not redactional, emphasizing its connection to 1:3ff and its consistency with Qohelet's language elsewhere:

   (a) the phrase "in all its toil" (בְּכָל־עֲמָלוֹ) in 1:3 is subsumed by "all" (הַכֹּל) in 1:2;

   (b) since both the generic particle הַכֹּל and the noun *hebel* contain a reference to human endeavor, there is a logical continuation from v. 2 to v. 3;

   (c) since 5:6a is composed by Qohelet, it is clear that he uses *hebel* in the plural; also, Qohelet's style frequently employs paranomasia (e.g., with עשה, עמל, קרה), making it not unlikely that he would compose something such as הֲבֵל הֲבָלִים; and

   (d) notwithstanding the possibility that 12:8 is a self-quotation of Qohelet, it serves to close the preceding unit, either as a reference to both "dust" and "wind" in 12:7, or to the two *hebel*-judgments in 11:8b and 11:10b.

Backhaus concludes that 1:2 and 12:8 serve a double function, both to join with the following and preceding verses, respectively, and to frame the whole.

HB refers primarily to things mentioned in its immediate context.[23] Thus, when Qohelet states in 3:19 that "*all* is *hebel*," he is referring specifically to the mortality of humans and animals.[24] In 2:11, כֹּל concerns the work accomplished by Qohelet the "king."[25]

Thus Lohfink and Fox argue correctly that 1:2, "All is *hebel*," is not a universal or cosmic statement,[26] but a statement which addresses human existence "under the sun,"[27] life in this temporal world. However, Lohfink additionally contends that the programmatic statement in 1:2 is qualified in 1:3 so that it pertains only to human *toil*.[28] He is correct that 1:2 also serves as an introduction to 1:3–11. However, to restrict the concern of 1:2 to the issue of toil is to misjudge the role of 1:2 as thesis and motto for the entire work. This is evident on several counts:

(1)   the statement in 1:2 is restated (almost verbatim) in 12:8, so that it serves as inclusio for the body of the book;

(2)   the phrase "Completely *hebel*, all is *hebel*" (1:2 and 12:8) is distinctive among the book's *hebel*-phrases by the intrusion of the frame-narrator ("says Qohelet"); this has the effect of heightening its emphasis;

(3)   this interruption of the sentence divides the *hebel*-judgment into two aspects: its intensity (*hebel* of *hebels*) and its universality (*all* is *hebel*);

---

[23] Lohfink, "Koh 1,2," 201–16; Fox, *Time to Tear Down*, 40–42. Qohelet uses כֹּל repeatedly to indicate the scope of his research: 1:2 "all is *hebel*"; 1:3 "all the toil" (cf. 1:7, 8); 1:13 "all that is done under heaven"; 1:14 "all the deeds"; 2:10 "all my toil"; 2:11 "all the work"; 2:14 "the same fate befalls all of them"; 2:16 "all will have been long forgotten"; 2:18, 19, 20, 22; 3:13 "all my/their/its toil"; 2:23 "all its days"; 3:14 "all that God does endures forever"; passim.

[24] Lohfink, "Koh 1,2," 204–6; cf. statements at Eccl 1:14; 2:11, 17; 9:2; and 11:8.

[25] Other statements which may appear to be of a broad reference, also are probably limited. For example, the references in 1:13–14 to "all that is done under heaven" and to "all the works that are done under the sun," are comments upon human effort, the primary concern of the book's first half.

[26] Barton also takes this perspective (*Ecclesiastes*, 70). Murphy (*Ecclesiastes*, 4) insists that God is excepted and so is the cosmos. On the other hand, according to James A. Loader (*Ecclesiastes: A Practical Commentary* [trans. John Vriend; Text and Interpretation; Grand Rapids: Eerdmans, 1986 (1984)], 20), Qohelet "intends an all-embracing declaration of nullity." Crenshaw (*Ecclesiastes*, 58) calls the statement "universal." Whybray (*Ecclesiastes*, 36) considers it to be an indication of the editor absolutizing Qohelet's thought, since Qohelet less absolutely characterizes specific aspects of human life as *hebel* and takes a more positive view of God's creation overall (Eccl 3:11).

[27] This phrase, occurring twenty-nine times and unique to Ecclesiastes among biblical writings, refers to the universality of human experience (cf. "under the heavens," Eccl 1:13; 2:3; 3:1; Gen 1:9; 6:17; Exod 17:14; Deut 2:25; Job 28:24; 41:11; Jer 10:11; Lam 3:66; Dan 7:27; 4 Ezra 7:6; Bar 2:2; Acts 2:5; 4:12; Col 1:23).

[28] Lohfink, "Koh 1,2," 211–12.

(4)   the key term of the phrase—*hebel*—is employed as a leitmotif throughout the book; and

(5)   aside from 1:2 and 12:8, Qohelet states on three other occasions that "all is *hebel*" (1:14; 2:17; 3:19) and further implies it by attaching *hebel* as a label to all kinds of situations and experiences (e.g., 1:13, 14a), the report of his investigations.[29]

Thus, whatever its origins, 1:2 serves appropriately as the book's motto, and "all" includes the entirety of those matters in human experience which Qohelet is about to describe. Within the body of Qohelet's work, it is generally true that כל is used restrictively in reference to the particular subject at hand. An additional important point about כל is that Qohelet frequently uses it hyperbolically. For example, 2:22–23:

> What do humans have for all their toil and the pursuit of their heart with which they toil under the sun? For in all their days is pain, and their business is a vexation; even at night their heart does not rest. This indeed is vapor (*hebel*).[30]

It is possible, likewise, that Qohelet is speaking hyperbolically in the framing statements (1:2; 12:8).[31] Regardless, it is clear that he is embracing all types of human experience as he has encountered it: everything Qohelet will talk about is *hebel* in one way or another.[32]

In sum, the opening declaration concerning *hebel* (1:2) refers to all that Qohelet will discuss in his book. However, the referent for *hebel* is ambiguous and a challenge to the reader: no assisting clues—no synonyms, contraries, or extensions—are given initially. The reader becomes aware, in retrospect, that Qohelet is here alluding to all the R values which he will develop for *hebel*. But that development, the result of his careful symbol-building process, follows only upon the completion of the work. At the outset lies a puzzle which the reader is invited to solve.

1:2–11 The Creation Is Weary

The declaration in 1:2, "Completely *hebel*, All is *hebel*," serves both as

---

[29] See Fox, *Time to Tear Down*, 161–63.

[30] Note the hyperbole of 1:8–11, and compare additionally the term כל at 4:4 and 8:17.

[31] Fox is among those who recognize 1:2 and 12:8 as framing statements (*Time to Tear Down*, 162–63, 332). However, since he understands *hebel* to always mean "absurd," he urges that הכל is not quite universal even of human experience because not everything Qohelet refers to is absurd (*Time to Tear Down*, 40–41).

[32] Qohelet is concerned about those things which affect human beings. His allusion to earth, sun, wind, and water in 1:4–7 are for purposes of comparison with human activity. Yet, as Whybray notes (*Ecclesiastes*, 49), that which "is done under heaven" refers to more than just human activity. God's activity, as it impacts human beings, is also of interest to Qohelet

thesis for the book and as the introduction to the first section, 1:3–11.[33] Qohelet begins to demonstrate his thesis by following it immediately with a question in v. 3:

> What surplus (יִתְרוֹן) is there for humans
> from all the toil which they toil under the sun?[34]

Here, Qohelet inquires whether there is an advantage to human toil (S)[35] and provides evidence in the subsequent poem (vv. 4–11).[36]

Qohelet thus raises his primary subject (S) for the first half of the book in v. 3: human toil. His first treatment of it will involve commentary on the workings of the world in general. On the one hand, this section (1:2-11) focuses upon human toil (עָמָל)—hard work—as opposed to other activities of human beings, such as pleasure and wisdom, each of which will be specifically

---

(e.g., 3:10–11).

[33] Seow, *Ecclesiastes*, 111; Backhaus, *Denn Zeit*, 326, 330.

[34] Although there are exceptions, many commentators agree that the question in 1:3 is rhetorical. Rhetorical questions may be defined as "asking a question, not for the purpose of eliciting an answer but for the purpose of asserting or denying something obliquely" (Corbett, *Classical Rhetoric*, 453). H. Louis Ginsberg, for example, proposes that Qohelet declares the world to be zero (*hebel*, v. 2), raises the practical question of what "plus" (יִתְרוֹן) there can be in acquiring worldly goods (v. 3), then settles the issue by proving the premise in vv. 4–11: the world is valueless. He believes the remainder of the answer is found at 2:24–26: "the only positive value is the enjoyment of one's gains" (*Studies in Koheleth*, 1–4; the quotation is from p. 4).

[35] The wisdom literature is full of rhetorical questions, and they make a significant contribution to the persuasiveness of a presentation. The agreement they accomplish between audience and speaker serves persuasion by strengthening the speaker's credibility (one who sees things as the audience does), by building a sequence of agreement which anticipates more, and by limiting the categories the audience is allowed to use in relating to the issue at hand (cf. Corbett, *Classical Rhetoric*, 453–54). Raymond Johnson includes an overview of rhetorical questions in the wisdom literature of the ancient Near East in his study of some thirty rhetorical questions in Ecclesiastes ("Rhetorical Question"). Johnson pays particular attention to the rhetorical effects of such questions (e.g., pp. 208–26). See also Kennedy, *New Testament Interpretation*, 57.

[36] Contra Graham Ogden (*Qoheleth*, 28), this is not the programmatic question for the entire book. It concerns toil (עָמָל), the primary focus of the book's first half. This is why the question (3:9; 5:15 [Eng. v. 16]; 6:8, 11) does not occur after 6:11 (although the term יִתְרוֹן itself is found in 7:12; 10:10, 11). However, Ogden is correct that Qohelet will acknowledge a יִתְרוֹן for wisdom (2:13; 7:12; 10:10), and that those in power, despite their oppressive behavior, do benefit a land (5:8 [Eng v. 9]). So there is a sense in which Qohelet does provide a response to his declarations, some of which are accomplished through rhetorical questions, about the null value of toil (1:3; 3:9), wisdom (6:8; cf. 7:11), and pleasure (2:2). See the discussion of Qohelet's rhetoric in Chapter 5.

addressed in 1:12–2:26.[37] On the other hand, the poem of 1:3–11 places toil—human effort in general, עָמָל more broadly considered which includes the attempt to accomplish pleasure and wisdom—alongside the restless activity of other participants in the created order under the sun.[38]

Qohelet proceeds in this section to decry the ceaseless activity of the natural world: the earth, sun, wind, rivers, and seas. He uses hyperbole to capture the reader's imagination: nothing ever changes, nothing is ever new. The activity of human beings is established as part of the larger problem, again eliciting Qohelet's hyperbole: words are wearying, the eye is not satisfied and the ear not filled (v. 8), some only mistakenly think they have found something new (v. 10), and no one ever remembers those who came before them.[39] The lack of satisfaction (שׂבע) for the eye and filling for the ear (מלא), the failure of activity to accomplish something new (חָדָשׁ), and no one being remembered (זִכְרוֹן)—these serve as contraries for *hebel* (P) to make the claim that, for the workings of the world (S), including human involvement in it, all is *hebel* in the sense of being insubstantial: the toil is futile (R).[40]

---

[37] The noun עָמָל denotes human effort, nearly always with a negative association of trouble and suffering (BDB, 765; Gordis, *Koheleth*, 205; Seow, *Ecclesiastes*, 104). As Seow emphasizes, "toil" is not just work (עֲבוֹדָה) or activity (מַעֲשֶׂה). The term is used in Ecclesiastes of a person's physical or intellectual effort to achieve some particular goal. For an example of the verb עמל used of intellectual effort, see Eccl 8:17.

[38] Some commentators have interpreted this poem as a celebration of the cosmos (N. Lohfink, "Die Wiederkehr des immer Gleichen: Eine frühe Synthese zwischen griechischem und jüdischem Weltgefühl in Kohelet 1,4–11," *Archivo di Filosofia* 53 [1985]: 125–49). R. N. Whybray insists that the description here does not emphasize the weariness of creation, but compares nature to human nature in order to point out the proper limitations of each (*Ecclesiastes*, 39–46).

[39] Similarly in 2:16 and 9:5, Qohelet complains that those who die are forgotten. The hyperbolic nature of the statement concerning memory seems evident from Qohelet's own appeals to the past, such as the boast that, as king, his greatness surpassed all that came before him (1:16), and the assumption required by 1:10 that one know what happened in the past in order to determine whether something new actually happened or not. This claim likely challenges traditional wisdom literature which celebrated the achievements of those sages who had gone before, e.g., *The Immortality of Writers* 3.2–3 (also 2.5ff), *Merikare* ll. 36–37, 63–64, 141–42, and *Papyrus Lansing* 9.3–4. There may also be a performance aspect to this memory, an assumption that the worthies who have preceded deserve reverence or "memorializing"; note, for example, how the root זכר involves reverent activity in Pss 103:18 and 109:16. One of the ironies in this hyperbole is that Solomon, the great king of Israel's past, is precisely one whom Qohelet *does* want his audience to remember, though not for the reasons kings normally seek fame.

[40] These are not primarily references to Qohelet's own eye, ear, and memory, but statements of the human condition: there is no satisfaction, no filling, no remembrance—just as there is no surplus (יִתְרוֹן, v. 3). It is vapor.

The futility of effort established in vv. 4–11 recalls the rhetorical question of v. 3 in which human toil was specifically addressed. Here we find the term יִתְרוֹן, the first of *hebel*'s contraries, and one of the most important for explicating the referent of *hebel*. A term possibly from the economic sphere, the word יִתְרוֹן suggests something which gives surplus: something left over that is enduringly advantageous to the possessor.[41] Human toil, Qohelet seems to say, is not like that.[42]

Summary of 1:2–11

In this section, then, the association between human toil and *hebel* is accomplished first by placing the rhetorical question of 1:3 (What surplus . . .?) immediately after the thematic and omnivalent statement of 1:2. In the poem that follows, human effort is intertwined with all the other fruitless activity of the world. The sense of 1:2–11 is: All is vapor = vain, futile. Both the world's activity generally and human toil specifically have vapor's quality of insubstantiality.[43] The function of *hebel* in this section is descriptive.[44]

---

[41] Mitchel J. Dahood, "Canaanite-Phoenician Influence in Qoheleth," *Bib* 33 (1952): 220–21. The word *ytrn* has been identified twice in Aramaic economic texts (J. B. Segal, *Aramaic Texts from North Saqqâra* [London: Egypt Exploration Society, 1983], nos. 19.2; 149.2). Although economic connotations are possible in Eccl 1:3; 3:9; 5:8 [Eng v. 9]; 5:15 [Eng v. 16]; 7:12, more inclusive references are found in 2:11, 13; 10:10, 11. The term יִתְרוֹן is employed for purposes of contrast when evaluating toil (e.g., 1:3; 2:11; 3:9; 5:15) and in those contexts serves as a contrary for *hebel*. Elsewhere, it is used positively of the advantage of wisdom (over folly, 2:13, compared with light vs. darkness; also 7:12; 10:10), of the advantage of a king for agricultural production (5:8), and of the potential advantage of snake charming (10:11). For Qohelet, certain things are recommended over others, as evident from his use of the *ṭôb*-saying (though sometimes used in parody), and other passages in which he gives genuine advice. Of toil, however, he can say, for example, that it will not *satisfy* the eye (cf. other *hebel*-guarding terms in the "toil" contexts); it may have some value but it accomplishes no "surplus." So E. H. Plumptre, who describes יִתְרוֹן as "the surplus, if any, of the balance-sheet of life" (*Ecclesiastes or the Preacher* [Cambridge: Cambridge University Press, 1881], 104). Cf. Seow, *Ecclesiastes*, 103–4.

[42] At least we expect a negative answer to the question of 1:3 which appears to be rhetorical: toil provides no surplus. Likewise, 2:2 questions the value of pleasure, and 6:8a the value of wisdom. However, Qohelet will eventually provide his own answer for each of these matters. See Douglas B. Miller, "What the Preacher Forgot: The Rhetoric of Ecclesiastes," *CBQ* 62 (2000): 228–29; Johnson, *Rhetorical Question*, 251–54; Fredericks, *Coping*, 53.

[43] "Vain" and "futile" are appropriate words to express the R value of *hebel* in this context. The quality of *hebel* that makes the connection with toil is its insubstantiality.

[44] There are certainly evaluative connotations here in a negative direction. Qohelet is disappointed that human struggle accomplishes nothing new, and so on. But *hebel* primarily communicates the fact of toil's limitation.

Elsewhere, specific declarations that toil is *hebel* are found at 1:12–15; 2:1–11; 4:4–6; 6:7–11 (cf. 3:1–13; contrast 2:18–23). In the sections to come, Qohelet will sometimes focus on toil in itself and sometimes use the term more generally of the *effort* to achieve pleasure or the *effort* to achieve wisdom.[45]

1:12–2:26 (9x) Royal Pursuits

Eccl 1:12 begins the magnificent "royal experiment" section of Qohelet's presentation in which he adopts the persona of Solomon.[46] This suits his purposes well, since the figure of King Solomon has associations with Qohelet's concerns here: the interrelated matters of wisdom, pleasure, and achievement. Through the medium of parody, he expresses his search for "all that is done under heaven."[47] His pattern is to present statements of inference, accompanied by supporting examples.

Qohelet here continues the symbol-building which he began in 1:3–11.[48] The comments of 1:13–14 and those which close the unit in 2:24–26 form a frame. At each end God is mentioned, though not in the interim.[49] The formula "all is vapor and a chasing after wind" is repeated at points of summation throughout (1:14; 2:11, 17, 26). The center of the unit is 2:9–11 where Qohelet brings together the three primary issues of his focus here—toil, pleasure, and wisdom—and declares them all to be insubstantial effort.[50]

---

[45] Or possibly, the effort to achieve satisfaction, etc., by means of pleasure or wisdom. Note how 2:1–11 is concerned with pleasure, yet Qohelet reports how he "toiled" to accomplish various pleasures. Also, in the treatment of wisdom in 2:12–17, Qohelet refers to the work (הַמַּעֲשֶׂה) done under the sun. And in the concluding treatment of toil in 2:18–23, he comments on toiling with wisdom.

[46] So Gordis (*Koheleth*, 204, 209), who contrasts Ecclesiastes with a true pseudepigraph such as the Wisdom of Solomon. The initiation of a new section is evident in 1:12 by the employment of the first person voice and autobiographical presentation throughout. The section is unified by the royal experiment and its conclusions.

[47] See previous discussion of הַכֹּל (above). The designation of Qohelet as king in this section and in 1:1 has led some commentators to consider the entire book to be a "royal testament."

[48] Qohelet immediately presents most of the subjects of prime importance to his treatise: (1) toil, particularly human inability to remedy wrongs (1:12–15, cf. 2:18–23; 7:13), (2) wisdom and knowledge (1:16–18; 2:12–17), (3) pleasure (2:1–3), (4) lasting achievement (2:4–11), (5) the God factor (1:13–14; 2:24–26), and (6) his recommended response (2:24–26).

[49] Seow, *Ecclesiastes*, 143. Cf. the similar theological framing at the beginning of the book's second half, 6:10–7:14.

[50] On the limits of this unit, see Whybray, *Ecclesiastes*, 46–47. The thematic structure of this section is chiastic in the following sequence:

1:12–18 *Qohelet Begins His Investigation (1x)*

In 1:14, Qohelet declares the outcome of his investigation proleptically when he says:

> I saw (רָאָה) all the works that are done under the sun;
> and look, all (הַכֹּל) is vapor (*hebel*) and a chasing after wind.

In this section, Qohelet introduces two new phrases which, in effect, apply the term הַכֹּל (discussed above) to the matter of human effort. These are "all that is done under heaven" (כָּל־אֲשֶׁר נַעֲשָׂה תַּחַת הַשָּׁמָיִם) in v. 13, and "all the works that are done under the sun" (כָּל־הַמַּעֲשִׂים שֶׁנַּעֲשׂוּ תַּחַת הַשָּׁמֶשׁ) in v. 14. These allude to "under the sun" in 1:3 and indicate that the scope of Qohelet's investigation, and that which he declares *hebel* in 1:14, embrace all which occurs in the human realm.[51] As indicated in 1:13, this will involve God's activity which affects human beings (cf. 3:10–11).

Qohelet also introduces in 1:14 a new synonym guardian of *hebel*'s R values which foreshadows Qohelet's conclusion to the entire section (1:12–2:26): "I saw all the deeds that are done under the sun; and indeed, all is vapor (*hebel*) and *a chasing after wind*." This is the first occurrence of this phrase (רְעוּת רוּחַ) which, along with its variant (רַעְיוֹן רוּחַ), accompanies *hebel*-statements eight times in the first half of the book (and the phrase occurs by itself at 1:17).

These equivalent phrases are used exclusively within texts concerned with human toil. They function as synonyms to *hebel*, and have a descriptive function. Like an attempt to capture wind, they comment upon effort whose goal is unattainable. They, like the contrary יִתְרוֹן in 1:3, relate human toil to the insubstantial quality of *hebel* (vapor). This insubstantial dimension of *hebel* is also guarded in 1:12–15 by extension—the comments concerning human inability in v. 15: "What is crooked cannot be straightened, and what is lacking cannot be counted." That is, human deeds are not wrong-rectifying.[52]

A Works
B Wisdom
C Pleasure/Works/Wisdom
B' Wisdom
A' Toil
C' Advice: pleasure/toil/wisdom

[51] Fox, *Time to Tear Down*, 40–41.

[52] The proverb in v. 15a may originally have been a saying directed toward recalcitrant students of the sages to the effect that some were hopeless and could not be instructed (Seow, *Ecclesiastes*, 146–47). *The Instruction of Any* (Egyptian) contains a proverb suggesting the opposite, that there is hope:

In 1:13, use of רָע indicates that Qohelet gives a negative evaluation to this situation. Thus, the use of *hebel* in this passage is multivalent. Though Qohelet begins here to suggest a foulness dimension for the term, he does not emphasize it as he will do later.

In 1:16–18 Qohelet alludes specifically to knowledge and wisdom. As with human effort generally, this pursuit, rather than accomplishing its goal (1:17b), produces pain (1:18). Thus, it is not the transience of human effort (S) but its emptiness or failure that is identified.

2:1–11 Pleasure (2x)

This section, a careful pastiche of aggrandizing statements typical of ancient Near Eastern royalty, is framed by *hebel* statements in v. 1b and v. 11.[53] Eccl 2:1–2 reads:

> I said in my heart, "Come now, let me test you with pleasure; see good." But look, this indeed was vapor (*hebel*). I said of laughter, "<What> does it boast?"[54] And of pleasure, "What does this do?"

And 2:11:

> Then I considered all the work that my hands had worked and the toil that I had toiled to do, and look! all was vapor (*hebel*) and a pursuit of wind, and there was no surplus under the sun.

The occurrence of the root עמל (toil) four times in vv. 10–11, and the related root עשה (to do, work) twice, underscores that the concern here involves human struggle. The *hebel*-statement in v. 1b is guarded by synonymous

---

The crooked stick left on the ground,
With sun and shade attacking it,
If the carpenter takes it, he straightens it,
Makes of it a noble's staff,
And a straight stick makes a collar (*AEL*, vol. 2, 145).

Qohelet uses the contrasting proverb in v. 15a to support his claim that human effort is sometimes of no use, possibly an allusion to the wise whose limits he will also address later.

[53] Seow, "Qohelet's Autobiography," 275–84, presents his thesis that the royal experiment section of Ecclesiastes is a parody of ANE political propaganda, viz., the pronouncements found on royal stelae.

[54] The form מְהוֹלָל, a *hapax legomenon*, is traditionally conjectured to mean "foolishness," a Poal participle from the root הלל III (cf. הוֹלֵלוֹת at Eccl 1:17 and 2:12; הוֹלֵלוּת at Eccl 10:13). Though such a meaning would fit in this context, it suits the syntactical construction better to repoint the MT from מְהוֹלָל to מַהוֹלָל (cf. Exod 4:2; Isa 3:15; 2 Chr 30:3 for similar patterns), or to actually emend the text to מַה הוֹלֵל (for analogous use of הלל, cf. Ps 5:6 [Eng. v. 5]). As a result, there are two rhetorical questions here (Seow, *Ecclesiastes*, 126). Both this proposal and the traditional conjecture provide that מהולל serves *hebel* as a synonym

extension: "What does it boast? What does this do?" Both of these rhetorical questions communicate the insubstantiality of human accomplishments of pleasure (vv. 1–2). The *hebel*-statement in v. 11 is guarded there by the synonym "chasing after wind" (רְעוּת רוּחַ) and by the negated contrary "surplus" (יִתְרוֹן) so that the subject is toil more generally. The latter echoes its occurrence in 1:3 where the topic of human effort and its insubstantiality was introduced.

Certainly Qohelet had something to show for his work: the parks, vineyards, etc. In contrast to some persons he will describe later, he *was* able to do what he wanted. Yet something was wrong. As in 1:12–18, to call these efforts *hebel* does not mean they were transient, that they slipped away. Thus he forces the reader to consider some other dimension of *hebel* here. Synonym, extension, and contrary indicate the quality of insubstantiality for both occurrences of *hebel*. Human toil, whether directed toward building projects and other aggrandizement, or pleasure in some other way, does not bring surplus.

2:12–17 Wisdom and Folly (2x)

Qohelet turns again to consider wisdom's situation.[55] Here and a few other places he uses what has been labeled a "*zwar-aber*" structure: on the one hand X, but on the other hand Y. He presents two matters which are true without resolving the tension between them.[56] Though it is true (*zwar*) that wisdom and knowledge bring some relative advantage (יִתְרוֹן) over folly just as light has over darkness (2:13), the other reality (*aber*) is that wise and foolish die alike (2:14) with no one to remember them (2:16). The effort to be wise accomplishes nothing more substantial than the great works of the king described beforehand.

In 2:15, Qohelet says:

> Then I said in my heart, "The fate of the fool will happen to me also; why then have I been so wise in excess?" And I said in my heart that this indeed is vapor (*hebel*).

The subject, for which *hebel* is the predicate, concerns wisdom and its entailments. The first guarding element for *hebel* in v. 15 is the use of the root יתר in the rhetorical question of v. 15a: יוֹתֵר (excess). This term alludes to the

---

to the effect that laughter accomplishes nothing.

[55] This section builds upon Qohelet's previous emphasis that human effort accomplishes insubstantial results and complements 1:16–18, also concerned with wisdom.

[56] H. W. Hertzberg, *Der Prediger* (KAT 17/4; Gütersloh: Mohn, 1963), 89–92. Hertzberg uses the term "*zwar-aber*" to mean that Qohelet introduces issue A (*zwar*) only to reject it on the basis of issue B (*aber*). It is thus used differently in the present study.

previous occurrences of יִתְרוֹן in 1:3 and 2:11 where the latter served as a contrary for *hebel*. This connection then qualifies the use of יִתְרוֹן just two verses earlier (2:13) where Qohelet states that there *is* a surplus for wisdom compared with folly. Ironically, Qohelet has been wise in excess (יוֹתֵר, 2:15) but *has* no excess, nothing left over, to show for it.

The additional point that there is "no remembrance" of the wise, and the resentful tone conveyed by the rhetorical questions in this section (vv. 12, 15, 16) anticipate the guarding terms for *hebel* found in 2:17, Qohelet's most bitter lament thus far:

> So I hated life, because the work done under the sun was evil to me; for all is vapor (*hebel*) and a chasing after wind.[57]

As with previous subjects, the phrase "chasing after wind" emphasizes wisdom's inadequacy. In this unit, then, Qohelet employs *hebel* to describe wisdom's insubstantial character.

However, now for the second time (2:17; cf. 1:13) Qohelet adds the word רָע (evil) to make an evaluative statement. Qohelet's declaration that "all" is *hebel* echoes his previous statements of universality which began with 1:2. Yet the basis of this pronouncement here is his particular experience with wisdom, and thus the terms רָע and שֹׂנֵא serve to guard *hebel*'s meaning of foulness. The wisdom done under the sun is both futile and disgusting, or, perhaps, the futility of wisdom is disgusting. *Hebel* here is multivalent, guarded by synonyms which draw upon two different aspects of vapor's qualities.

2:18–23 Toil (3x)

In this important passage, Qohelet employs *hebel* three times to further emphasize the foulness of toil (S). He now is concerned not only for the lack of substance which his own efforts achieve, but is chagrined by the unfairness of what benefit may be acquired by another. According to 2:18:

> I hated all (the wealth from) my toil[58] in which I had toiled under the sun,

---

[57] The juxtaposition here of the phrase הַמַּעֲשֶׂה שֶׁנַּעֲשָׂה תַּחַת הַשָּׁמֶשׁ (the work done under the sun) with the phrase הַכֹּל הֶבֶל (all is vapor) demonstrates again that Qohelet's concern is with the realm of human experience in this world.

[58] This is a case in which עָמָל indicates the products of Qohelet's toil, those things which may be passed along (Fox, *Time to Tear Down*, 99–100). It is very interesting that Qohelet adopts here the first person form of address. By describing the situation in terms of his own affairs, he heightens the emotional impact of the unfairness of the situation. If he would have described the circumstances as a third party observer of such a situation, the impact would be much less. For the audience would see that no harm had come to the person passing along the inheritance (they were dying anyway and could no longer use it) and would be more prone to celebrate the fortune of the one who had come into some unexpected

seeing that I must leave it to the human who comes after me.

The situation is emphasized by the rhetorical question in 2:22 which declares the uselessness of toil.[59] In addition, the language of hate (v. 18), despair (v. 20), pain and vexation (v. 23) indicates that *hebel* is not simply a descriptive term. Rather, Qohelet is using it here to pass negative judgment. As was indicated by the use of רַע in 1:13 and 2:17, things that are *hebel* are sometimes things that *ought not* to be. It is not simply that toil has *nothing* to show for itself. It is rather, as with wisdom (1:16–18; 2:12–17), that it also has disgusting and frustrating results.

In 1:13, Qohelet boldly announced that God has given humans an "evil business." As he surveyed the inconsequential results of human effort from 1:14 to 2:17, we see his frustration slowly build. His use of *hebel* is primarily descriptive, but in 1:18 he points out the pain and vexation which accompany wisdom, and in 2:17 he expressed his hatred of life because the situation of human work was "evil."

Here in 2:18–23 his frustration reaches one of its boiling points. Again there is an expression of hatred (v. 18) and despair (v. 20) until finally he announces (v. 21) that this situation is הֶבֶל וְרָעָה רַבָּה (vapor and a great evil), the first time he couples the synonym רַע with the *hebel*-phrase. He then concludes the section with additional references to pain, vexation, and *hebel* (v. 23).

It is important to recognize that Qohelet's style is to make both descriptive and evaluative statements on the basis of his own authority. When he says he hated his toil, it means that the toil was hate-worthy. When he says he despaired concerning his toil, it means that the toil was despair-inducing. Thus, through the use of רַע as synonym, but primarily through extension, Qohelet indicates that *hebel* here has a referent of foulness.

2:24–26 Enjoy Life! (1x)

At the conclusion of this section (1:12–2:26), Qohelet gives the reader his first declaration of advice on how to respond to his analysis of life. Although he has assessed pleasure and wisdom as empty, and toil's products as a foul situation, he nevertheless recognizes value in all three, for their source is God's hand. This he describes in vv. 24–26 along with a double rhetorical question:

---

wealth. Qohelet's way of presenting this allows full expression to the frustration of the one who has done all the labor.

[59] As Ogden has noted, this alludes to the question of profit or surplus raised about toil in 1:3, even though יִתְרוֹן is not used here (Graham S. Ogden, "Qoheleth's Use of the 'Nothing Is Better'–Form," *JBL* 98 [1979]: 345).

There is nothing better for the human than[60] to eat and drink and see itself good in its toil.[61] This also, I saw, is from the hand of God; for who can partake[62] or who can enjoy[63] apart from <him>?[64] For to a human who is in favor with him, he gives wisdom and knowledge and joy; but to the one who is offensive he gives the business of gathering and heaping, only to give to one who is approved of God.[65] This indeed is vapor (*hebel*) and a pursuit of wind.

As has happened several times already, *hebel* is accompanied by the synonym "chasing after wind" (1:14, 17; 2:11, 17), a comment that its subject achieves insubstantial results. However, the subject of the *hebel*-statement here, the designation of זֶה, is a matter of controversy among commentators.

---

[60] Because other אֵין טוֹב expressions in Ecclesiastes declare that experiencing "good" is dependent upon the advice that follows (to enjoy, 3:15, to eat, 8:15), we expect something similar here: Qohelet is calling for enjoyment. On the grounds of haplography, scholars sometimes emend the text here to supply a *mem* of comparison: from בָּאָדָם שֶׁיֹּאכַל to בָּאָדָם מִשֶּׁיֹּאכַל (so Fox, *Time to Tear Down*, 189). That is, the Hebrew phrasing seems to require something similar to what is found in analogous passages, such as כִּי אִם (3:12; 8:15) and מֵאֲשֶׁר (3:22). However, the variety of Qohelet's phrasing to express the same point is instructive. The versions likely reflect an acknowledgement of the actual meaning rather than a different Hebrew source (see discussion in Seow, *Ecclesiastes*, 138–39).

[61] Cf. the Egyptian wisdom text, *The Admonitions of Ipuwer* 8.6–7, dated ca. 13th century B.C.E.:
Lo, a man is happy eating his food.
Consume your goods in gladness, while there is none to hinder you.
It is good for a man to eat his food.
God ordains it for him whom he favors (*AEL*, vol. 1, 157).

[62] The verb אכל (eat, partake) in v. 25 should be taken in a general sense here as a reference to participation or enjoyment (cf. 5:17–19 [Eng. vv. 18–20]; 6:1–2). It serves as a synonym for שׂמח.

[63] Various proposals have been given for the term יָחוּשׁ (2:25). LXX, Theod., and Syr. apparently read ישׁתה "to drink," likely due to scribal dittography or an emendation to replace an unknown term. The Targum derives the form from חושׁ "to fear." חושׁ (and its by-form חוּשׁ) may also mean "to suffer" or "to consider." It is most probable that the rhetorical questions here are intended to justify the statement in v. 24, a role they frequently play in Ecclesiastes (cf. 3:21, 22; 5:5 [Eng v. 6]; 7:16, 17). Double questions of the מִי-type elsewhere in the HB, and not only in poetry, are most often synonyms of one another (cf. 1 Sam 18:18; 25:10; 2 Kgs 19:22; Isa 29:15; Ps 24:3; Job 21:31; 26:4). This is also true in Ecclesiastes (6:8, 12; 8:1). Thus the proposed Akkadian cognate, *ḫašāšu* "to rejoice" fits well here (so Murphy, *Ecclesiastes*, 24–25).

[64] Emending מִמֶּנִּי to מִמֶּנּוּ with most commentators, so eight Hebrew MSS, LXX, and other versions. It is unlikely that Qohelet is quoting God here, or that he is referring to himself. Scribal confusion between *yod* and *waw* is not uncommon.

[65] Cf. Prov 13:22; 17:2; and the Late Demotic Egyptian wisdom text, *Papyrus Insinger*, dated to approximately the first century B.C.E. At line 4.9, the latter says: "The impious man leaves his savings at death and another takes them" (*AEL* 3:188).

Possibilities include:

(1)   The enjoyment Qohelet is recommending here. That is, even this (a relative good) must be subsumed under the label of futile effort (not ultimately satisfying). This position is defensible, but Qohelet makes no similar declarations elsewhere about the advice that he offers. Those commentators who have taken it this way often consign v. 26a to an orthodox glossator.[66]

(2)   The futile "gathering and heaping" of the "sinner" whose toil ends up for the benefit of the morally "good" who are blessed by God.[67] This reflects a pietistic reading which is problematic for the book as a whole.

(3)   The urge to be "good." It is possible to read the subject of *hebel* as the attempt to seek God's favor in order to achieve the benefits described in v. 26. Such concerns are addressed elsewhere in the book (e.g., 9:2) but seem not to be the focus here.

(4)   Qohelet's concerns in the time poem of Eccl 3 which follows immediately. Yet, an introductory role for a *hebel*-statement, though possible (analogies include Eccl 4:7; 5:15 [Eng. v. 16]; and 8:10, 14), is rare.

A fifth option for *hebel*'s subject is to be preferred:

(5)   Toil in general, a summation of 1:12–2:26. The "sinner" (חוֹטֵא) is anyone out of favor with God, and this one's toil ends up for the benefit of the one God (arbitrarily) prefers.[68] This position takes חוֹטֵא and טוֹב not as moral categories concerning which Qohelet proclaims divine justice, but as labels for those in or out of God's favor.

Since God is in the business of enabling certain ones to enjoy their life, one should take full advantage of any enjoyment that is available. But toil is

---

[66] So Barton, *Ecclesiastes*, 84–85. Barton believes the *hebel*-saying was original and followed v. 25.

[67] So Tg.

[68] The חוֹטֵא (trad. "sinner") does not necessarily refer here to one who is morally offensive. Nor is the one "good before God" necessarily righteous. The fortunate beneficiary may be a fool (2:19), and the unfortunate one who toils and then hands it over may toil with wisdom (vv. 19b, 21). חטא refers to one who offends, but not always morally (cf. 1 Kgs 1:21; Eccl 10:4). See Fox, *Time to Tear Down*, 189–91. There may seem a tension between v. 26a (God gives wisdom to the one in favor) and v. 19 (the recipient of goods may be a fool). However, Qohelet may be responding to a traditional saying (cf. Job 27:13–17; Prov 13:22; 28:8) so that his emphasis is upon the perceived injustice in v. 26b. Murphy also understands these verses to emphasize the divine freedom (*Ecclesiastes*, 26–27), and claims that elsewhere Qohelet rejects any distinction between the lot of the good and the bad (4:1–3; 7:15; 8:10–14; 9:1–3). Also Seow, *Ecclesiastes*, 141–42, 157–58. Gordis notes that, in contrast to טוֹב and חוֹטֵא, צַדִּיק and רָשָׁע are used by Qohelet as conventional terms of piety and lack thereof (*Koheleth*, 227).

hebel, i.e., insubstantial, futile, because God is arbitrary.[69] We may recognize here another example of *zwar-aber*: on the one hand, there is nothing better than to find good in one's toil; on the other hand, God is arbitrary in passing out the rewards.

In 2:18–23, Qohelet emphasized his negative evaluation of toil's insubstantiality. Here in 2:24–26, he states further that toil is insubstantial because God's gifts are given without consideration of that toil. Even more, vv. 24–26 serve as a conclusion to 1:12–2:26 as a whole. They make reference to God's involvement, alluding to the bad business (עִנְיָן) God gives to humans (cf. 1:13; 2:23). This allusion suggests that here too *hebel* has a negative evaluative dimension.

Summary of 1:12–2:26

Qohelet began in 1:2–11 with the insubstantiality dimension of *hebel*. Here in this unit, he has focussed separately on toil, pleasure, and wisdom, yet each is interconnected with the other. In the process, he has demonstrated that *hebel* has an evaluative function as well as a descriptive one: some things designated as *hebel* are foul. This began with the hint concerning "bad business" in 1:13, was mentioned again in 2:17 and developed explicitly in 2:21, and then was hinted again in 2:26. He has presented a wide range of human effort, described and judged it as insubstantial and some aspects as foul, and has given his first words of advice.

3:1–22 (1x) God's Relation to Time and Eternity

A new unit is indicated by the poem of 3:1–8 which follows the summary conclusion to the royal investigation (2:24–26). There, Qohelet affirmed the divine freedom. He now examines God's relation to timing in the activities of life. Although there are connections to the previous section,[70] this section is unified by its attention to the sovereignty of God in the determination of events. Introduced in 3:1–15, this is developed in the area of judgment in 3:16–22. The unit is concluded in 3:22 by a summary statement which parallels that of 2:24–26.

3:16–22 God's Judgment Tests Humans (1x)

In the context of judgment and justice, Qohelet turns in this section to address the human physical condition (the subject of *hebel* here), and this

---

[69] Seow suggests that God is here being compared to an arbitrary ruler who gives to his favorites as he pleases, but neglects those who are out of favor (Seow, *Ecclesiastes*, 25–26).

[70] 3:16–22 resumes the issue of fate raised in 2:12–17, and the conclusion regarding pleasure in 3:22 both reinforces 3:13 and echoes 2:24–26. Note also the transition provided

constitutes his most direct treatment of it.[71] Qohelet closes the section with an allusion to one particular human weakness which will dominate the second half of the book: the limitation of knowledge. In the midst of this appraisal, Qohelet inserts a *hebel*-statement surrounded by guarding elements (3:19–20):

> For the fate of human offspring and the fate of animals is the same fate: as one dies, so dies the other. They all have the same wind (רוּחַ), and the human has no advantage over the animal; for all is vapor (*hebel*). All go to one place; all are from the dust (עָפָר), and all return to dust.

Qohelet's comments here on the quality of the human constitution are a shift away from human efforts and experiences. He insists that there is no advantage to being human: humans and animals share the same רוּחַ (wind, breath, or "spirit"), have death as the same fate, and that no one can determine whether, after that event, there is some distinction between them. Therefore, he concludes and specifically states, the human has no advantage (מוֹתָר, from יתר), over the animal. To this contrary, he adds a synonym: dust (עָפָר).[72]

Although Qohelet has no well-developed "anthropology" in the modern sense of that term, his use of *hebel* to describe humanity is readily apparent. He has now applied the insubstantiality quality of *hebel* to a second distinct subject.[73] Just as human effort fails to yield a surplus, so humans themselves, as dust, are perishable and lack enduring substance.

---

by the infinitives in 2:26 to those in the poem of 3:1–8.

[71] The phrase וְעוֹד רָאִיתִי (and, further, I have seen) indicates a shift of focus, yet with continuity to the previous. It connects with the use of ראה in 3:10, and will close the unit in 3:22. Qohelet continues alluding to death, climaxing with the final poem in 12:1–7.

[72] The imagery in 3:19–20 is strongly punctuated with the word כֹּל ("all"):

- all have the same רוּחַ ("wind," or "spirit"),
- all is *hebel*,
- all go to one place,
- all are from the dust, and
- all turn to dust again.

[73] Here the imagery of dust (עָפָר) alludes to human creation: ". . . then the Lord God formed the man (אָדָם) from the dust (עָפָר) of the ground, and breathed into his nostrils the breath (נְשָׁמָה) of life" (Gen 2:7). Jer 10:14–15 is also of interest: "Everyone is stupid and without knowledge; goldsmiths are all put to shame by their idols; for their images are false, and there is no breath (רוּחַ) in them. They are *hebel*, a work of delusion; at the time of their punishment they shall perish." Qohelet's use of the terms "dust" (עָפָר) and "wind" (רוּחַ) in 3:20–21 serve to associate *hebel* with human mortality. While the more common Hebrew terms for air inside the human body are רוּחַ and נְשָׁמָה (both also used anthropomorphically of God; cf. Pss 18:16; 33:6; Isa 11:4), *hebel* may also have the sense of "breath" (*B. Bat.* 75a; *Šabb.* 88b). On these matters, see Seybold, "הֶבֶל," 318.

Summary of 3:1–22

The first half of this unit gathers together, without using *hebel*, Qohelet's conclusions concerning the insubstantiality of human effort, and the difficult circumstances which God has prescribed. In the process, Qohelet emphasizes the permanence of God's work, which, in the unit's second part, becomes a contrast to the insubstantial *hebel* dust of the human condition.

4:1–16 (4x) Toil in the Midst of Oppression

In between two sections which reflect on the deity (3:16–22; 4:17–5:6 [Eng. 5:1–7]), the verb שׁוּב ("*Again* I saw . . .") signals the start of a new section (4:1–16), this one devoted to self-serving toil in the midst of oppression.[74] Qohelet's use of *ṭôb*-sayings here recalls his advice in 2:24, 3:12, and 3:22 that "there is *nothing better* than" to enjoy oneself,[75] and anticipates his deliberation on the *knowledge* of goodness in 6:10–7:14 (the start of the book's second half with its special concern for human knowledge).

This unit proceeds in a chiastic structure, marked by *ṭôb*-sayings in four of its five subunits.[76] It is unified by the theme of self-serving toil in the midst of oppression, and by the presence of טוֹב woven throughout. *Hebel* is found in the second, third, and final subsections.[77]

---

[74] The conclusion of the unit in 3:22 parallels that of 2:24–26, the ending of the royal experiment section. This and the reference to "time" in 3:17 and the continued development of God's role, connect 3:16–22 with 3:1–15, and make it unlikely that the comments on oppression in 4:1–3 are a continuation of 3:16–22 (so Fox, *Contradictions*, 199–200, contra Robert Gordis, *Koheleth*, 238–39, and Crenshaw, *Ecclesiastes*, 101–7). Although 3:16, like 4:1–3, concerns corrupted power, the focus in ch. 3 remains upon the role of God.

[75] Qohelet's concept of enjoyment is communal, a rejection of an individualistic self-gratification; cf. his evaluation of pleasure in 2:1–3.

[76] The first two subunits end with a *ṭôb*-saying, the final two begin with a *ṭôb*-saying; only the center section has none, although it asks the rhetorical question, "Why am I depriving myself of good (טוֹב)":

A The oppressed abandoned (4:1–3)
B Toil in competition (envy) (4:4–6)
C Toil for no one else (4:7–8)
B' Toil in cooperation (two better than one) (4:9–12)
A' The oppressed youth abandoned (4:13–16)
For further discussion of this chapter and its ethical implications, see Douglas B. Miller, "Power in Wisdom: The Suffering Servant of Ecclesiastes 4," in *Peace and Justice Shall Embrace: Power and Theopolitics in the Bible* (ed. Ted Grimsrud and Loren L. Johns; Telford, Pa.: Pandora Press U.S., 1999), 145–73.

[77] A diversity of proposals for the interrelationship of these subunits, or lack thereof, have been made by commentators, e.g., Gordis, *Koheleth*, 238–46 (who considers vv. 1–3 part of the previous section); Loader, *Ecclesiastes*, 47–57; Barton, *Ecclesiastes*, 113–22 (who

Qohelet observes the situation of the oppressed, which is so horrible that he lifts up those who were never born as most to be congratulated. As he looks around, he sees no one attempting to comfort the oppressed; instead, they are toiling out of envy of others, i.e., in competition with them. While laziness (a second option) is foolishness, contentment is the third and best option. He sees people toiling for no one else's benefit (center of the chiasm). He commends life in companionship (cooperation) for its many advantages (e.g., toil is put to good use). He concludes his meditation with an episode about an oppressed youth who came forth to serve with wisdom; but this royal one is merely rejected and abandoned, left alone himself.

4:4–6 Toil in Competition (1x)

The second subsection, which (like 4:1–3) ends with a *ṭôb*-saying, takes up a new dimension of the toil issue: the envy which motivates those who labor or, alternatively, the envy which results from another's labor. The grammatical construction may be interpreted either way.[78] In either case, a lack of contentment with one's own state is being presented, so that both possibilities would fit the pericope. However, the first possibility, that of toil motivated by envy, seems to work better in the larger context with its emphasis on community in relation to oppression.

Those who might help the ones "with no one to comfort them" (4:1) are busy toiling in competition with others. They do not help those in need, and, in regard to their own benefit, accomplish nothing either. In both cases, this toil produces nothing of value; thus "chasing after wind" (insubstantial, twice in the unit) accompanies the *hebel*-statement.

These persons need to see that laziness, which brings destruction (v. 5), is not the only alternative to competitive labor.[79] Qohelet advises contentment

---

isolates vv. 13–16); and Whybray, *Ecclesiastes*, 81–91 (who isolates both vv. 1–3 and vv. 13–16). Fox is one who does see some pattern among the subunits, calling them a "loose thematic cluster" (*Time to Tear Down*, 217). Graham Ogden, who would also isolate 4:13–16, argues that vv. 1–12 be divided into three subsections ending in a "better"–saying (vv. 1–3, 4–6, 7–9), with vv. 10–12 an explanatory addition to the third subsection ("The Mathematics of Wisdom: Qoheleth IV 1–12," *VT* 34 [1984]: 446–47). Dominic Rudman has recently defended the thematic unity of the entire chapter ("A Contextual Reading of Ecclesiastes 4:13–16," *JBL* 116 [1997]: 57–73).

[78] As Seow points out (*Ecclesiastes*, 179), it is not clear whether the קִנְאַת־אִישׁ is the result or the cause of human strivings (see the use of קִנְאָה to mean rivalry in Isa 11:13 and *B. Bat.* 21a; cf. Eccl 9:6).

[79] The phrase "folding the hands" is idiomatic of idleness, an idleness that brings poverty according to Prov 6:10; 10:18; 24:33, and others. This saying may be intentionally ambiguous. The phrase "eating his flesh" could mean that the fool, despite idleness, is able to have some food (so Lohfink, *Kohelet* [4th ed.; NEchtB Altes Testament; Würzburg: Echter,

(v. 6): rest (נַחַת)[80] with "a handful" rather than two with strife.[81]

4:7–8 Toil for No One Else (2x)

> Furthermore, I saw vapor (*hebel*) under the sun: the case of one, without a second, who has not even son or brother; and there is no end to all his toil, yet his eyes are never satisfied with riches. "For whom am I toiling and depriving my self of good?" This indeed is vapor (*hebel*) and an evil business.

Beginning with the *hebel*-statement in 4:7, at the center of the larger unit's structure, Qohelet again continues his symbol-building. First, he describes a person who toils "without end" (קֵץ, a contrary) and without "satisfaction" (שבע) in riches (a second contrary) so that the R value of *hebel* in v. 7 relates to *hebel*'s insubstantiality.[82]

Then as he continues, Qohelet extends the analysis: the toiler, while not benefiting self or anyone else, seems unable to stop.[83] The situation (S), more broadly evaluated, then, is (v. 8b) "vapor and an evil business" (הֶבֶל וְעִנְיָן רָע). The addition of the synonym phrase "evil business" communicates that Qohelet

---

1993], 36), or could indicate that the fool's idleness is self-destructive. In regard to the first of these possibilities, the verb אכל is often used with בָּשָׂר to communicate about humans eating food (Exod 12:8, 46; 16:12; 29:32; Lev 7:18; Num 14:11; Deut 12:20; Ezek 4:14). Though בָּשָׂר (flesh) elsewhere in Ecclesiastes refers to the human body, this may be an instance of Qohelet adapting a traditional saying to his own purposes. As for the second possibility, the saying would refer to self-cannibalism. Seow notes that the noun בָּשָׂר with a suffix in the HB never refers to one's food, but to the body or part of a body. Also, "eat the flesh" is used idiomatically of humans being destroyed (Ps 27:2; Isa 49:26). Thus, Seow argues that there really is no ambiguity; the saying communicates only the self-destructiveness of the fool (Seow, *Ecclesiastes*, 179). Even if the saying of v. 5 has some ambiguity, it seems that Qohelet is setting off two extremes (those consumed with work out of envy vs. those who are idle), and is proposing a third alternative.

[80] The term נַחַת does not indicate inactivity, but rather the absence of strife or danger (cf. Isa 30:15; Prov 29:9; Eccl 6:5; 9:17). Thus, it does not refer to the fools who "fold their hands" in v 5.

[81] The Targum explains this verse to mean that a handful of food with enjoyment is better than toil. However, Prov 15:16–17; 16:8; 17:1 employ a similar construction to praise having a small amount of material things rather than to have a large amount along with some particular problem, viz. trouble, lack of justice, strife (Seow, *Ecclesiastes*, 188).

[82] Although Qohelet is not making general declarations about toil here, he uses קֵץ and שבע to evaluate this specific situation just as *hebel* is used to evaluate it.

[83] Again a rhetorical question is employed. The speaker is not identified—possibly Qohelet (Barton, *Ecclesiastes*, 64, 115). Most commentators believe, however, that this is a statement by the toiler, or a question which Qohelet is challenging the toiler to make (see Gordis, *Koheleth*, 97; Hertzberg, *Prediger*, 114–15). Perhaps by keeping the speaker unidentified, the reader is subtly invited to make the question his or her own (Johnson, "Rhetorical Question," 160). In any case, the answer to the question is a negative one.

is not only being descriptive, but is pronouncing a negative evaluation.[84] Qohelet now declares toil which is done for personal benefit to be *hebel*, just as previously he used *hebel* for that toil which results in benefit for another (2:18–23).

The comment concerning wealth anticipates the discussions in 5:9–11 [Eng. vv. 10–12] and 5:12–16 [Eng. vv. 13–17]. But the focus in this subunit, as with the section as a whole, is concerned with self-serving effort as opposed to work which is of benefit to others. Ironically, in pursuit of riches, the toiler has been deprived of good, the good Qohelet is about to describe in 4:9–12. In addition, no one else has gotten any good out of it either, particularly, we might recall, the oppressed ones with which Qohelet introduced this section (4:1–3) and who experience their own dose of evil (רָע, v. 3).

In sum, the two occurrences of *hebel* in 4:7–8 are complementary: the first describes the insubstantiality of the labor, and the second evaluates the situation as foul. It is notable that the work Qohelet describes in the following section (4:9–12), characterized by mutual assistance, is not declared to be "vapor"or "evil."

4:13–16 The Oppressed Youth Abandoned (1x)

The chiastic structure of 4:1–16 returns in the final subunit to the issue of oppression, and here Qohelet once again picks up the subject of wisdom. Starting as in the previous subunit with a *ṭôb*-saying, Qohelet tells the story of a young but wise commoner,[85] a former prisoner, who came forth to reign with wisdom but was subsequently forgotten.

Proposals for this story may be considered in two groups. Both agree that v. 13 presents a contrast between a young, wise commoner and an old, foolish king. The first reads that the youth came from prison, usurped the king and ruled wisely in his place, yet was later dishonored by a fickle public.[86]

---

[84] The רָע phrase echoes 1:13, with allusions also to 2:23, 26; 3:10 and (anticipating) 8:16. The phrase is also used in 5:13 [Eng. v. 14], where it appears to refer to a specific incident rather than being a general evaluation of human existence.

[85] The term מִסְכֵּן (only here and in 9:15–16; cf. מִסְכְּנוֹת in Deut 8:9) in postbiblical Hebrew indicates a person of lower social status but only secondarily of impoverishment in terms of wealth (cf. Jastrow, 807–8). The Akkadian *muškēnu/maškēnu*, from which it is likely borrowed, indicates a status of dependency upon the state (E. A. Speiser, "The Muškênum," in *Oriental and Biblical Studies* [ed. and intro. J. J. Finkelstein and M. Greenberg; Philadelphia: University of Pennsylvania Press, 1967], 332–43). The term יֶלֶד is used most often of a young child, so that here youth is set in contrast to old age, and common status in contrast to royalty (so Rashbam).

[86] I.e., there was only one youth. Some such as Emmanuel Podéchard (*L'Ecclésiaste* [EBib. Paris: Gabalda, 1912], 332-33) would delete הַשֵּׁנִי (second v. 15) as a gloss.

Variations to this thesis urge that the wise youth was himself deposed by a second youth (הַשֵּׁנִי, v. 15b),[87] or that the wise youth succeeded the king without usurping him (הַשֵּׁנִי as "successor"),[88] or that there were actually three youths.[89]

The second thesis interprets that the wise youth came from prison to a position of *advisor* (הַשֵּׁנִי) to the king before succeeding him.[90] As with the first proposal, this youth who gave much to his people, was largely unappreciated and his memory unheralded. Whether or not the tale involves allusion to legend or history, most agree it is best read as a parable or an example story of the "rags to riches" type.[91]

Thus, with either proposal, Qohelet tells of a poor one who came to a royal office and ruled wisely, yet the public for whom he served failed to give him appropriate honor (cf. 9:13–18). As is axiomatic for a wise ruler in the ancient Near East, his reign must have included justice for oppressed ones like those mentioned in the initial subunit (4:1–3). His time in prison suggests his own experience of oppression, for prisons were often the repository for economic and political outcasts.[92]

However, this royal figure is cast aside by fickle followers, oppressed and isolated once again through rejection and lack of support.[93] His attempts to

---

[87] E.g., Seow, *Ecclesiastes*, 185, and Ellermeier, *Qohelet*, 217–32.

[88] So Gordis, *Koheleth*, 245.

[89] Fox, *Time to Tear Down*, 226.

[90] Rudman, "Contextual Reading," 66–73, who develops the work of Graham Ogden, "Historical Allusion in Qoheleth IV 13–16?" *VT* 30 (1980): 309–15. See also Miller, "Power in Wisdom," 159–65, and Addison G. Wright, "The Poor But Wise Youth and the Old But Foolish King (Qoh 4:13–16)," in *Wisdom, You Are My Sister* (CBQMS 29; Fs. Roland E. Murphy; ed. Michael L. Barré; Washington, D.C.: Catholic Biblical Association, 1997), 142–54.

[91] So Murphy, *Ecclesiastes*, 42. It is part of Qohelet's rhetoric to allude to various life situations, whether those of himself or of others. Plausible allusions to biblical figures, such as Joseph and Daniel, have been suggested by proponents of either proposal. Fox believes that the tale was recognizable to Qohelet's audience and argues that "the audience must be able to grant the factuality of the episode in vv. 13–14 in order for the twist in vv. 15–16 to be effective" (*Time to Tear Down*, 228).

[92] Virtually all commentators take הסורים as a by-form for האסורים; elsewhere an omission of aleph may be noted by comparing 2 Kgs 8:28 and 2 Chr 22:5 (see GKC §35d). This reading is supported by the ancient versions (except Tg.). On the character of ancient prisons of this region, see Karel van der Toorn, "Prison," in *ABD* 5:468–69.

[93] The interpretation of v. 14 and its relationship with v. 13 is a matter of difficulty. Some understand v. 14 as a reference to the commoner introduced in v. 13a while others read it as a description of the king mentioned in v. 13b: one who came forth from prison to reign, though in his kingdom (the commoner's or that of the king) he was born poor (רָשׁ as adj. or ptc.). See Murphy, *Ecclesiastes*, 41. However, it is also possible that v. 14 contrasts the commoner (who came forth from prison) with the king who was born into his kingship and

promote a just community end in expulsion from his community.[94] The "chasing after wind" synonym accompanies the *hebel*-statement because the efforts of such a wise one are of no lasting result. In the context of the chapter, 4:13–16 qualify the wise examples described in 4:9–12.[95] Wisdom again proves insubstantial, this time due to human fickleness.

Summary of 4:1–16

Qohelet begins this unit with a stark presentation of those abandoned to oppression, and labels the situation an "evil work." He next introduces the insubstantiality of the one toiling out of envy. The unit's center laments that toil for one's own self accomplishes nothing for self or anyone else. Since he has already despaired concerning toil passed along to those who come after (2:18–23), Qohelet goes on to build his case for a communal orientation in contrast to the solitary life. Lest there seem to be cause for optimism, however, he reminds the reader in conclusion that those seeking to serve others through wisdom may themselves be abandoned and left alone.

Through *hebel*-statements, Qohelet declares toil from envy and obsessive toil to be futile and the latter to be foul. After proposing an alternative lifestyle, he cautions that wise living is also *hebel*, futile due to human fickleness.

In the midst of building his *hebel*-symbol, Qohelet is also making a case for the life he commends, however qualified. Prior to this unit, Qohelet had given advice on three occasions: 2:24, 3:12, and 3:22. After establishing that toil and pleasure are insubstantial, at these points Qohelet urged his audience to enjoy life and find satisfaction in their labor. Now in ch. 4, he commends that this be done in a context of common care and mutual effort.

---

then impoverished (רָשׁ as a perfect 3ms verb). So Seow (see discussion *Ecclesiastes*, 190–92).

[94] As with other ambiguities in this subunit, the object of displeasure in v. 16 is not certain. Most interpret this as a reference to a second (or third) upstart youth who takes over for the wise youth (Seow, *Ecclesiastes*, 185; Ellermeier, *Qohelet*, 217–32; Fox, *Time to Tear Down*, 226). Thus, the throne room represents a revolving cycle, and the fickle crowd rejects a wise king as quickly as a foolish one.

[95] So Wright, "Poor But Wise Youth," 150–54. It is interesting to compare this royal figure with the servant of Yahweh found in Deutero-Isaiah. In that context, too, royalty is alluded to (42:1–4, establishing justice; 52:15; 53:12, recognized among kings and great ones), the servant is abused (50:6–9; 52:14; 53:3, 7–8), and the mission of that one seems at first of no effect (42:4; 49:4; 50:7; 53:3, 10–12). Unlike the prophet, Qohelet expresses no confidence in the ultimate success of his "wise youth." He is simply a further instance of wisdom's failures.

4:17–5:6 [Eng. 5:1–7] (1x) Relations with God

A new unit is indicated by a switch to the imperative mood and by a change of subject. As in 3:1–22, Qohelet turns to issues concerning God, this time in regard to matters of speech. While his advice in the previous unit was of the "wisdom sentence" variety, here he uses direct commands.

4:17–5:6 [Eng. 5:1–7] Words before God (1x)

Dealing with the deity is one of Qohelet's main concerns, and once again he emphasizes the importance of respecting the distance between humanity and God. Thus he counsels discretion, integrity, and reverence.[96] He is especially concerned with the matter of speech, and uses nearly all the devices of his repertoire to heighten the impact of his counsel.[97] Among these are the negative example of the fool (4:17 [Eng. 5:1]; 5:2, 3 [Eng. vv. 3, 4]), characterizations of the deity (5:1, 3 [Eng. vv. 2, 4]), a *ṭôb*-saying (5:4 [Eng. v. 5]), a rhetorical question (5:5 [Eng. v. 6]), a *hebel*-saying (5:6 [Eng. v. 7]), and direct exhortation (5:1, 3, 6 [Eng. vv. 2, 4, 7]). The rhetorical question of 5:5 [Eng. v. 6] appears to sum up the sense of this section: there is no reason to arouse God's anger at one's words and to have one's works destroyed as a result.[98]

Within this discussion of careful speech is an especially challenging *hebel* text (5:6 [Eng. v. 7]), the only place outside the framing statements in the book where *hebel* is in the plural:

כִּי בְרֹב חֲלֹמוֹת וַהֲבָלִים וּדְבָרִים הַרְבֵּה
כִּי אֶת־הָאֱלֹהִים יְרָא׃

For with many dreams and vapors (*hebel*'s) and a multitude of words; thus, fear God.

---

[96] Seow, *Ecclesiastes*, 197

[97] Cf. Eccl 12:13, "Fear God." A number of texts in the HB reflect a relationship between fear of the divine and circumspection of speech: Job 1:9 and 4:6, Job fears God and does not sin with his lips; Ps 34:11–13, fear of the Lord involves keeping one's tongue from badness, deceit; Ps 36:1–3, the wicked do not fear God, their words are mischief and deceit; Prov 8:13, the fear of Yahweh is to hate badness, including perverted speech.

[98] This sentiment is a common one in ancient Near Eastern wisdom. Note the following:

Offer to your god,
Beware of offending him . . . .
He gives power in a million forms,
He who magnifies him is magnified.
(*Any*, 7.13–16; *AEL* 2:141)
Do not make many words.
Do not talk much before your master.
(*Ankhsheshonq*, 14.12; 17.25; *AEL* 3:170, 173)

The sense of the complicated syntax is reflected in the above literalistic translation. Various proposals have been offered for this verse. Some would rearrange the words,[99] or emend in various ways,[100] although the integrity of MT is supported by LXX and other versions and is supported by various commentators.[101]

Seow points out that חֲלוֹם (dream), which occurs twice in this unit (5:2, 6 [Eng. vv. 3, 7]) but nowhere else in the book, can express that which is unreal, worthless, or short-lived, i.e., insubstantial or transient (Job 20:8; Ps 73:20; Isa 29:7; Sir 34:1–2 [LXX]).[102] He also cites wisdom texts from Egypt and elsewhere in Mesopotamia that use dreams as an image of that which is illusory or ephemeral. Thus he proposes a hendiadys of *hebel* and חֲלוֹם in v. 6 [Eng. v. 7]: "vacuous dreams" or the like. It would be the same as saying, "this is *hebel* and a dream." In Seow's proposal, the second occurrence of כִּי is adversative, and the second *waw* may then be understood as resumptive or adjunctive:[103]

> For with many dreams-and-vapors there is (also) a multitude of words; rather, fear God.[104]

This proposal makes good sense of the immediate text, and fits well into the larger picture of Qohelet's symbol-building with *hebel*. As predicate terms of a metaphorical relation, both חֲלוֹם and *hebel* may have referents of either insubstantiality or transience. To determine which applies here, it remains to

---

[99] So Barton, *Ecclesiastes*, 124–25.

[100] So *HALOT*, vol. 1, s.v. "חֲלֹם," cj. emending "dreams" (חלמות) to "madness" (הללות) in 5:2. Some have sought to relate v. 6 with v. 2 to the effect that a kind of hallucination or bad dream results from extreme duress (v. 2); the further consequence (v. 6) is then emptiness with verbosity. Note, for example, the Akkadian wisdom text cited by A. Leo Oppenheim (*The Interpretation of Dreams in the Ancient Near East [TAPA* 46; Philadelphia: American Philological Society, 1956], 227):
Remove [wo]e and anxiety from your heart,
[wo]e and anxiety create dreams!
Various proposals have been made concerning the range of possibilities with *waw*. Charles Whitley, for example, offers that the second waw is asseverative, "there are *indeed* many words" (Charles F. Whitley, *Koheleth: His Language and Thought* [BZAW 148; Berlin: Walter de Gruyter, 1979], 49–50).

[101] Gordis defends the MT, proposing to take בְרֹב to mean "in spite of": "In spite of all the dreams, follies and idle chatter, indeed, fear God" (*Koheleth*, 249–50).

[102] Cf. M. Ottosson, "חֲלֹם" *TDOT* 4:432. Rabbi Hanan (*Ber.* 10b, in reference to Eccl 5:6) counsels that even if a man should learn in a dream he will die on the morrow, he should not cease to pray, an apparent recognition that dreams are unreliable or possibly deceptive.

[103] Ronald J. Williams, *Hebrew Syntax: An Outline* (2d ed.; Toronto: University of Toronto Press, 1976), §440–41.

[104] Seow, *Ecclesiastes*, 197–200. Cf. Zech 10:2, a hendiadys of חֲלוֹם and שָׁוְא.

identify their subject. It would appear to be the activity of fools—particularly their loquacity—who are given as a negative example on three occasions (4:17 [Eng. 5:1]; 5:2, 3 [Eng. vv. 3, 4]).

The sense of 5:2 [Eng. v. 3], then, would be as follows: just as the dream (insubstantial) comes with much business, likewise the fool's voice (which is insubstantial) is accompanied by a lot of words.[105] Building on the dream image of v. 2 [Eng. v. 3], *hebel* is paired with "dreams" in v. 6 [Eng. v. 7] to reinforce the emptiness of words: in the midst of insubstantial (R) foolish activity (S), one finds excess speech. Unlike the fool, the one who fears God will keep words to a minimum.

Summary of 4:17–5:6 [Eng. 5:1–7]

This section resumes Qohelet's concern for relations with God, primarily in regard to speech. Here *hebel* is guarded with a synonym, "dreams," as well as through extension, particularly the fool as negative example, and the details on problems of speech. While the insubstantiality referent is primarily a descriptive one in this presentation, the element of negative evaluation is not completely absent. In 4:17 [Eng. 5:1], Qohelet comments that the fool does עֵר, while 5:6 [Eng. v. 7] warns against the mouth leading to sin (חטא) and cautions that God may bring destruction upon the work of those who speak improperly. Since these are things for which people have choices, at least some things that are *hebel* and עֵר can be avoided.

5:7 [Eng. 5:8]–6:9 (4x) Enjoyment Instead of Greed

A focus on greed and true satisfaction characterizes this unit, a return to an issue which surfaced briefly at 4:8a. As Fredericks has proposed, the structure is chiastic.[106] It begins, as did 4:1–16 and the subunit 3:16–22, with the issue of oppression. It should not be surprising that oppression occurs,

---

[105] There appears no suggestion of transience in the passage, that anything discussed here will be short-lived.

[106] Daniel C. Fredericks, "Chiasm and Parallel Structure in Qoheleth 5:6–6:9," *JBL* 108 (1989): 17–35. Fox outlines according to chiasm in *Contradictions*, 213, but not in his later revision (*Time to Tear Down*, 235). Yet his discussion of the section is essentially the same in both. The position adopted here is closer to that of Fox in *Contradictions*, although, unlike either Fox or Fredericks, it includes 5:7–8 [Eng. vv. 8–9] in the larger unit. Seow also includes the latter verses (*Ecclesiastes*, 217), but otherwise is closer to Fredericks than the following:

    A 5:7–11 [Eng. vv. 8–12] Wealth Brings No Satisfaction
    B 5:12–16 [Eng. vv. 13–17] Money Easily Lost
    C 5:17–19 [Eng. vv. 18–20] Best to Find Good in One's Work
    B' 6:1–6 Money Easily Lost (God's Role)
    A' 6:7–9 Toil Brings No Satisfaction

Qohelet says, as he goes on to insist that money will not satisfy. Further, wealth is easily lost. Enjoy the gifts God has given, he adds, for a stranger may come and take it all away, and life is not worth living without some enjoyment.

5:7–11 [Eng. vv. 8–12] Money Brings No Satisfaction (1x)

This subunit begins with two verses which have been problematic. Verse 7 again raises the concern that the poor are being oppressed and that justice and right are being violated. Given the system of officials in existence, the reader should really not be surprised, however.[107] It is possible, then, to read this as ironic or cynical: of course the officials will not really do anything about the problem. On the other hand, it may be that Qohelet is pointing to the officials as the very source of the problem: they look out for each other as they allow the poor to be oppressed.[108]

Qohelet moves in vv. 9–11 [Eng. vv. 10–12] to challenge the notion that such kings and princes, with their wealth and powerful position, have what everyone should be striving for (cf. 4:6). These lovers of money and wealth, who will oppress to get them, will never be satisfied (שׂבע) by them (v. 9 [Eng. v. 10]). Qohelet then asks a rhetorical question (v. 10 [Eng. v. 11]) to the effect that there is also no true advantage (כִּשְׁרוֹן) for those with wealth. Those who possess wealth find that the more they have, the more it is out of their reach; they can only see it.

Thus, שׂבע (satisfaction) and כִּשְׁרוֹן (gain) serve as contraries to emphasize that wealth (S) is *hebel* in the sense of being futile (insubstantial). Laborers have sweet sleep even in relative poverty, while the "satisfaction" (שׂבע) of the wealthy will not let them sleep (v. 11). Qohelet uses שׂבע ironically in v. 11 to claim that wealth actually makes life worse—there is no true satisfaction by that means.[109]

---

[107] The term גָּבֹהַּ (from גבה, to be high) is taken by most commentators as a reference to a government official. However, James Kugel points out that גָּבֹהַּ never means this in Hebrew, but rather an "arrogant one" ("Qohelet and Money," *CBQ* 51 [1989]: 35–38). Thus 5:7 [Eng. v. 8] may refer to the upper class or classes rather than government officials specifically.

[108] In either case, the sense of v. 8 is also a difficulty. The MT is possibly corrupt here, though the versions essentially support it. Various emendations have been proposed to make sense of it. Several of these support the basic sense that government bureaucracy brings both advantage and disadvantage. See the commentaries for discussion.

[109] The author likely is intentionally ambiguous here. "שׂבע of the wealthy" refers both to the fact that too much food (אכל in v. 10) causes them to remain awake (due to digestive problems), and to the anxiety caused by material wealth. A Sumerian proverb says, "He who eats too much will not (be able) to sleep" (Edmund I. Gordon, *Sumerian Proverbs* [Philadelphia: University of Pennsylvania Musem, 1959], 97, cited in Seow, *Ecclesiastes*, 220)

6:1–6 Wealth Easily Lost (God's Role) (2x)

In 6:1–6, Qohelet presents the situation of those who are not able to enjoy things, the very things which God gave them and which they should enjoy.[110] 6:2 lists the person's good things ("wealth, possessions, and honor"), and yet these are enjoyed by a stranger instead. Qohelet expresses his abhorrence of such a scenario by declaring it to be רָע (evil, 6:1) and then also הֶבֶל וָחֳלִי רָע (*vapor* and an evil sickness, 6:2). Life should not be this way, and Qohelet does not hesitate to hold God accountable for it: God has given good things to this person but has not enabled (שׁלט) the person to enjoy them.[111]

The referent for *hebel* in 6:2 is not immediately apparent. A possible contrary is שׂבע (no satisfaction) in 6:3, which might suggest something related to insubstantiality. However, Qohelet is not evaluating material possessions here and the degree of satisfaction they provide. Rather, he is describing one who is deprived of the satisfaction they bring by having them taken away, an exception to the general rule of God's benevolent giving described in 5:17–19 [Eng. vv. 18–20]. Because he considers this to be repugnant, he introduces the unit with רָע in 6:1, and couples *hebel* in 6:2 with חֳלִי רָע (evil sickness). The referent of *hebel* in 6:1–3 is therefore foulness and the subject is the situation being described.[112]

In 6:3b, Qohelet introduces a comparison: a stillborn child is better off than a person so deprived of material goods. Eccl 6:3–5 reads:

---

[110] Bo Isaksson (*Studies in the Language of Qoheleth with Special Emphasis on the Verbal System* [Studia Semitica Upsaliensia 10; Uppsala: Almqvist and Wiksell, 1987], 122). Eccl 5:17–18 [Eng. vv. 18–19] states the general rule (for all people), while 6:1–2 addresses the individual exception to the rule. The perfect verbs of the former indicate what *is*, the imperfect of the latter what *could be*. However, it seems unlikely that Qohelet is saying that the general rule is that everyone has an abundance to enjoy. Rather, it is the general rule that it is fitting for people to enjoy what God has given.

[111] Compare the corresponding use of שׁלט in 5:18 [Eng. v. 19]. In ch. 6, Qohelet describes the circumstances by raising two matters traditionally associated with blessedness in ancient Near Eastern culture—having many children, and long life—and declaring them to be worthless without enjoyment. Such things are no compensation for one made destitute.

[112] The subunit 5:12–16 [Eng. 5:13–17], which corresponds to 6:1–6 in the chiasm of 5:7–6:9 [Eng. 5:8–6:9], does not involve *hebel*. However, it addresses a situation similar to that described in 6:1–3: the "evil" situation that a person toils and achieves wealth but then loses it (interestingly, it likewise refers to the birth of a child). 5:15 [Eng. v. 16] reflects that Qohelet uses רוּחַ with a referent of insubstantiality but not of foulness. The מַה־יִּתְרוֹן (what surplus?) rhetorical question in that verse concerns toil and makes clear that "toiling for wind" means toiling with nothing accomplished. The situation, the fact that someone has toiled with nothing gained, is רָעָה חוֹלָה (evil, a sickness); but Qohelet does not declare such a situation itself to be "wind" like he declares such situations to be *hebel*. Thus, in 5:15, Qohelet does *not* say, "This is wind and an evil sickness." But in 6:2 he can and does say of the same kind of situation, "This is vapor (*hebel*) and an evil sickness."

If a man should beget a hundred, and live many years—even great be the days of his years—but he is not satisfied from good things, then even though it has no burial,[113] I say that a stillborn child is better off than he.[114] Even though it comes in vapor (*hebel*) and goes in darkness,[115] and in darkness its name is covered,[116] though it has not seen the sun[117] or known anything,[118] yet it finds more rest than the other.[119]

In v. 6, Qohelet combines hyperbole (live a thousand years) with a rhetorical question to clinch his point: all people go to the same place when they die (the netherworld). This continues Qohelet's theme of human frailty (cf. 3:20).

The use of *hebel* in v. 4, Qohelet's second use of it in this subunit, requires extended comment.[120] First, it is possible that here Qohelet is employing *hebel* in the material sense of breath or vapor, a usage which would

---

[113] The stillborn has no burial (or perhaps burial marker), a matter related to its name being covered (v. 4).

[114] There are two difficulties of syntax in v. 3: וְרַב and וְגַם־קְבוּרָה. Various emendations have been offered though the versions affirm the MT. See the commentaries for discussion. The *waw* in וְרַב is explicative (even). Since רַב can have the sense of quality as well as quantity (cf. Ps 31:20; 48:20), it appears to be used here as a play on the use of רַב in 6:1—the years are great, but also remember that badness is great. As regards the second issue, the use of גַם is concessive, which corresponds to its use in v. 5: "though (גַם) it has not seen the sun or known anything, yet it finds rest rather than he."

[115] In 6:4, MT וּבַחֹשֶׁךְ יֵלֵךְ, LXX ἐν σκότει πορεύεται (= וּבַחֹשֶׁךְ הוֹלֵךְ as in 2:14), and 4QQoh^a has הלך. Likely both LXX (participle) and 4QQoh^a (probably the perfect, since the participle is written הוֹלֵךְ in 6:6) are an attempt to conform to the corresponding verb בָּא (which may be perfect or participle). The MT should be retained as the *lectio difficilior*.

[116] The reference to the name of the stillborn being "covered" is a reference to death and/or nonexistence, with the result that none remembers it. Murphy, (*Ecclesiastes*, 54) cites the opening lines of the *Enuma Elish* and also refers to Isa 40:26 and Ps 47:4 where naming is associated with creation and existence (Gen 1:5, 8, 10; 2:19, 23). Qohelet comments several times on the lack of remembrance which the living have of those past (1:11; 2:16; 9:15). Fox rejects these comparisons on the ground that the stillborn would not have a name. He argues that 6:4 describes the unfortunate person of 6:3a (*Time to Tear Down*, 243).

[117] Light is associated with life, while death is indicated by darkness. See, e.g., Job 3, esp. vv. 4–6, 16, 20–21; note also the references to "rest" in Job 3:13, 17, 26.

[118] ידע has no object here. It refers to the stillborn's general lack of awareness.

[119] And rest *is* a possibility for the living, as Qohelet indicates in 4:6. For the syntax of the final phrase of v. 5, cf. Prov 26:12b, תִּקְוָה לִכְסִיל מִמֶּנּוּ, "a fool has more hope than he" (Arnold B. Ehrlich, *Randglossen zur hebräischen Bibel* [vol. 7; Leipzig: Hinrichs, 1914], 79).

[120] Although Fox interprets v. 4 as referring to the person of v. 3a, and then v. 5 as referring to the stillborn, it is more likely (with most commentators) that vv. 3b–5 all refer to the stillborn. It is extremely awkward to read vv. 3b–5 with such an alternation in antecedents for the pronouns. The advantage of Fox's reading for his thesis is that it allows him to interpret *hebel* here as a reference to the person unable to enjoy wealth, etc., to say that such a person "comes into a life of absurdity" and returns to darkness at death; the stillborn, he says, never reaches the realm of absurdity (*Time to Tear Down*, 243).

be unique to Ecclesiastes (yet see p. 131, note 135). Several texts in the HB make reference to wind or breath in connection with early human life. For example, Qohelet himself comments in Eccl 11:5:

> Just as you do not know how the wind (רוּחַ) comes to the bones in the mother's womb, so you do not know the work of God, who makes everything.

This reference to the mystery of birth (cf. Ps 139:14–16; Job 10:10–11) recalls the "breath of life" described in the creation account of Gen 2:7, although there נְשָׁמָה is the term used for "breath."

In Isa 26:18, wind is referred to in connection with the birthing process:

> We were pregnant, we writhed,
> We gave birth, as it were, to wind (רוּחַ).
> We could not accomplish deliverance for the earth,
> Nor were inhabitants of the world fallen (i.e., born).

The passage is an extended image meant to express the failure to accomplish anything substantial. However, at the literal level of the image, there may be a reference to vapor which surrounds the fetus in the womb. In this case, the birth process brought forth the vapor only; no child was actually present.

Further, in a text mentioned previously, *Lev. Rab.* 29:8,[121] Rabbi Ḥiyya comments that marriage partners are foreordained to marriage while they are yet vapor (*hebel*) in the womb of their mother. To summarize, Qohelet's use of *hebel* in 6:4 may, like the texts just cited, reflect a material use of the term *hebel* as a vapor, either the breath of life within the emerging child, or as "wind" within the womb.[122]

The other viable ways of construing *hebel* in 6:4 posit that here, as elsewhere in Ecclesiastes, the term is used metaphorically. The existence of a stillborn child could be considered to have a fleeting duration. However, no guarding terms in the subunit point in this direction. Another possibility would be the insubstantiality or frailty of the stillborn. This dimension of human life was described in Eccl 3:20 using *hebel* and עָפָר (dust).

As with other passages, the phrases and words associated with *hebel* here must be carefully considered. In this case, חֹשֶׁךְ and the similar "not seeing the sun" (v. 5) are crucial.[123] There is a symmetry between *hebel*, in which the child comes, and חֹשֶׁךְ, to which the child goes. The root חשׁךְ in Ecclesiastes

---

[121] A discussion in Chapter 3 of Ps 62:10 [Eng. v. 9], humans are only vapor (*hebel*).

[122] In the former case, of course, the use of *hebel* would allude to God's involvement.

[123] It is plausible that Qohelet is saying the stillborn comes out of nothing and goes into darkness in the sense of dissolution. In support of this is the stillborn's lack of burial or burial marker, so that it is not remembered, and the idiom "covering the name" which indicates nonexistence. However, "darkness" (חֹשֶׁךְ, v. 4), is not used elsewhere in this sense.

refers variously to literal darkness (2:13), the ignorance within which fools exist (2:14), an experience of destitution (5:16 [Eng. v. 17]), "days of darkness" beyond the time of youth (11:8), and the experience of decline in old age (12:2–3).

Qohelet's previous use of darkness to indicate both death and ignorance is consistent with similar metaphorical associations elsewhere in the Hebrew canon.[124] The additional description that the unborn does not know anything (v. 6), and *hebel*'s referent of ignorance elsewhere[125] makes it plausible that *hebel*'s referent in this case has the sense of ignorance or mystery.[126] Considering Qohelet's penchant for multiple valencies, it is not unlikely that he is seeking to develop some combination of considerations in the present context. He can use *hebel* for breath of life, darkness for death, and both for mystery.

It is important to note what Qohelet has accomplished rhetorically for *hebel* with this brief narrative. Connecting the term with life's incipience, as he does here, allows Qohelet to present the phenomenon of *hebel* "under the sun" as totally pervasive: it is there at the beginning of even the briefest life (6:4), infuses all of life among those given breath (7:15; 9:9), and is that which awaits one at death (11:8).

The first occurrence of *hebel* in 6:1–6 decries the foulness of experience for those deprived of good things. The second use of the term points to the insubstantial and mysterious origins and destiny of human life by reference to a stillborn child.

---

[124] On ignorance, cf. Job 22:15; 42:3; Ps 82:5; on death, cf. 1 Sam 2:9; Ps 88:13 [Eng. v. 12] (Helmer Ringgren, "חָשַׁךְ," *TDOT* 5:252–58).

[125] While there are no explicit associations between darkness and *hebel* in texts outside of Ecclesiastes, a connection between *hebel* and ignorance is found in at least five texts, of which Job 35:16 is representative:

Job opens his mouth in *vapor* (*hebel*),
he multiplies words without knowledge.

Other texts include Ps 94:11 and Job 27:12. The ignorance of false gods is emphasized in Jer 10:8 and 23:16 (*hbl* verb).

[126] There are several ways one might explain *hebel*'s referent of "mystery" on the basis of its material sense. Just as material vapor may appear to be something substantial when in fact it is not, so that which appears to be knowledge may actually be error. Another way to construe the imagery for *hebel* in this connection is by analogy with fog-like vapor which may obscure what is behind it. Likewise, the mind may unclearly "see" and make an error. Seybold, for example, concludes that Qohelet in 6:4 draws upon the "concealing sphere of vapor" ("הֶבֶל," 319). Finally, just as vapor is insubstantial, so the mind may have difficulty "grasping" certain mysterious phenomena. Whether one takes this connection with *hebel* on the basis of vapor's insubstantiality, its obscuring properties, or its illusory nature, it is the author's use of the metaphor or symbol, guarded by contextual clues, which we are attempting to determine. The rationale is not requisite to this determination.

6:7–9 Toil Brings No Satisfaction (1x)

The rhetorical power of this section (6:7–9) is enhanced by a *ṭôb*-saying, two rhetorical questions, and by allusions to previous themes: the lot of the wise, the fool, and the poor; the sight of the eyes; desire (נֶפֶשׁ); and death vs. life. As he brings together the results of his previous discussions, Qohelet particularly focuses on the three aspects of human effort which have been his primary targets.

In v. 7, he addresses toil (עָמָל): for all the effort, nothing ever gets filled, that is, satisfied. Qohelet has several times used food and eating imagery metaphorically of consuming in general.[127] He does so here as well, referring to the mouth and to נֶפֶשׁ, which may be taken as "life," "throat," or "desire," among other things. The lack of filling (מלא) here appears to be an alternative way of expressing the lack of satisfaction mentioned earlier (1:8; 5:9 [Eng. v.10]; cf. 4:8 which also mentions toil and נֶפֶשׁ). However, the term נֶפֶשׁ as "throat" may also allude both to the insatiability of death, that is, Sheol, and to the oppression of rich over poor (Isa 5:4; Prov 27:20; cf. Hab 2:5; Ps 73:9).[128] Just as in the first section of this unit (5:7–11 [Eng. vv. 8–12]), Qohelet is making a connection between insatiable greed and the oppression (עֹשֶׁק רָשׁ, 5:7 [Eng. v. 8]) which results from it.

The second issue summarized here is wisdom (v. 8). There is no surplus to being wise, a theme addressed several times previously (esp. 1:16–18; 2:12–17). Continuing the imagery of oppression, this verse mentions the afflicted (עָנִי) who have even less chance than the wise to gain an advantage.

Finally in v. 9, Qohelet addresses pleasure. This may be discerned from his reference to the eyes, which are associated with pleasure in 2:10 and 5:10 [Eng. v. 11] and with lack of satisfaction in 1:8 and 4:8. In 5:10, within the subsection which corresponds structurally to 6:7–9, there is also the imagery of eating/consuming (אכל), another reason to suppose that the use of נֶפֶשׁ, in both 6:7 and 6:9, includes the sense of appetite or desire. It is better to experience pleasure with what one has, than to allow one's (insatiable) desires to wander.[129]

Qohelet's use of *hebel* in vv. 7–9, then, expresses his major conclusion that human effort (toil, wisdom, pleasure) is insubstantial, a futile and lost cause. To communicate this, he employs a favorite contrary regarding wisdom,

---

[127] Positively, 2:24–25; 3:13; 5:17–18; 8:15; 9:7; in negative context, 5:10, 16; 6:2.

[128] See discussion in Seow (*Ecclesiastes*, 226–27) who cites Ugaritic texts employing *npš* in descriptions of Death's insatiability.

[129] So, e.g., REB, NIV, NRSV, NAB, NJB. Yet also, since both the verb הלך (go) and the term נֶפֶשׁ (life, desire, throat) have associations with death, it is possible that there is a secondary allusion here to the death which comes from oppressors with insatiable desires (so Seow, *Ecclesiastes*, 227).

יוֹתֵר (excess, leftover, v. 8), and adds a new application of another: toil does not fill (מלא) the mouth (v. 7).[130] In addition, he presents his final use of the synonymous wind phrase: human effort is vapor (*hebel*) and a chasing after wind (v. 9).

Thus, this subunit serves as a conclusion to the larger unit which repeatedly addresses the matter of desires unfulfilled, while it emphasizes true enjoyment instead of greed (cf. 4:1–8). These verses likewise bring the book's entire first half fittingly to a close in their three-part address of human effort.

Summary of 5:7 [Eng. 5:8]–6:9

In this unit, Qohelet declares that wealth does not satisfy, so it is not worth pursuing. Further, wealth is easily lost. In the center of the unit, he commends enjoyment, particularly finding "good" in one's work. Yet sometimes the gifts of God are taken away. This is so terrible, he insists that it would be better not to be born than to live without enjoyment.

Although *hebel* is used in the book's first half to assess the quality of the human condition as insubstantial in 3:19–20 (dust), Qohelet's primary concern has been with human effort broadly understood: toil (incl. various entailments), pleasure, wisdom, wealth, foolish activity, and speech. This effort is assessed as *hebel* in the sense of being insubstantial. While this use of *hebel* is essentially descriptive, certain situations, as well as various complications involving human effort, are also declared to be *hebel* in its foul dimension: the business (in general) God has given humans (1:12–15), a common fate for the wise and the fool (2:15–16), inappropriate benefit from the toil of another (2:18–23), obsessive toil (4:8), and the loss of goods (6:1–2).[131] It thus becomes evident that at least some statements involving *hebel* are also declarations of negative evaluation.

Finally, in the center three subunits of the first half's closing section (5:12 [Eng. 5:13]–6:6), Qohelet reports seeing רָע (evil, 5:12 [Eng. v. 13]), טוֹב (good, 5:17 [Eng. v. 18]), and then רָע (evil, 6:1) once again. This prepares the reader for a discussion of goodness in 6:10–7:14. While a number of other themes introduced in the book to this point will be picked up again in the second half, Qohelet makes a significant transition here from an emphasis on human effort to a focus on human understanding.

6:10–7:14 (3x) No One Knows What Is Good

A theological introduction (6:10–12) and conclusion (7:13–14) frame a series of proverbs as this unit launches the second half of Qohelet's work (cf.

---

[130] Cf. especially the lack of filling (מלא) and satisfaction (שבע) expressed in the book's introduction, 1:7–8.

[131] To these could be added Qohelet's statements involving רָע without *hebel*: oppres-

the framing of 1:12–2:26).[132] A parody on the verbosity of those who are confident in their knowledge, these verses serve as a fitting introduction to a major theme of this part of the book: the limitation of human knowledge.

6:10–12 Human Limits (2x)

These verses introduce the unit and serve as a transition from what has preceded. Human knowledge is severely limited, as Qohelet is about to demonstrate. Yet among that which humans *do* know are conclusions from the book's first half, viz., that humans are weak (v. 10, not able to dispute with the one stronger, i.e., God, an allusion made in 7:13–14),[133] and many times verbosity simply increases *hebel* instead of giving help (v. 11). Just as 6:7–9 served both as a conclusion to its own unit and as a conclusion to the book's first half, so 6:10–12 both introduces the book's second half and introduce a unit with a specific focus on "goodness."[134]

The use of *hebel* in 6:11 has the sense of insubstantiality, and the subject is words:

> Certainly there are many words (which) increase vapor (*hebel*)
> —what excess (יֹתֵר) is there for the human?

The insubstantiality referent is evident from the allusion to 4:17–5:6 [Eng. 5:1–7] (the insubstantiality associated with words) and from the contrary יֹתֵר (excess, advantage, v. 11). The rhetorical question here in v. 11 (מַה־יֹּתֵר, what excess?) is the same one used in 6:8 (just previously) in connection with the futility of wisdom.[135]

This subunit's second use of *hebel* (v. 12) is found within the first of two rhetorical questions which highlight Qohelet's new theme of knowledge:

---

sive acts by the powerful upon the weak (4:1–3), and wealth lost (5:12–16 [Eng. vv. 13–17]).

[132] Allusions to the deity are oblique in 6:10: "one who is stronger," "already been named," "it is known." The structure of the unit:

    A 6:10–12 Human Limits
    B 7:1–12 Good and Better
    A' 7:13–14 God's Work Limits Humans

[133] Reading the Qere with Syr., Tg. and some Heb. MSS See the commentaries for textual issues with v. 10. Cf. Job 9:4–5; 14:20; and Qohelet's discussion of humans as dust at Eccl 3:20.

[134] Note that the remainder of the unit, 7:1–14, appears to have its own inclusio, viz., the double use of טוֹב (good) and יוֹם (day) in both vv. 1 and 14. Yet there are even stronger correspondences between 6:10–12 and 7:10–14, reflected in the verbs היה and יכל, and the terms יֹתֵר, צֵל, and אַחֲרָיו.

[135] Qohelet ironically claims that there is a verbosity which actually increases *hebel* in its attempt to overcome it. Seybold ("הֶבֶל," 319) notes the possible allusion to the material sense of "breath" when Qohelet uses *hebel* here in connection with many words (cf. 7:6).

For who knows what is good for humans while they live the few days of their vapor (*hebel*) lives,[136] which they spend like the shadow (צֵל)?[137] For who can inform humans what their future will be under the sun?[138]

Who knows? Who can inform? *Hebel* in this subunit is guarded by a new synonym, צֵל (shadow), here with the referent of "brevity."[139] *Hebel* and צֵל occur together with this sense in Ps 144:4 to comment upon the shortness of the human lifespan, and they will be paired again at Eccl 8:13. The extensional phrase "few days" also indicates that the intended referent here involves transience. Thus a new R value for *hebel* has been introduced by Qohelet and an additional way that *hebel* may be used to describe the human condition (S): its short duration.

The issue of humanity's transience recalls the portion of the *Gilgamesh Epic* in which Gilgamesh says the following to Enkidu:

Only the gods live forever under the sun.
As for mortals, numbered are their days;
Whatever they achieve is but the wind! (*šāru*)[140]

In sum, Qohelet emphasizes human weakness in this opening subunit, with the accent on matters related to knowledge. Humans are unable to dispute (דין) with one stronger, their words bring no advantage and increase *hebel* (insubstantiality), and no one really knows what is good for humans during their *hebel* (transient) life.

---

[136] יְמֵי־חַיֵּי הֶבְלוֹ. A similar construction is found at 9:9, כָּל־יְמֵי חַיֵּי הֶבְלֶךָ (all the days of your vapor life), although without the guarding terms found here. For the shortness of the human life span, see also Eccl 2:3 and 5:17 [Eng. v. 18].

[137] The verb עשה (to do, make) with "days" means "to spend days," a usage found among the postbiblical Hebrew literature. In addition, a similar idiom is found in Egyptian and Akkadian material (see Seow, *Ecclesiastes*, 233). Most commentators understand the phrase וְיַעֲשֵׂם כַּצֵּל (and he does them like the shadow) to be equivalent to a relative clause, i.e., "the human" is the subject of the verb. Gordis (*Koheleth*, 264) argues that עשה has a similar sense in Ruth 2:19 and also cites examples in rabbinic texts. The NAB takes God as the subject of עשה, causing the days to pass swiftly.

[138] Seow (*Ecclesiastes*, 234) makes a convincing case that אַחֲרָיו here means "future" or "destiny" on the basis of cognate Ugar. *uḫry* and Arab. *uḫrāy* (both mean "destiny" or "end").

[139] צֵל may be used metaphorically in several ways, one of which is to indicate protection (cf. Job 40:22; Hos 14:8). It may also be used of insubstantial things, e.g., Job 17:7, where Job complains, "My eye has also grown dim because of grief, and all my members are as a shadow," or "have wasted like a shadow" (see commentaries for textual issues). It is also used of transience. See Job 8:9; 14:2; Ps 102:12 [Eng. v. 11]; and 1 Chr 29:15, where the simile "our days on earth are like a shadow (צֵל)" is clarified by the statement "we are sojourners" (גֵּרִים).

[140] OB 3.4.6–8 (translation adapted from E. A. Speiser, *ANET*, 79).

7:1–12 Good and Better (1x)

Moving now to develop his theme of human knowledge of the "good" (טוֹב, *ṭôb*), Qohelet in this section presents a series of proverbs and *ṭôb*-sayings which take up such traditional wisdom topics as the name (reputation), wisdom, pleasure, the fool, restraint, and inheritance. Throughout, it is important to keep in mind Qohelet's previous insistence that many words increase *hebel* (6:11), and that no one knows what is good (6:12).

In the very middle, 7:6bß, Qohelet pronounces the conversation to be *hebel*. As Murphy notes, one's interpretation of *hebel* here is determined by the construal made of the entire chapter.[141] Crenshaw understands this section as a series of Qohelet's teachings on what is relatively good; the *hebel*-statement indicates that even wisdom cannot always be relied upon.[142] Fox sees the *hebel*-statement as part of Qohelet's self-directed irony; he is qualifying the certainty of his own teaching.[143] Lohfink, on the other hand, interprets the statement as part of a pattern throughout the section of subverting traditional wisdom teaching.[144]

While the perspective of Lohfink seems superior here, the referent of insubstantiality for *hebel* in 7:6b is the same within each of the several proposals. The use of *hebel* is an allusion to 6:11, where Qohelet declares there is no advantage (יֹתֵר) for words. So here he gives examples of such worthless words (S) which simply increase vapor.[145]

Summary of 6:10–7:14

Qohelet moves into the second half of his book with a transition from human effort to the limitation of human knowledge, themes which overlap. His focus in 6:10–7:14 is on the confidence of human speech in relation to what is good and better. An R value newly used with *hebel*, but one which will recur, is that of transience, applied here to the short duration of human existence (6:12). *Hebel* is also used with the R value of insubstantiality in an assessment of human words (6:11; 7:6).

7:15–29 (1x) Wisdom and Righteousness

As the previous unit (6:10–7:14) ended with a call to "see what God has done" (7:13), so this unit begins with a statement concerning what Qohelet has

---

[141] Murphy, *Ecclesiastes*, 64.

[142] Crenshaw, *Ecclesiastes*, 132–39.

[143] Fox, *Time to Tear Down*, 250.

[144] Lohfink, *Kohelet*, 49–50. This latter orientation is also adopted by Murphy (*Ecclesiastes*, 62–63) and Seow (*Ecclesiastes*, 242–43).

[145] It is possible that the subject for *hebel* is the "laughter of fools" (cf. 2:2), also in v. 6. However, the subunit taken as a whole calls the words of the wise into question; Qohelet

seen—thus qualifying him to reflect upon it—and a concluding reference to God's activity (7:29). This section is unified by Qohelet's concern with matters of wisdom and righteousness in response to the human condition as he has been describing it: insubstantial in its makeup and limited in knowledge, transient in duration, and inextricably bound up in the bad aspects of life under the sun. In the first subunit (7:15–18), Qohelet urges the reader to act in moderation concerning righteousness and wisdom. The second subunit (7:19–22) reflects on the wisdom and righteousness of others. The final verses (7:23–29) concern the elusiveness of wisdom and righteousness, and the threat of folly and wickedness.[146]

7:15–18 Choosing Righteousness and Wisdom (1x)

In 1:2 Qohelet declared that "All is *hebel*." Since then, he has taken the reader through his "journal," describing and lamenting the things he has "seen."[147] In 7:13–14 he urged the reader to "see" that God is responsible for both good and bad days. Now, he will describe something else he has encountered (7:15):

> I have seen both[148] in my *vapor* days (בִּימֵי הֶבְלִי):
> There are righteous people who perish in their righteousness,
> and there are wicked people who prolong in their destructiveness.

This situation becomes the basis for his advice concerning wisdom and

---

questions the extent to which their elocutions are superior to the verbiage of fools. Qohelet never recommends folly, but addresses folly here in order to challenge the limits of wisdom.

[146] Interpreters have discerned different subunits in this section. Fox rearranges the text, moving 7:19 into a subunit with 7:11–12, leaving 7:13–18 + 20–24 as a main section with the following subunits: 7:13–14; 7:15–18 + 20; 7:21–22; and 7:23–24. He considers 7:25–8:1a to be the following section (*Time to Tear Down*, 256–65). Murphy divides this section into two units, 7:15–24 and 7:25–29 (*Ecclesiastes*, 68–78). Seow considers 7:15–29 to be one unit, divided into subunits of 7:15–22 and 7:23–29 (*Ecclesiastes*, 266).

[147] On Qohelet's use of ראה, see Michel, *Eigenart*, 24–29, 35–38; Fox, *Time to Tear Down*, 72 n. 1; Antoon Schoors, "Words Typical of Qohelet," in *Qohelet in the Context of Wisdom* (ed. Antoon Schoors; Leuven: Leuven University Press, 1998), 26–33. Seow ("Qohelet's Autobiography," 285–86) notes the prevalence of this verb in Ecclesiastes and compares it to the *Gilgamesh Epic* which begins as a report from "he who saw all" and "knew everything" who now begins to communicate his wisdom; likewise Qohelet.

[148] Though Qohelet's repeated use of כל continues to recall his theme that "all is *hebel*," more specifically הַכֹּל here refers to "both" elements of the contrast which Qohelet now discusses (cf. the inclusio with 7:18). That is, as is typical, כל concerns that which follows it (see discussion of Eccl 1:2 above), and Qohelet is here presenting two cases he has seen (Rüdiger Lux, "Der 'Lebenskompromiß'—ein Wesenszug im Denken Kohelets? Zur Auslegung von Koh 7,15–18," in *Alttestamentlicher Glaube und Biblische Theologie* [ed. J. Hausmann and H.-J. Zobel; Stuttgart: Kohlhammer, 1992], 267–78). Lux argues for a chiastic structure in vv. 15–18.

righteousness in the following verses (7:16–18).[149]

The construction with *hebel* is similar to that found in 6:12, יְמֵי־חַיֵּי הֶבְלוֹ (the days of [the human's] vapor life), and perhaps is elliptical for it. The issue in 6:12, indicated by guarding terms, is human transience. So it is possible that human transience is *hebel*'s referent here.

However, it is notable that this time no guarding terms are evident for *hebel*, whether in connection with transience or any other R value. His comment involving *hebel* in v. 15a does not concern the case he is citing in v. 15b, something which is happening to other people. He does not lament that this circumstance is bad, as he will in 8:10–14, for example. Nor does *hebel* apply to the advice Qohelet is giving (Do not be excessively wise, righteous, wicked, or foolish), as if this advice was insubstantial or transient. Rather, it is the "days of *my hebel*," *Qohelet's* vapor days.

Further, if Qohelet is *only* alluding to the brevity of his life here ("I saw this during my brief existence"), it would actually weaken his position rhetorically, raising the possibility that he simply had not lived long enough to see the final outcome of the scenarios he will describe.

Thus, it is better to conclude that Qohelet is using *hebel* omnivalently, alluding in a general way to insubstantiality, foulness, and transience altogether. In the course of his vaporous existence (futile/painful/brief), he has seen certain phenomena. Outside of the statement of thesis in 1:2, this is the first omnivalent employment of *hebel* in the book (cf. 9:9; 11:8). Previously he has developed a variety of referents for *hebel*. Now, using the *hebel*-symbol, he is able to encapsulate them all.

Summary of 7:15–29

In this section, Qohelet gives advice concerning the mysteries of wisdom and righteousness. His single use of *hebel* in this section, in the subunit 7:15–18, is not used to describe or evaluate the situation he is discussing.

---

[149] These verses have been the subject of much comment since they seem to counsel the reader to refrain from being overly wise or righteous. R. N. Whybray ("Qoheleth the Immoralist? [Eccl 7:16–17]," in *Israelite Wisdom* [Fs. Samuel Terrien; ed. John G. Gammie, et al.; New York: Union Theological Seminary, 1978], 191–204) has argued that Qohelet is counseling against hypocrisy here, but the support he offers is dubious. Qohelet is here addressing the one who "fears God," יְרֵא אֱלֹהִים (v. 18). It appears likely that by using this phrase, rather than the term צַדִּיק (righteous), which he uses in vv. 15–16, Qohelet indicates those who seek to serve God in sincerity. The terms "wicked" and "righteous" are terms of performance (cf. 7:20 which indicates that everyone will sometimes fall short in this regard). So Qohelet is counseling against an extreme perfectionism on the grounds that even if people were to accomplish it, they would not thereby achieve any complete security from harm. Rather they risk being confounded (שׁמם), possibly here indicating depression (cf. Ps 143:3–4; see Seow, *Ecclesiastes*, 267–68).

Rather he employs it in an omnivalent reference to his own life, subsuming all the valencies he has established for the term.

The remainder of the unit (7:19–22) continues the concern with righteousness and wisdom, this time that of other people, and then concludes with the difficulty of obtaining wisdom/righteousness and the threat of folly/wickedness (7:23–29).

8:1–17 (3x) Even the Wise Do Not Know

This unit is framed by references to the wise and their futile quest for knowledge. The rhetorical question in v. 1 (Who knows . . . ?) anticipates the statement and question in v. 7 (the human does not know, for who can inform . . . ?), and the conclusion in v. 17 (even the wise do not know).[150] The first subunit (8:1–9) emphasizes human limitations, particularly in regard to power and knowledge; the second (8:10–15) the lack of proper reward; the concluding verses (8:16–17), insist that God's ways are mysterious, even to the wise.

8:10–15 Unjust Rewards (3x)

This paragraph has taxed the ingenuity of commentators and requires extended comment.[151] *Hebel* is found three times in 8:10–15: once in v. 10, and twice in v. 14. In the former, the syntax of the MT is difficult and there are textual problems as well.

I saw the wicked <brought> to burial, and they proceeded from a holy place,[152]

---

[150] On the structure of this unit, see Graham Ogden, "Qoheleth IX 1–16," *VT* (1982): 158–60, and Antoon Schoors, *The Preacher Sought to Find Pleasing Words: A Study of the Language of Qoheleth* (Orientalia Lovaniensia Analecta 41; Leuven: Peeters, 1992), 107–8.

[151] Part of the challenge is knowing where to divide the thought from the previous verses. Most commentators (so Barton, Fox, Gordis, Scott, Crenshaw, Ogden, Whybray) divide between vv. 9 and 10. The late adverb וּבְכֵן begins v. 10, and probably means "after," "then," or "thereupon" (cf. GKC §119ii; Schoors, *Pleasing*, 102). It is transitional but maintains a connection with what came before (cf. Esth 4:16; Sir 13:7). As regards *hebel*, the question is whether this connection between vv. 9 and 10 suggests that the *hebel*-statement in v. 10b evaluates the thought of only these two verses, or if it connects also with vv. 11ff. However, such determination is not critical to the issue since Qohelet's discussion in vv. 11–15 is a continuation of the problem of human wrong and retribution begun in the previous subunit (8:1–9; esp. v. 6).

[152] This reading assumes קבר מובאים instead of MT קברים ובאו. This is reflected by SyrH. and Copt. (so Seow, *Ecclesiastes*, 284; Gordis, *Koheleth*, 295; Whitley, *Koheleth*, 74–6). The LXX is similar, but reflects plural קברים:

καὶ τότε εἶδον ἀσεβεῖς εἰς τάφους εἰσαχθέντας,
καὶ ἐκ τόπου ἁγίου ἐπορεύθησαν
And then I saw the wicked brought into the tombs,
and out of the holy place they departed.

Fox follows LXX (*Time to Tear Down*, 283). However, the plural (τάφους) is best explained but those who did justly were forgotten in the city.[153] This indeed is vapor (*hebel*). Because sentence against a bad work is not executed speedily, therefore the heart of human offspring is fully set to do badness. If a sinner does badness a hundred times and prolongs (days), yet I know that it will be good for those who fear God, because they fear before him, and it will not be good for the wicked; like the shadow,[154] neither will they prolong days, because they do not have fear before God. There is a vapor (*hebel*) that is done on earth, that there are righteous people who are treated according to the work of the wicked, and there are wicked people who are treated according to the work of the righteous. I said that this indeed is vapor (*hebel*). And I praise enjoyment, for there is nothing better for humans under the sun than to eat, and to drink, and to enjoy, for this will go with them in their toil through the days of life God gives them under the sun.

Essentially four readings have been offered for v. 10:

(1)   the wicked entered the holy place and boasted that they acted righteously,[155]
(2)   the wicked were buried and everyone praised them,[156]
(3)   the wicked were buried and their wickedness forgotten,[157] or

---

as the result of dittography of the *mem*. Driver (largely following Burkitt) would emend קברים to קרבים (metathesis), and read, "And then I have seen wicked men approaching and entering the holy place . . ." (G. R. Driver, "Problems and Solutions," *VT* 4 [1954]: 230–31; F. C. Burkitt, "Is Ecclesiastes a Translation?" *JTS* 23 [1922]: 25–26). However, this is not reflected in any of the ancient versions.

[153] Following MT. LXX reads,

καὶ ἐπῃνέθησαν ἐν τῇ πόλει, ὅτι οὕτως ἐποίησαν. καί γε τοῦτο ματαιότης.

And they were praised in the city, for thus they had done. And indeed this is vanity. This reflects וישתבחו (and they were praised) instead of MT וישתכחו (and they forgot). However, MT (as emended in v. 10a) makes sense as retained. Qohelet is complaining that the wicked receive a proper burial, while the righteous are neglected. This lament is found also on the lips of Job (21:32–33).

[154] There is a complication in v. 13 regarding the word "shadow" (צֵל). As mentioned previously, in the HB it is used metaphorically with referents of transience, insubstantiality, and protection. Here, the syntax gives the initial impression that the simile's subject is the hypothetical "prolonging of days" by the wicked one, and that the referent for צֵל is extended duration. Thus Barton explains that shadows become long in the evening, but the sinner will not reach the evening of life (*Ecclesiastes*, 154). Though the syntax of the verse is unusual, the more common referent of transience for צֵל is retained by the following translation: "And it will not be good for the wicked; like the shadow (transient), neither will they prolong days, because they do not have fear before God" (similarly Fox, *Time to Tear Down*, 282). Thus the subject of the simile is the wicked, and צֵל is guarded by the contrary "prolong," negated by "not" (לֹא). However, by either explanation, צֵל is used to reinforce the declaration that the life of the wicked will be shortened.

[155] So Driver, "Problems and Solutions," 230.

[156] Following LXX.

[157] This understands וְיִשְׁתַּכְּחוּ בָעִיר אֲשֶׁר כֵּן־עָשׂוּ as, "and they forgot in the city that they

(4)   the wicked were buried and those who acted righteously were forgotten.[158]

Qohelet then comments that this is *hebel* (v. 10b). The first reading declares the unchecked hypocrisy of the wicked, while each of the subsequent readings understands the author to be juxtaposing the honorable burial of the wicked with something inappropriate: the wicked were praised, or their wickedness was forgotten, or the righteous were neglected. While the fourth proposal may be most convincing, all four recognize injustice as Qohelet's focus of concern. The first possible subject of *hebel* in v. 10, then, is the injustice emphasized in this same verse.

However, it has also been argued that *hebel* predicates what is described in v. 11 (and perhaps also what follows), a rare *hebel*-statement at the *beginning* of a discussion.[159] The crux is the uncertain role of אֲשֶׁר in v. 11. Fox contends that אֲשֶׁר is the nominalizing particle (= namely), so the *hebel*-phrase goes with what *follows* it. He translates vv. 10b–11a:

This too is an absurdity [*hebel*]:
the sentence for a wicked deed is not carried out quickly.[160]

Although such a use of אֲשֶׁר is unusual for Ecclesiastes, it does occur a few verses later in this unit (8:14a).[161] Fox insists that otherwise אֲשֶׁר has no legitimate function here on the basis that causal אֲשֶׁר is never prospective. He compares the syntax to that of אֲשֶׁר in 8:14, and, as a phrase, to the statement in 5:15 [Eng. v. 16], וְגַם־זֹה רָעָה חוֹלָה (and this indeed is a bad thing, an illness). He acknowledges that a *waw* before גַּם would be expected here, and suggests it was lost through haplography.

---

had done thus" (i.e., wickedly). So NJB.

[158] This reading understands וְיִשְׁתַּכְּחוּ בָעִיר אֲשֶׁר כֵּן־עָשׂוּ as, "and they forgot in the city those who had done justly" (so Sym., ὡς δίκαια πράξαντες); Murphy, *Ecclesiastes*, 80–81; Whybray, *Ecclesiastes*, 136; Whitley, *Koheleth*, 74–76; Fox, *Time to Tear Down*, 282–84; Seow, *Ecclesiastes*, 284–86, 294; NJPS). Although כֵּן is not used elsewhere in Eccl with this sense, it is a well-established usage, e.g., Gen 42:11; 1 Sam 23:17. Also, it anticipates the discussion of righteous and wicked to follow. Fox (*Time to Tear Down*, 284) proposes that this "forgetting" in the context of death indicates an abandonment, a neglect of proper burial for the righteous (cf. Ps 9:19 [Eng. v. 18]; Isa 49:15). This would make sense of the reference to the city (they inappropriately lie dead without attention for a time), and would provide that the passage not be in tension with Qohelet's emphasis elsewhere that *everyone* is forgotten (1:11; cf. 2:16) in a broader sense.

[159] Fox, *Time to Tear Down*, 284–85, who cites 4:7; 5:15; and 8:14 as analogies; also Gerrit Wildeboer, "Der Prediger," in *Die fünf Megillot* (ed. K. Budde, et al.; KHC 17; Freiburg: Mohr, 1898), 151.

[160] Fox, *Time to Tear Down*, 282. Although a general statement, it is likely that its implications include the deity's lack of action.

Thus we are left either with an unusual *hebel*-statement (at the *outset* of a discussion),[162] or a rare use of causal אֲשֶׁר (at the beginning of a sentence).[163] As for prospective causal אֲשֶׁר, while this is unusual, it is not unprecedented.[164] In Gen 42:21, Joseph's brothers say to one another,

(1)   "Truly we are guilty concerning our brother.
(2)   Because (אֲשֶׁר) we saw his distress when he pleaded with us and we would not listen,
(3)   therefore (עַל־כֵּן) this distress has come to us."

The structure corresponds to that of Eccl 8:10b–11:

(1)   v. 10b "This indeed is vapor.
(2)   v. 11a Because (אֲשֶׁר) sentence against a bad work is not executed speedily,
(3)   v. 11b therefore (עַל־כֵּן) the heart of human offspring is fully set to do badness."[165]

Since the thesis of Fox leaves v. 11b as a somewhat awkward paren-thesis, it seems better to conclude that v. 11a and v. 11b are linked as cause and effect.[166] On the other hand, the analogous structure in Gen 42:21 indicates that even though אֲשֶׁר is causal, the preceding *hebel* phrase may still be related to it. That is, the statement in v. 11 supplements the primary subject of *hebel* in v. 10a. As Fox notes, the meaning of *hebel* is the same whether applied to 8:10a or 8:11–13 since both describe an unjust situation.[167]

Qohelet laments (v. 11) that justice comes slowly, a circumstance that actually encourages more wrong to be committed. Verses 12 and 13, on the other hand, express the speaker's confidence that it will not always be this way: those who fear God will find good, and those who do not will be cut short.[168]

---

[161] The term אֲשֶׁר occurs eleven times in 8:10–15.

[162] So Fox (*Time to Tear Down*, 284-85) and H. Louis Ginsberg ("The Structure and Contents of the Book of Koheleth," in *Wisdom in Israel and in the Ancient Near East* [VTSup 3; ed. M. Noth and D. W. Thomas; Leiden: Brill, 1955], 144).

[163] So most commentators, e.g., Zimmerli, *Predigers*, 215; Lauha, *Kohelet*, 153.

[164] Contra Fox, *Time to Tear Down*, 285; Michel, *Eigenart*, 224.

[165] Analogous syntax to initial causal אֲשֶׁר followed by עַל־כֵּן is found in the following texts: 1 Kgs 9:9/2 Chr 7:22 (עַל אֲשֶׁר); Jer 44:23 (...וָאֲשֶׁר... מִפְּנֵי אֲשֶׁר); Ezek 44:12 (יַעַן אֲשֶׁר).

[166] So Schoors, *Pleasing*, 140–41.

[167] *Time to Tear Down*, 285. He adds that v. 11 is probably a reference to both human and divine justice, although it is not a claim that such justice is *always* delayed. In the case of the person whose burial was described in v. 10, judgment happened so slowly that he died first.

[168] Schoors (*Pleasing*, 141–42) argues convincingly (contra Michel, *Eigenart*, 223) for a parallel causal use of אֲשֶׁר in the second half of both vv. 12 and 13. As most commentators agree, Qohelet is citing his tradition here concerning the wicked (cf. Pss

Then v. 14 seems to return to the theme of vv. 10 and 11, a lament that the righteous and the wicked receive treatment opposite to that which is appropriate to their deeds. The section concludes with Qohelet's advice to enjoy the life that God gives under the sun.

The tension here is that Qohelet seems both to lament the reversal of appropriate rewards, and to express confidence that such will not always be the case. For that reason, many commentators have discerned the hand of a later "corrective" editor in vv. 12–13 who insists that God's justice, though perhaps delayed, will indeed be accomplished.[169] But note, first, that v. 12 likewise acknowledges the slowness of justice (the "sinner" prolongs days), and second, that texts more commonly attributed to the primary author of Ecclesiastes also affirm the certainty of God's judgment.[170] Thus, if vv. 12–13 were added by a later hand, there is a certain consistency with the original author's statements taken as a whole.

Others suggest that the sense of vv. 12–13 is concessive: "*I have heard* that it will go well for those who fear God and that the wicked will be punished, but such is not actually the case."[171] This is possible, yet the confidence in God's judgment Qohelet expresses elsewhere makes it unlikely that he is completely rejecting that here.

A third possibility involves the case made for an R value of transience in each of *hebel*'s occurrences. With this understanding, the unjust situations in vv. 10–11 and v. 14 are declared by Qohelet to be short-lived. These verses would thus be in harmony with vv. 12–13 which declare that God-fearing ones will be vindicated and the life of the wicked cut short. This thesis allows that צֵל (shadow, v. 13) serves as a synonym for *hebel*, along with the phrase "will not prolong days," to convey transience (as similarly in 6:12).[172] Thus, the sense of the passage is coherent, the tension resolved.[173]

There are at least two difficulties with this thesis. First, the injunction to "enjoy life," found in v. 15, always responds in its other occurrences to situations which Qohelet appraises *negatively* (cf. 2:24; 3:12, 22; 5:17–18 [Eng. vv. 18–19]; 9:7). While it is possible that the resolution proposed here would still leave Qohelet with some level of frustration, it seems to significantly minimize it and soften the need for his appeal in v. 15.

37:1–2, 35–38; 39:5–7 [Eng. vv. 4–6]).

[169] There is tension even within vv. 12–13, for v. 12 (and 7:15) seems to concede that the wicked may prolong their lives, while v. 13 denies this possibility.

[170] For example, 5:5 [Eng. v. 6], and, with less consensus, 3:17.

[171] Gordis, *Koheleth*, 184, 297; Murphy, *Ecclesiastes*, 85.

[172] The other metaphorical possibilities for צֵל do not appear plausible in this context: insubstantiality, protection (cf. Eccl 7:12).

[173] Farmer, *Who Knows?* 181–83; Fredericks, *Coping*, 88–90.

A more serious difficulty with the transience proposal is that it proposes a use of *hebel* here which differs from its use to predicate similar issues. In 2:12–17, after Qohelet calls wisdom's accomplishments insubstantial, especially the common fate of wise and fool, he then calls the entire situation evil (רָע). So, when Qohelet presents the circumstance of v. 10, we expect him to be quite upset about it. According to the transience thesis, he is no longer so upset at such things because he realizes they are only temporary.

Further, in 9:1–3 which closely follows 8:10–15, we find that Qohelet *is* still wrestling with this. There he again declares the common fate of the wicked and righteous to be evil (רָע). This common fate, the final injustice, is not something which Qohelet will simply entrust to time as a healing agent.

It seems better to view 8:10–15 as a *zwar-aber* situation.[174] On the one hand, Qohelet sees the injustices and inequities of life. On the other, his tradition tells him that God is just: the wicked will not ultimately prosper, and it will be good for the righteous. He quotes the tradition, not to mock it, but because he believes it—yet he also refuses to downplay injustice.

Each use of *hebel* in vv. 10–15 is accompanied by terms which suggest the three different R values used elsewhere in the book. We expect Qohelet to declare the injustice in v. 10 to be evil. In fact, the foulness R value of *hebel* in that verse is suggested by the double use of רָע in v. 11 to describe deeds done on earth, just as Qohelet has used *hebel* with רָע elsewhere to describe foul matters (1:14; 2:15, 17, 19, 21, 23; 4:7, 8). It would initially seem likely, then, that when Qohelet employs *hebel* twice in v. 14—as a kind of inclusio, describing the same injustice he introduced in vv. 10–11—that those occurrences of *hebel* likewise involve foulness.

Yet in vv. 12 and 13, other potentially guarding terms are evident. When Qohelet describes the wicked as a shadow (צֵל) in v. 13, we should recall that he used that term in 6:10–12 to guard a sense of transience for *hebel*.

The declaration "I know" in v. 12 (cf. 3:14) invites comparison with the limits on human knowledge which Qohelet has declared previously (3:21; 6:12) and which he is particularly highlighting within the 8:1–17 unit as a whole. That is, much cannot be known—including the puzzle of injustice—but he does know that proper rewards will eventually obtain. The unit begins in 8:1 with the double rhetorical question: "Who is so wise?[175] And who knows the

---

[174] So Hertzberg, *Prediger*, ad loc. As mentioned previously, and somewhat different than Hertzberg, this is understood as a style by which Qohelet introduces two conflicting realities both of which he recognizes but does not resolve. Other possible examples include the fact that wisdom is valuable, and yet the wise and foolish share the same fate (2:13–14; cf. 9:16–18), and the fact that life should be freely enjoyed, and yet God holds all accountable (11:9).

[175] MT כְּהֶחָכָם (like the wise) is best understood as an incorrect division of consonants from original כֹּה חָכָם. Elsewhere in Ecclesiastes, the article with כְּ is always syncopated. This

פֵּשֶׁר (solution, interpretation) of a thing?" It closes in 8:17 with statements that no one can "find" (מצא) or "know" (ידע) the work of God. In the middle subunit, Qohelet follows his declaration of knowledge with a double employment of *hebel* as bookends around the enigma of present concern: the human experience of injustice.

In sum, Qohelet in 8:10–15 is holding forth a *zwar-aber*, something unresolved: he sees injustice—this is foul; he also believes in God's justice—the two together produce an enigma or mystery, something the human mind is too insubstantial to fathom. Finally, his confidence in the tradition makes it possible that experiences of injustice are transient. The multivalency of the *hebel*-symbol enables Qohelet to hold diverse elements in paradox.

Qohelet concludes the subsection in v. 15 by his now-familiar exhortation to enjoy life. While there may be some reason to hope for a better future, the present is still foul: appropriate rewards are often inaccessible. He therefore commends enjoyment in the midst of the present circumstances.

Summary of 8:1–17

The center of this unit employs *hebel* three times in the same subunit (8:10–15). The significance for Qohelet's symbol-building is that Qohelet for the first time combines the R values of foulness and mystery, and for the first time his multivalent use of *hebel* combines three R values at once, including transience as well.[176]

9:1–10 (3x?) Enjoy Life Now

The discussion presented in 9:1–10 has three major points: (1) all will die, righteous and wicked alike, (2) the advantage of the living over the dead is that the living know they will die and can still partake of their "portion," and (3) as a consequence, those among the living should enjoy the life God has made available to them. These verses express more directly and extensively than elsewhere Qohelet's connection between the reality of death and the response of the living which he commends. The insistence that all mortals will face death (9:1–6) is followed by a call to enjoy life (9:7–10).

9:1–6 Same Fate for Righteous and Wicked (1x?)

In 9:1–3, Qohelet laments that death is the fate for righteous and wicked alike (cf. 2:12–17; 3:17–22; 8:10–15).[177] The deeds of the wise and the

---

emendation is supported by Tg., Vulg., and Syr., and perhaps also by LXX (see discussion at Seow, *Ecclesiastes*, 277).

[176] Note that this is different from the omnivalent use of *hebel* in 7:15; in that context there are no guarding terms related to the subject.

[177] The initial כִּי is asseverative ("indeed") and has only a loose relationship with what precedes.

righteous, in their variety, are under God's control and guarantee no outcome different from that of anyone else.[178]

The syntax of vv. 1–2 is difficult. LXX, Syr., and Sym. have the equivalent of *hebel* instead of הַכֹּל at the beginning of v. 2, which provides a more smooth reading than that of the MT. Though some commentators emend the MT to *hebel*, citing scribal error,[179] the versions do not give evidence of a consistent *Vorlage* and may simply reflect their own emendation to resolve the Hebrew syntax.[180]

If 9:1b–2a is emended from הַכֹּל כַּאֲשֶׁר to read הָבֶל: בַּאֲשֶׁר (so *BHS*), it may be translated as follows:

> . . . both love and hate[181] the human does not know. Everything before them <is a vapor (*hebel*) in which[182]> the same fate comes to all, to the righteous and to the wicked . . .

If the emendation is adopted, the reference to a common fate, and the statement זֶה רָע (this is evil) at the beginning of v. 3, echoes the disgust Qohelet similarly expressed in 2:15–17 and the failure of wisdom described there. One referent for *hebel* here would thus be foulness. The proximity of 9:1–2 to 8:16–17, which insists that God's ways are mysterious to human beings, the use of *hebel* in 8:10–15 in regard to similar fates for righteous and wicked, and the phrase "does not know (ידע)" in 9:1 support a second *hebel* referent here of mystery (insubstantiality of thinking). Humans are largely ignorant of what God is doing in their lives, except, of course, the final goal common to all. If the MT is retained, it may be read as follows:

> . . . both love and hate. People do not know everything that is before them. Everything is (the same) as for everyone: there is one fate for the righteous and the wicked . . .[183]

---

[178] The terms "love" and "hate" are paired twice in this subunit, in verses 1 and 6. Their polarity in 3:8 indicates a "proper time for both," not that one is virtuous and the other not. Note that things which Qohelet elsewhere condemns (such as עֲשֻׁקִים "oppressions," 4:1) are not found in the poem of 3:1–9. Thus, the point both in ch. 3 and in 9:1–6 is the variety of human actions. People do not know what the consequences will be for their actions; these are in the hand of God (under God's power). Alternatively, some commentators understand love and hate in 9:1 (but not 9:6) as a reference to God's response to human activity (so Tremper Longman III, *The Book of Ecclesiastes* [NICOT; Grand Rapids: Eerdmans, 1998], 227).

[179] Barton, *Ecclesiastes*, 158; Fox, *Time to Tear Down*, 291–92.

[180] Syr. appears to have a conflate reading, *hbl' kl* = *hbl hkl* (Fox, *Time to Tear Down*, 291) and the LXX shows evidence of an inner Greek error (Seow, *Ecclesiastes*, 299).

[181] The sequence . . . גַם . . . גַם indicates "Both . . . and . . ." (Williams, *Hebrew Syntax*, §378).

[182] Alternatively, "because."

[183] So Crenshaw, *Ecclesiastes*, 160; Seow, *Ecclesiastes*, 298–99; Murphy,

Even without the term *hebel*, it is evident from Qohelet's statement in 9:3—This is עָר!—that he considers this to be wrong. As he has said elsewhere, it is not right that the same fate comes to all persons regardless of their character and behavior.[184]

In the midst of his lament on human epistemological limitations, Qohelet has consistently acknowledged certain things that humans do know.[185] In 9:1–6 there appears to be deliberate irony: the living know that they will die. Yet this is important knowledge, for it enables humans to make the most of their time among the living, as the advice which follows (9:7–10) indicates (cf. 11:8).

9:7–10 Make the Most of Enjoying Life (2x?)

In 9:7–10, Qohelet is once again giving his recommendations on how one should live in response to the circumstances of this existence. In light of death's certainty, he counsels enjoyment and, in v. 9, he adds:

> Enjoy (ראה, lit. "see") life with the wife whom you love, all the days of your vapor (*hebel*) life (כָּל־יְמֵי חַיֵּי הֶבְלֶךָ) that are given you under the sun, all the days of your vapor (*hebel*; כֹּל יְמֵי הֶבְלֶךָ)[186] because that is your reward in life and in your toil at which you toil under the sun.

As in 7:15, *hebel* is employed here in 9:9 without guarding terms as it predicates "life" (S). The context could suggest life's brevity, for (1) the phrase "all the days of your vapor life" is similar to the phrase found in 6:12, and (2) 9:10 reminds the audience that they are on their way to Sheol wherein there is no "work or thought or knowledge." Yet, unlike at 6:12 where guarding terms clarified the sense of life's transience, here the speed of the journey to the end is not indicated.

It is better to see this statement as the counterpart to 7:15 where Qohelet alluded to his own vapor days. Here he addresses the reader about "*your* vapor

---

Ecclesiastes, 91.

[184] Qohelet comments very similarly at 2:12–17, 7:15–18, and 8:10–15. Additional presentations on evil matters are found at 1:12–15 God's evil business; 2:18–23 the foolish heir; 4:1–3 oppression; 4:7–8 the workaholic; 5:12–16 [Eng. vv. 13–17] and 6:1–6 wealth easily lost; 7:23–29 the dangerous woman; and 8:5b–9 human ignorance and weakness. There is also more to come at 9:11–12 time and chance, 10:5–7 the overturning of social position, 10:12–15 the result of fools' talk, 11:1–6 trouble which affects economics, and 12:1 old age.

[185] For example, the advice to enjoy (3:12), certain factors related to God (3:14), the reality of human weakness (6:10), self-awareness (7:22), that there is a judgment (8:6; 11:9) and a reward for those who fear God (8:12). In addition, the epilogue affirms that Qohelet taught people knowledge (12:9).

[186] The repetition of כֹּל יְמֵי הֶבְלֶךָ is almost certainly the result of dittography. It is omitted by LXX^A, Tg., OL, Jerome, and several Heb. MSS The subject predicated is the earthly existence of those being addressed, whether by a single or double occurrence of *hebel*.

life." The life Qohelet has been describing as *hebel* involves not only brevity, but insubstantial and foul matters as well. By leaving the term "unguarded" here, Qohelet allows *hebel* to symbolize all that he has been constructing. As he did at 7:15, Qohelet makes this statement of the vapor nature of existence in close connection with his advice on how to respond to it.

Summary of 9:1–10

This section emphasizes death, one of the few things about which humans can be sure. In 9:2, *hebel* (if so emended) expresses both the mystery and foulness of injustice concerning a common fate for all. In 9:9, it makes an omnivalent reference to the life Qohelet has been describing.

11:7–12:8 (5x) Conclusion: Youth and Old Age

Some interpreters include 11:7–8 with the previous unit, 11:1–6.[187] On the one hand, vv. 7–8 have connections with what precedes. 11:7 begins with a *waw*, and the term טוב occurs in both vv. 6 and 7. Further, v. 6 makes reference to "morning" and "evening," imagery which makes an interesting juxtaposition with the references to light and darkness in 11:7–10.

On the other hand, the connections between vv. 7–8 and what follows are stronger. These include references to enjoyment and memory (cf. 11:9; 12:1), further examples of the root טוב, and further images of light and darkness (12:1–3). 11:7–10 is a call to appreciate and make the most of one's youth right now, while 12:1–7 provides the justification for this warning. The entire section (11:7–12:7) moves from youth, to old age, to death. The reference to the "Creator"[188] in 12:1 corresponds to the cycles of the created order with which Qohelet began in 1:3–11.

Thus, there is a definite shift of focus from concern with the future's unknowability, to a discussion of the character of youth and the admonitions which follow from it. The celebration of youth and the call to enjoy it (11:7–10) are followed by the poem on old age and the death of the cosmos (12:1–7). The final poem provides a framing analogous to the opening poem in 1:3–11, as the restatement of theme in 12:8 serves as inclusio with 1:2.

11:7–10 Rejoice in Your Youth (2x)

This section gives further evidence of Qohelet's delight in multivalent imagery. Here he plays off light and life with darkness and death. This has analogies with 6:4–5 which also uses the absence of the sun and darkness in connection with death and nonexistence.[189] The imagery of light, or seeing

---

[187] So Michel, *Eigenart*, 210.

[188] See commentaries for discussion.

[189] While חֹשֶׁךְ (darkness) indicates mystery in 6:4a, death is the context, and "covering the name" (6:4b) indicates nonexistence (see previous discussion).

light, for life and the living is a common one in the ancient Near East, while the absence of light is correspondingly used of death.[190]

However, light and darkness imagery may also be used in other ways, as Qohelet has previously demonstrated. In 2:13–14 light and darkness are used of ignorance, and in 5:16 [Eng. v. 17] Qohelet employs darkness for oppressiveness. Further, in the poem on old age which immediately follows, Qohelet uses imagery of darkness to represent the difficulties of the later years (12:1–3), while death itself is represented in different terms (12:5b–7).

Thus, the present context allows that "darkness" could refer either to death,[191] or to problems during life,[192] or to both.[193] At any rate, the whole of 11:7–12:7, which moves through youth and old age to death, suggests that it is the time at the end of life to which Qohelet alludes. Here he is counseling those in their prime to make the most of the opportunities, to "rejoice while young."[194] Soon these will exchange the time of youth (יַלְדוּת) and dark hair

---

[190] Cf. Pss 49:20 [Eng. v. 19]; 58:9 [Eng. v. 8]; Job 3:16; 10:21–22; 17:13; 18:18; Prov 20:20; *Gilgamesh* 7.4.36–39; OB 10.1.11–14.

[191] So Gordis, *Koheleth*, 334.

[192] So Seow (*Ecclesiastes*, 369–70) who interprets that for Qohelet, darkness may dominate even before death.

[193] So Murphy, *Ecclesiastes*, 116. The difficulty here is determining who is being considered in vv. 7–8. The youth is addressed in v. 9, but the comments in vv. 7–8 apply equally well to those who have already lived "many years" who should still "rejoice in them all" (i.e., during them all). In what sense, for such a person, would the "days of darkness" yet to come be anything but death itself? On the other hand, if it is really the young who are being considered in vv. 7–8, contemplating the possibility of a long life, then "days of darkness" could refer to either the problems of life in general, the physical decline of the later years, death, or some combination of these.

[194] It is best to understand יִשְׂמָח וְיִזְכֹּר (11:8) as jussives which anticipate the imperatives of the same roots in 11:9 and 12:1, contra Ellermeier (*Qohelet*, 303–6) and Lauha (*Kohelet*, 204–8) who take them as indicatives. The idioms "follow the ways of your heart and the sight of your eyes" appear to contradict Num 15:39. Some LXX MSS attempt to resolve the tension by additions to the verse. However, parallels in other ANE wisdom suggest that this was simply a way of expressing enjoyment, which Qohelet elsewhere commends, and not a challenge of the proscription in Numbers. See discussion in Seow, *Ecclesiastes*, 349–50. As an example of the idiom "follow your heart," cf. the Egyptian sage Ptahhotep (11th maxim):

> Follow your heart as long as you live,
> Do no more than is required,
> Do not shorten the time of "follow-the-heart,"
> Trimming its moment offends the *ka*.
> Don't waste time on daily cares
> Beyond providing for your household;
> When wealth has come, follow your heart,
> Wealth does no good if one is glum! (*AEL* 1:66)

(שַׁחֲרוּת)[195] for days of darkness.

The second occurrence of *hebel* in this unit, at 11:10, will be considered first. Here, transience is the referent.[196] Youth (S) is not detestable (foulness), nor is Qohelet lamenting that the prime of life is a mystery or amounts to nothing (insubstantial). Rather, he *celebrates* youth and urges the young person to make the most of it while possible. It is *hebel*, transient, gone all too soon.

Qohelet guards this value of *hebel* through the discussion as a whole (extension) rather than by specific synonyms or contraries. The coming days of darkness suggest the shortness of the present. The exhortation to the youth to rejoice while young alludes to the time when this will no longer be possible, a prospect developed in 12:1–7. Thus, in v. 10, it is the transience of youth and black hair that motivate the urgent imperatives to "banish anxiety" and "put away badness from your body."[197]

The situation for *hebel* in v. 8b is not so clear, specifically the "all that comes" (כָּל־שֶׁבָּא) which serves as *hebel*'s subject. That which "comes" could refer to the "days of darkness," whether life's oppressions, old age, or death which follows. If the subject is oppressions or old age, *hebel* could have a referent of mystery; injustice is a mystery for Qohelet, and, in contrast to the joys of youth, it is unclear why the old must suffer as they do. If the subject is death, then insubstantiality ("nothingness") is the most likely referent.[198]

---

[195] The *hapax legomenon* שַׁחֲרוּת is problematic. Syr. renders it *l'ydt'* (ignorance) and LXX has ἄνοια (folly), a term which elsewhere (Prov 14:8; 22:15) translates MT אִוֶּלֶת. Vulg. has *voluptas* (desire). Apparently this was a rare and difficult term. Scholars have divided over whether the root שחר here indicates "blackness," i.e., of hair = youth (i.e., in contrast to gray hair = old age; so one version of Tg.; Murphy, *Ecclesiastes*, 112–13; Crenshaw, *Ecclesiastes*, 181, 184; Gordis, *Koheleth*, 337; NJPS; NJB), or "dawn," i.e., of life = youth (Ibn Ezra; Seow, *Ecclesiastes*, 350–51; NRSV; NAB). There is cognate evidence that would allow for either "blackness" or "dawn," but in either case, commentators agree that the term refers to youth. It is interesting to note how the blackness imagery would allow for a poetic contrast between youth and the days of darkness to come. Perhaps again Qohelet is artfully developing more than one sense for one of his terms. See discussion at Seow, *Ecclesiastes*, 350–51.

[196] There is general agreement on the meaning of *hebel* in this context (e.g., Murphy, *Ecclesiastes*, 113; Gordis, *Koheleth*, 337). Fox: "*Hebel* here denotes ephemerality, for that is the only quality of youth that makes pleasure-seeking pressing. At the same time it connotes illusoriness and thus absurdity, because the very brevity that makes it precious also makes it deceptive; and what deceives the mind is absurd" (*Time to Tear Down*, 319); previously Fox had insisted that absurdity is suggested here, "for it is unreasonable that the best part of life is so brief" (*Contradictions*, 279–80).

[197] As previously, Qohelet commends enjoyment (e.g., 3:22; 5:17–19 [Eng. 5:18–20]; 8:15). As in 5:17 [Eng. 5:18] and 9:10, the shortness of the opportunity contributes to the urgency of Qohelet's advice.

[198] Those who understand death as the subject include Gordis, *Koheleth*, 335; Barton, *Ecclesiastes*, 184; Whybray, *Ecclesiastes*, 161; Scott, *Proverbs, Ecclesiastes*, 253–54; and

However, because of close proximity, it is likely that *hebel* in v. 8 has some connection with the subject of *hebel* in v. 10: "youth." *Hebel* in both verses, then, could include transience as referent. This understanding has affinities with the proposal of Seow. He notes that in Ecclesiastes, human beings are often the subject of the verb בוא, including the other two occurrences of שֶׁבָּא (5:14–15 [Eng. vv. 15–16]). Seow interprets the statement of v. 8b to say that any person or generation which comes is soon on its way out, not permanent but transient.[199]

It is somewhat surprising, however, that Qohelet would not employ the phrase כָּל־הָאָדָם, as he did before (3:13; 5:18 [Eng. 5:19]; 7:2; cf. 12:13), if he wanted to restrict his *hebel*-judgment to human beings alone. Since he has guarded *hebel* in ch. 11 only by extension and has indicated the subject through the phrase כָּל־שֶׁבָּא, it is best to take the *hebel*-statement in 11:8 broadly, that is, to be an allusion to the work's primary thesis that הַכֹּל הָבֶל (All is *hebel*, omnivalent). Because Qohelet has already demonstrated multivalent uses of *hebel* in his symbol-building, it is not surprising to find it here also.

12:1–8 A Poem about the End

From early in the history of interpretation, the poem of 12:1–7 has been understood as an allegory of old age.[200] Recently, scholars have been reviewing this traditional understanding. Although a bit tricky at points, many of the images do make apt connections to that time of life.[201] For example, the darkening of light in v. 2 may be associated with the dimming of eyesight, the women who cease grinding in v. 3 could be teeth, the low sound of grinding might represent a loss of hearing, and so on.

However, there are parts of this section which need not (12:3a, 4a) or cannot (12:5a) be interpreted allegorically.[202] One of the earliest challenges to allegory was made by Charles Taylor who argued that 12:2–5 is a dirge on the occasion of death.[203] Other proposals advocate for the image of a house in disrepair—a parable for the failure of human efforts in this world[204]—or as a

---

Fox, *Time to Tear Down*, 317, who understands *hebel* to mean "absurd" as does Crenshaw, *Ecclesiastes*, 183. Ogden (*Qoheleth*, 195) urges for "incomprehensible" as the referent.

[199] Seow particularly notes the "generations" of 1:4 who come (בוא) and go (הלך), just as "all" come (בוא) in 11:8 and go (הלך) to the house of eternity in 12:6 (*Ecclesiastes*, 348–49).

[200] So Tg., *Eccl. Rab.*, and *Šabb.* 131b–132a.

[201] Gordis acknowledges various difficulties with sustaining the allegory (*Koheleth*, 338–40).

[202] Seow, *Ecclesiastes*, 372.

[203] Charles Taylor, *The Dirge of Coheleth in Ecclesiastes XII* (London: Williams & Norgate, 1874).

[204] J. F. A. Sawyer, "The Ruined House in Ecclesiastes 12: A Reconstruction of the

symbol for death.[205] Others believe a rainstorm is being described,[206] or a dark, wet winter's day,[207] in both cases considered metaphors for death.

Fox evaluates three interrelated levels from which to interpret the poem: the literal, the allegorical, and the symbolic.[208] On the literal level, he follows the suggestion of Taylor that this section describes a funeral.[209] Allegorically, he acknowledges images which reflect the disability of the aged.[210]

At the symbolic level, Fox proposes that the poem draws upon apocalyptic terminology, a dimension which accounts for otherwise puzzling aspects.[211] Rarely would a community grieve so deeply the death of one individual, nor do the heavenly lights literally go dark at someone's demise. The darkening of the luminaries, the gathering storm clouds, universal silence, and the references to "the day," are thus eschatological language, similar to various other biblical passages which describe the endtime—a disaster of cosmic magnitude. Fox interprets these references, not as prophecy, but as a way of evoking "the unimaginable experience of one's own death."[212]

Seow, however, places emphasis on the cosmic. He notes, for example, that the Hebrew word for "tremble" (זוע) in 12:3 indicates not feebleness but

---

Original Parable," *JBL* 94 (1975): 519–31. According to Sawyer, the parable original to Qohelet was later allegorized incompletely by editors, causing an inconsistency in the text's present form (523–25, 30–31). Seow posits in response that Qohelet himself took an old poem, one with allegorical elements, and adapted it to his purposes in a new context. Several extant poems from ancient Egypt and Mesopotamia reflect the theme of decline upon the approach of old age, with both literal and metaphorical elements (Seow, *Ecclesiastes*, 372–74).

[205] Hagia Witzenrath, *Süß ist das Licht...Eine literaturwissenschaftliche Untersuchung zu Kohelet 11,7–12,7* (Arbeiten zu Text und Sprache im Alten Testament 11; St. Ottilien: EOS, 1979), 44–50.

[206] E.g., Michael Leahy, "The Meaning of Ecclesiastes 12,1–5," *ITQ* 19 (1952): 297–300.

[207] Loretz, *Qohelet*, 189–93.

[208] M. Fox, "Aging and Death in Qohelet 12," *JSOT* 42 (1988): 55–77; idem, *Time to Tear Down*, 333–49.

[209] Taylor, *Dirge*; also Seow (*Ecclesiastes*, 379–82) who notes several images in the poem which have possible funerary associations.

[210] However, Fox emphasizes that the purpose of the poem is not to inform (his audience would surely know that old age involved such matters), but to "instill an attitude toward aging and (more important) death" (Fox, *Time to Tear Down*, 349).

[211] The patristic commentator Gregory Thaumaturgus (*Metaphrasis*) suggested something similar (cited in C. L. Seow, "Qohelet's Eschatological Poem," *JBL* 118 (1999), 212 n. 16) as does Lohfink (*Kohelet*, 84).

[212] Fox (*Time to Tear Down*, 340–42) cites Jer 25:10–11a; Ezek 32:7–8; Joel 2:2a, 6, 10b (cf. Zeph 1:15); and Isa 13:9b–10, among others. In these messages, he considers it likely that the prophets drew upon the language and imagery of mourning practices. The quotation is from p. 343.

terror. The reference to women grinding at the mill who are diminished in number (12:3) is reminiscent of end-time descriptions in the New Testament (Matt 24:40–41; Luke 17:34–35). According to Seow, "the author has superimposed on the metaphors of old age another level of signification, drawing upon the imageries of cosmic doom, to depict the end of human existence."[213] The extinguishing of the lamp means that humanity's lamp will be forever extinguished, a strong symbolic denial of immortality. The references to "dust" and "wind/breath" in 12:7 indicate that the gift of life for humanity is hereby withdrawn, returned to its Creator. For Seow, "The point is that everything is ephemeral and beyond human control."[214]

At any rate, from earliest times on into the present, interpreters have understood the end of human life to be a concern of the poem in 12:1–7, something heightened but not negated by the recogniztion that cosmic references are also included. Such a focus serves as a fitting corollary to the exhortation to young people in 11:7–10. It is striking that Qohelet does not describe the "golden years" of life in terms of wisdom, veneration, or honor, assessments typical of the wisdom tradition (Prov 20:29; Job 12:12; 15:9–10; Sir 25:3–6). Instead it is a time of discomfort, declining faculties, and impending death. Particularly noteworthy is the statement in 12:7, "and the dust (עָפָר) returns to the earth as it was, and the wind/breath (רוּחַ) returns to God who gave it." Both the terms "dust" and "wind" recall Qohelet's presentation of human frailty in 3:18–22. The human condition (S) is insubstantial which causes it to be transient from a cosmic perspective.

Yet it is also clear that for Qohelet these aspects of old age are disappointing. He begins by describing such a time as "evil days" (יְמֵי הָרָעָה, 12:1), an allusion to the connection between *hebel* and רַע found in previous passages.[215] Thus, a referent of foulness is also indicated here for *hebel* in regard to the human condition, and all three qualities of *hebel* are joined multivalently.

The relationship between the threefold use of *hebel* in 12:8 and the poem of 12:1–7 is analogous to *hebel*'s role in 1:2 in regard to the poem which immediately follows. The statement of 1:2 serves both as motto for the book

---

[213] *Ecclesiastes*, 380. Seow's discussion of this poem is expanded in his article, "Qohelet's Eschatological Poem."

[214] *Ecclesiastes*, 382.

[215] All the "days" of human existence are *hebel* for Qohelet, and twice he has employed *hebel* omnivalently in reference to them (7:15; 9:9). Elsewhere he has described both their general transience and that of youth in particular (5:17 [Eng. v. 18]; 6:12; 11:10; cf. 2:3), and at other times, like here (12:1), he mentions coming days in which there will be no delight since they are רַע, evil (cf. 2:23; 5:16 [Eng. v. 17]; 7:14; 11:8). Sawyer ("Ruined House," 523) understands the evil days in 12:1 to be a general reference rather than to the time of old age.

and as comment upon the subject of toil in the immediate context. So in 12:8, the inclusio restatement of theme serves as a comment upon the material which immediately *precedes* it.[216] Thus *hebel* addresses old age and the demise of humanity just presented in 12:1–7.[217]

12:8 Restatement of Thesis (3x)

We come now to the concluding pronouncement of Qohelet's presentation (12:8):

הֲבֵל הֲבָלִים אָמַר הַקּוֹהֶלֶת הַכֹּל הָבֶל:

"Completely *vapor!*" says (the) Qohelet, "All is *vapor.*"

This reprise of 1:2 serves as a reminder to the reader that all which Qohelet has been describing of life under the sun may be appraised as vapor (*hebel*). It is a summons to recall each of the examples and assessments given by the author which are consummated in this statement.

There is perhaps nothing more fitting for gathering the diversity of *hebel*'s referents than Qohelet's concluding discussion of youth, old age, and death, including the death of humanity. It emphasizes that youth is transient (11:7–10), and old age is filled with a foul degeneration of faculties (12:1–7), so that one must enjoy while one can (5:17–19 [Eng. vv. 18–20]; 9:7–10); that death involves a common fate for all which is unjust (2:15–16; 3:18–21; 9:1–6, 11–12; cf. 8:10–14), and yet the dead may be congratulated because of oppressions among the living (4:1–3); that the insubstantial nature of human effort is brought into relief by death's reality (2:12–17; 2:18–23; 5:12–16 [Eng. vv. 13–17]; 6:1–9; cf. 4:7–8), as is human knowledge in particular (7:1–6; 10:12–15; cf. 3:9–11; 6:10–12; 7:13–14; 8:1–9, 16–17; 9:13–18; 11:1–6). Finally, the insubstantial nature of human beings (3:16–22) is raised to a cosmic level with the demise of humanity (12:2, 7; cf. 1:4–6).

Summary of 11:7–12:8

In this concluding section of his work, Qohelet takes up *hebel* once again after leaving it since 9:9.[218] Here the subject of *hebel* is the human condition, notably its transience (11:10). The poem on the end of life, which ends the main section of Ecclesiastes, additionally highlights the foulness (12:1) and insubstantiality dimensions (12:2–7) of human existence. Finally, the comment concerning "all that comes" (11:8) and the restatement of theme (12:8) also represent omnivalent references to all that Qohelet has called *hebel* in the book.

---

[216] Backhaus, *Denn Zeit*, 330.

[217] Interestingly, Qohelet begins and ends his book with poems which draw strikingly upon creation imagery.

[218] As in 11:8, his use of *hebel* in 9:9 omnivalent.

CHAPTER SUMMARY AND CONCLUSIONS

Qohelet's Use of *Hebel*

The variety of Qohelet's uses of *hebel*—whether of single referent, multiple valencies, or omnivalency—is summarized in the table on the facing page.[219] "M-V" indicates multivalency, "O-V" indicates omnivalency.

Qohelet's Program

According to the scenario proposed by this study, Qohelet pondered just what image might best represent life as he had experienced and deliberated upon it. Instead of symbols used elsewhere, he chose *hebel*, a vapor or breath. This term had a certain history of metaphorical usage, yet also lent itself to further tropical exploration.

Qohelet wields *hebel* as a "master's" metaphor to communicate what he knows of life through other means. He presents *hebel* omnivalently in his thesis statement (1:2), then immediately begins to demonstrate how, in various ways, life is vapor. While his primary concern in the first half of the book is the insubstantiality dimension of *hebel* in relation to human effort, he also introduces foulness early, and continues to develop it.

In the book's second half, Qohelet continues with the insubstantiality referent as he sharpens his focus upon human words and thought. The foulness of human experience is again important, and he also adds the transience dimension of *hebel* as he expounds on the shortness of human life. Along the way he includes omnivalent uses of *hebel* in 7:15, 9:9, and 11:8 before restating his thesis in 12:8 that "all is *hebel*."

Thus, Qohelet constructs his symbol with individual foci (transience, insubstantiality, or foulness), occasionally combines several of these with a given subject (e.g., 1:14; 8:14), and is able to allude to all three together when he wishes to do so.

Indicators that *Hebel* Is a Tensive Symbol

Several considerations indicate that Qohelet is employing *hebel* as a tensive symbol in the book. First, Qohelet begins and ends his deliberations with a very general statement: "All is vapor" (1:2; 12:8). This alerts to the possibility of *hebel* as symbol, depending upon the way it is used. Very quickly we recognize that *hebel* is not being used to mean vapor in a literal sense, and further exploration reveals that none of the known stock metaphorical meanings of the term fit every case (false gods, pagan nations, immorality).

---

[219] Another summary, organized by subunit sequentially through Ecclesiastes, is found in Appendix I. For an overview of the subjects Fox proposals for *hebel* in Ecclesiastes, see *Time to Tear Down*, 35–42.

Subjects of *hebel*	Insubstantial	Transient	Foul	M-V	O-V	Eccl Texts
Toil Toil	futile					(1:2) 2:11, 26
Works	futile		disgusting	x		1:14
Toil (wealth from)			disgusting			2:19, 21, 23
Toil (from envy)	futile					4:4
Toil (obsessive)	futile					4:7
Toil (obsessive)			disgusting			4:8
Money	deficient					5:9[10]
Pleasure Pleasure	futile					2:1
Wisdom Wisdom	futile					4:16
Wisdom	futile		disgusting	x		2:15, 17
Foolish Activity	futile					5:6[7]
Toil/Wisdom/Pleasure	futile					6:9
Human Condition General Condition	frail					3:19
Stillborn Child	mystery					6:4
Words	futile					6:11; 7:6
General Condition		brief				6:12
Time of Youth		brief				11:10
Human Condition and the Cosmos	frail	coming to an end	disgusting			(12:8)
Inability to Enjoy General Inability			disgusting			6:2
Unjust Rewards			disgusting			8:10
Unjust Rewards	mystery	temporary	disgusting	x		8:14 (2x)
Same Fate for All	mystery		disgusting	x		9:2 [txt. em.]
All of Life All/All that Comes					x	1:2 (5x); 11:8; 12:8 (3x)
"My/Your Days"					x	7:15; 9:9 (2x)

As we next consider metaphorical possibilities, and become alert to synonyms, contraries, and extension which authors normally employ with metaphor, we recognize that both the contexts in which *hebel* is found and the terms associated with it are quite diverse. While specific metaphoric meanings fit quite well in a given context, none will work throughout. Various abstract senses for the term, though unprecedented among *hebel*'s known usage, are possible but raise other difficulties, as discussed in Chapter 1.

Thus we come to the possibility of *hebel* as tensive symbol in Ecclesiastes. In further support of this thesis, we note that the term is occasionally used in contexts with multivalency, that several omnivalent occurrences of the term are evident in between the opening and closing thesis statements (related to "all," "days," and/or "life."), and that there is a plausible development or crafting of the term as symbol which has been suggested in the summary statements of this chapter. To summarize this crafting, in the first half of the book, each use of *hebel* is carefully guarded, only two qualities of vapor are involved (insubstantiality and foulness), and in most cases there is only a single referent for each use of the term.

In the book's second half, we recognize a third quality (transience), a more free use of extension rather than synonyms or contraries to guard the term, omnivalent uses for the first time since 1:2, and more complex multivalency. In sum, we learn that not everything is *hebel* in the same way, yet all is *hebel* in one way or another, and sometimes in more than one way.[220]

Description and Evaluation

Qohelet's statements involving *hebel* are, on one level, primarily statements of description related to the qualities of insubstantiality and

---

[220] Presumably, Qohelet was aware of such wisdom symbols as "Lady Wisdom" and "The Way." Likewise, he did not choose the tree as his central image (Ps 1), and he uses Solomon only as a foil. The work of Leo Perdue has demonstrated how the literature of wisdom participates in mythic systems. Perdue explores Qohelet's work in terms of significant metaphors within the mythic systems in which wisdom is rooted: cosmological traditions of the deity in terms of fertility, artistry, word, and struggle; anthropological traditions of humans in terms of ruler and slave (Leo G. Perdue, *Wisdom in Revolt*, 32–72, and idem, *Wisdom and Creation*, 325–42). These are important studies in Ecclesiastes scholarship. It is especially interesting to consider *hebel* in relation to the term רוּחַ (1:2, 6 passim) which elsewhere in the HB represents the animating power of God to sustain both human life (Job 27:3; Isa 42:5; Zech 12:1) and creation (Ps 104:29–30). On the other hand, in contrast to the emphasis of Perdue, it seems that the cosmological and anthropological metaphors of the wisdom tradition are not at the heart of Qohelet's rhetoric. This does not mean that Qohelet is not working with them, nor that such an analysis is unimportant for understanding his thought. Rather, his rhetorical purposes employ these indirectly and employ others, particularly *hebel*, quite directly. See Perdue's discussion of Ecclesiastes, *Wisdom and Creation*, 193–242.

transience. There is nothing inherently bad about insubstantiality. Marsh-
mallows, balsa wood, and a cool, gentle breeze on a hot day all have a charm in
their insubstantiality. And some things are fine if they are short-lived. A
headache, disappointment, and rainy days are endurable when fleeting.

Of course, Qohelet is not talking about such things. He addresses things
which he believes should *not* be insubstantial or transient, and thus there is an
evaluative implication to such descriptive *hebel*-statements. Qohelet wishes
that the period of youth would endure longer, wisdom has limits which one
could wish were otherwise, and so on. He wants to alert his audience to these
realities of life so that they can adjust their choices accordingly.

Qohelet gives warning concerning things which are deceptive. It may
seem that hard work and wisdom would guarantee security, that pleasure would
give lasting satisfaction, but this is not true. Thus an aspect of his instruction is
alerting his readers regarding deception. Yet it is interesting that he does not
guard *hebel* with terms we noted elsewhere in the HB, e.g., שֶׁקֶר (lie) or אָוֶן
(deceit), although "dreams" are used (Eccl 4:17–5:6 [Eng. 5:1–7]; cf. Zech
10:1–2). His warnings about deceptive things come mostly through description.

But there are other matters which Qohelet addresses for which he
employs *hebel* as a term of direct negative judgment. In these contexts, he
applies some evaluative guarding terms, particularly the synonym רָע (evil).
These are issues he also wants his audience to recognize: matters which are
mysterious, unjust, or absurd. While he is not so fatalistic as some
commentators assume, his advice for response to such realities is restrained
(e.g., Eccl 4:1–16).

Qohelet thus employs *hebel* both to describe certain important realities
and to pronounce judgment upon matters he finds revolting. The dimension of
his rhetoric which provides for his positive counsel will be described in the
following chapter.

Finally, there is a complex cognitive content to *hebel* as symbol,
although the attempt to summarize it demonstrates the qualitative superiority of
the symbol itself: the human situation in this world is such that effort does not
always accomplish, experiences do not satisfy, security is elusive, some things
are frail and do not last, yet others are frustratingly mysterious, and others are
disgusting.

Incorporating the Insights of Other Approaches

We conclude this chapter by noting that the symbol thesis argued here
has the merit of incorporating important insights of several other proposals into
a coherent understanding of Qohelet's use of *hebel*. As with the abstract sense
approach, it provides a rationale for the relationship between the framing
statements (1:2; 12:8) and Qohelet's use of *hebel* in the rest of the book. Like
the multiple senses approach, it acknowledges a certain spectrum of usage for

hebel in its diversity of contexts. Like the metaphoric approach, it recognizes that Qohelet is using *hebel* as a metaphor and must be interpreted by alertness to guarding elements. Some things are insubstantial, others are wrong and foul, still others are transient. None of these three metaphors *by themselves* applies to *all* of human experience, and yet with this symbol, Qohelet can demonstrate that "all is *hebel*" in one way or another.

The final chapter of this study addresses specific implications of the symbol thesis for Ecclesiastes scholarship.

Chapter 5

IMPLICATIONS

This concluding chapter briefly assesses the significance of the symbol thesis for *hebel* in Ecclesiastes. Three areas are considered: the integrity of the book, its rhetorical strategy, and the place of Qohelet among the sages.

THE INTEGRITY OF ECCLESIASTES

The integrity and coherence of Ecclesiastes have often been challenged on the basis of the tensions perceived within it.[1] Three types of these may be identified: Qohelet's observations of human experience, his use of *hebel*, and the book's injunctions.

Three Areas of Tension

The first of these concerns Qohelet's observations of life. Qohelet investigates and finds things which seem inconsistent with each other, or are in tension with what he "knows" from his tradition. For example, he expresses confidence that justice will happen, yet also questions whether justice occurs on earth (3:17–21; 8:10–14). Some passages challenge the value of life while others affirm it (2:17; 11:7–10). God is arbitrary, even capricious, and gives humans a "bad business," yet is also the source of good gifts (1:13; 3:13). God's ways are unknowable, and human knowledge is restricted, yet Qohelet makes confident assertions about God in several areas (7:13–14; 9:1–2; 11:5).

---

[1] According to the Talmud, "The Sages wished to hide the Book of Ecclesiastes [i.e., withdraw it from canonical status], because its words are self-contradictory; yet why did they not hide it? Because its beginning is words of the Torah and its end is words of the Torah" (*Šabb.* 30b).

The second area of tension has been the focus of the present study. Qohelet appears to use *hebel* with a diversity of meanings, especially as one attempts to relate the individual occurrences of the term with the thematic statement of 1:2 and 12:8 that "all is *hebel*." Qohelet regrets the fact that wise and fool share the same fate and calls this *hebel*, yet the period of one's youth which he praises is also called *hebel*. Since Qohelet also declares to be *hebel* other things which are likewise disparate, it is a problem to reconcile this diversity with the book's thesis statement.

Finally, there is the matter of the book's injunctions. Qohelet gives advice which is often difficult to reconcile with either his observations of life, or his assessments of those observations. For example, the author declares that pleasure does not satisfy, yet exhorts his readers to eat, drink and enjoy, and claims that life without enjoyment is not worth living (2:1–2, 24–26; 6:1–6). He insists in several ways that wisdom fails, yet elsewhere commends wisdom (2:15–16; 6:8; 7:16, 19; 8:17; 9:11, 16–18). Toil is a bad thing and accomplishes little, yet his readers should find satisfaction in it (2:20–24; 3:13, 22; 5:14–15 [Eng. vv. 15–16]). Qohelet insists that the same fate comes to all, righteous and wicked (2:14; 9:2–3), urges his reader to be neither excessively righteous nor excessively wicked (7:16–17), laments that the wicked and righteous sometimes receive the opposite of what they deserve (7:15; 8:14), and yet exhorts the reader to fear God (5:6 [Eng. v. 7]; cf. 7:18; 8:12; 12:13).

Previous Proposals for Resolution

Some commentators have simply given up hope for true coherence, either in regard to the thematic statement (Qohelet simply uses *hebel* inconsistently throughout), or more radically concerning the unity of Qohelet's entire thought. Yet others have offered a variety of proposals for resolving the tensions just described.

One approach assumes that additions of some sort have been made to the text of an original author. Commentators then attempt to identify which parts of the book are "original" and which are editorial modifications. For example, it could be that the impiety of certain remarks motivated the addition of counter statements designed to soften Qohelet's tone.[2] Carl Siegfried's proposal is the most extreme of this type, dividing the present form of the work among a total of nine hands, including various glossators, editors, and epilogists in addition to the original author.[3] Yet it remains unclear why Ecclesiastes, if so

---

[2] Recent commentators taking some form of this approach include Barton, *Ecclesiastes*, Galling, "Prediger," and Lauha, *Kohelet*.

[3] Carl G. Siegfried, *Prediger und Hoheslied* (HKAT 2:3,2; Göttingen: Vandenhoeck and Ruprecht, 1898).

unorthodox, would have been deemed worthy of such editing,[4] or why the editing was done so unsuccessfully.[5]

A number of the rabbis as well as more recent commentators have argued that there are no true contradictions in Ecclesiastes. Many of the earliest attempts to justify the book's apparent inconsistencies designated portions of the book as applicable to one particular group or another. For example, the commendation of food and drink in 5:17 [Eng. v. 18] could be considered valid only for a fool, even though the text gives no such indication.[6] Certainly it strains credulity to resolve all of the contradictions in this way.

Another version of this approach has been the "yes-but" (*zwar-aber*) pattern of argumentation. Hertzberg notes, for example, that in 2:13–14 Qohelet raises the advantage of wisdom only to qualify it (cf. also 4:13–16; 8:12–14; 9:4–5, 16–18). While Hertzberg identifies this pattern more than a dozen times in the book, many of these are debatable and the proposal has been controversial despite its merits.[7] In many cases, for example, the initial "*zwar*" element proposed by Hertzberg continues to be recognized as true by Qohelet and is not simply presented so that he can refute it.[8]

Another way of resolving the tensions is to propose that the author is in dialogue (disputation) with another person,[9] or that he quotes traditional sayings only to challenge them.[10] The general question of quotations in Ecclesiastes has been the study of several scholars.[11] Its major difficulty is that

---

[4] The assumption of Solomonic authorship is one explanation, though this was not enough to ensure canonization for the Wisdom of Solomon.

[5] It is sometimes suggested that the additions were originally scribal comments that were eventually incorporated into the main text.

[6] Ibn Ezra and, more recently, Mordechai Zer-Kavod, *Qohelet* (Jerusalem: Mosad ha-Rab Kook, 1973), 32-33. The Talmud cites a similar resolution for Prov 26:4–5 as precedent (*Šabb.* 30b).

[7] Hertzberg, *Prediger*, 29–30.

[8] Fox, *Time to Tear Down*, 16–17.

[9] An early maneuver, this has been most recently argued by T. Anthony Perry, *Dialogues with Kohelet: The Book of Ecclesiastes, Translation and Commentary* (University Park: Pennsylvania State University Press, 1993). Interestingly, Raymond Johnson notes the lack of accusatory rhetorical questions in Ecclesiastes. Their absence reduces the plausibility of a forensic style for the book (Johnson, "Rhetorical Question," 209).

[10] So Gordis, *Koheleth*, 95–108, and as far back as Gregory Thaumaturgus (ca. 213–270), the earliest extant Christian treatment of Ecclesiastes. See review in Murphy, *Ecclesiastes*, l.

[11] Gordis, ibid.; Michael V. Fox, "The Identification of Quotations in Biblical Literature," *ZAW* 92 (1980): 416–31; R. N. Whybray, "The Identification and Use of Quotations in Ecclesiastes," *Congress Volume: Vienna, 1980* (VTSup 32; Leiden: Brill, 1981), 435–51.

in most cases it is impossible to substantiate that a quotation actually exists.[12]

Finally, James Loader has developed a thesis by which he accounts both for the tensions in Ecclesiastes and for its organizational plan. He proposes twelve structural units which involve ten categories of opposing thought patterns.[13] "Polar structures" are "patterns of tensions created by the counterposition of two elements to one another."[14] While many would agree with Loader's insight that there are polarities of thought within the book, the response to his overall argument has not been enthusiastic. Loader's scheme has been criticized for a lack of clarity regarding what constitutes a "polarity" or a "tension." In addition, several polarities he proposes appear not to be so, some of the tensions he proposes are actually resolutions Qohelet has made, and many of the titles he gives to pericopae are suspect.[15]

Position of the Present Study

Regarding the first area of tension, Qohelet's observations of life, Fox has argued well that Qohelet identifies paradoxes of human experience and most often refuses to resolve them.[16] Similarly, Edwin Good, in his study of irony in the Old Testament, urges that despite a lack of formal structure for the book, life's incongruities are the unity around which Qohelet's work is centered.[17] Qohelet, then, considers how one might best exist without denying these realities, though they appear in opposition to one another. Tensions at this level of the book do not represent an incoherence in the author's mind nor a failure in his attempts to express himself. Rather, they represent the

---

[12] Some suggestions are generally accepted, e.g., 4:8, "For whom am I toiling?" Whybray ("Identification," 438-51) recognizes eight traditional sayings in the book. In contrast to others who take the quotation theory, he concludes that in every case Qohelet quoted them with *approval*, though in some cases this approval was qualified. Those with unqualified approval occur at 7:5, 7:6a, 10:2, and 10:12, those with qualified approval at 2:14a, 4:5, 4:6, and 9:17. Whybray notes that the following may also be quotations of traditional sayings: 6:7, 7:7, 7:8, 11:1, and 11:4.

[13] James A. Loader, *Polar Structures in the Book of Qohelet* (BZAW 152; Berlin: Walter de Gruyter, 1979), ix–x, 111–16.

[14] Ibid., 1.

[15] For example, 1:12–2:26 is termed "worthlessness of wisdom," yet it also contains discussions of remembrance, pleasure, death, and toil. The last section (11:7–12:8) is titled "toil and joy," yet the major issue here is youth and old age.

[16] Like Loader's "polarities and tensions" and Hertzberg's "*zwar-aber*" approach, Fox holds that Qohelet identifies tensions in human experience. Unlike them, he generally refuses to harmonize or resolve the tensions. Fox reads Qohelet as maintaining the coexistence of apparently contradictory realities while declaring that life as a whole is therefore "absurd," Fox's translation of *hebel* (*Time to Tear Down*, 16–17).

[17] "Limits," 172–73, 194–95.

problematic circumstances to which the book is addressed.

As for the second area of tension in Ecclesiastes, the symbol thesis for *hebel* argued in the present work demonstrates how Qohelet can use the term in a variety of contexts, with several different referents, and yet not be contradictory when he says that "all is *hebel*." Apparent inconsistencies in the way *hebel* is used are actually due to the multivalency of this tensive symbol. Qohelet introduces the symbol and demonstrates how various aspects of human experience are *hebel* in one way or another. The symbol thesis therefore resolves the supposed incoherence in Qohelet's use of this key term.

Thus, the present study finds acceptable solutions to the first two areas of concern. The third area, however—the matter of reconciling Qohelet's advice with the rest of the work—remains to be addressed. This will now be attempted in summary form by a proposal for the book's rhetoric.

THE RHETORIC OF ECCLESIASTES

This section begins by discussing the occasion of the book, followed by a proposal for Qohelet's three-fold rhetorical strategy. After locating the place of the *hebel*-symbol within this strategy, the section concludes with a brief consideration of the nature of Ecclesiastes.[18]

Occasion of the Work

Despite allusions to Solomon in a work dated centuries after his time,[19] Ecclesiastes is not a true pseudepigraph, for Solomon is impersonated only in

---

[18] For further development of the following issues related to the rhetoric of Ecclesiastes, especially of the three-fold strategy itself, see Douglas B. Miller, "What the Preacher Forgot."

[19] Linguistic considerations remain the most significant evidence for determining the date of Ecclesiastes, and several major studies have recently addressed this issue: Bo Isaksson, *Studies in the Language of Qoheleth*; Daniel C. Fredericks, *Qohelet's Language: Re-evaluating Its Nature and Date* (Ancient Near Eastern Texts and Studies 3; Lewiston, N.Y.: Edwin Mellen, 1988); Antoon Schoors, *Pleasing*; C. L. Seow, "Linguistic Evidence and the Dating of Qohelet," *JBL* 115 (1996): 643–66. The discovery of 4QQoh[a] at Qumran places the *terminus ad quem* of Ecclesiastes at roughly the middle second century B.C.E. (James Muilenburg, "A Qohelet Scroll from Qumran," *BASOR* 135 [1954]: 20–28). Consideration of orthography, diction, and the presence of two Persian words not extant elsewhere prior to the fifth century B.C.E. point to a time of composition somewhere between 500 and 175 B.C.E. While the majority of scholars currently date the book to the third century (e.g., Zimmerli, *Predigers*, 123–24; Bo Isaksson, *Studies in the Language of Qoheleth*, 17), significant evidence for the Persian period, the fifth century B.C.E., has recently been offered (James L. Kugel, "Qohelet and Money," 47; C. L. Seow, "The Socioeconomic Context of 'The Preacher's' Hermeneutic," *PSB* 17 n.s. [1996]: 168–95). Fredericks tries to push the

the opening portion of the book.[20] Some characteristics of the book's author may be conjectured on the basis of internal evidence. The epilogue (12:9–14) describes Qohelet as one among the sages, a teacher who edited proverbs and sought to carefully articulate the truth. Qohelet's comments suggest that he knows poverty and oppression primarily as an observer (4:1–3; 5:7 [Eng. v. 8]). The difficulties he describes as applying to himself are those of the relatively wealthy: all the wealth, accomplishments, and pleasure do not satisfy (1:12–2:26), the one who inherits from him may be a fool (2:18–20), he has been unable to achieve the wisdom he spent time and effort to seek (7:23–24; 8:16–17).

However, there are also indications that Qohelet identifies with problems common to the middle and lower classes. He employs the first-person voice in 2:18–23 when speaking of work and inheritance, exhibits intense emotion with regard to oppression in 4:1–3, and hints that his audience fits somewhere within two economic extremes (5:11 [Eng. 5:12]; 10:5–7; cf. 10:20). Thus, we may understand him to be of at least moderate means, and it is not possible to discount that he is a relatively wealthy citizen. Regardless, the frustrations he expresses and the extent to which he identifies with the problems of his audience suggest that he has a tremendous sympathy for those struggling with daily living.

Finally, it would appear that Qohelet is past the time of youth. His investigations, including matters most appropriate to the more elderly, are assessed from a retrospective vantage point. His exhortations in 11:7–10 are addressed to the young, while the final poem involving old age implies more familiarity with that stage of life than is suggested for at least some of his audience. Qohelet's repeated comments on the subject of death may also reflect the concerns of an older person. The epilogist's reference to "my child" in 12:12 is, of course, a motif of the sages, yet reflects the reality that experienced ones such as Qohelet instructed those of less experience.

Regarding the implied author's locale, "house of God" (4:17 [Eng. 5:1]) is a common Hebrew expression for the temple, as is "holy place" (8:10).

---

date as far back as the eighth century B.C.E. (*Qohelet's Language*, 263). At the other extreme, C. F. Whitley dated Ecclesiastes to ca. 150 B.C.E. (*Koheleth*, 132–48).

[20] This possibility of Solomonic authorship is rejected by most scholars for three primary reasons: (1) the book is ascribed to "Qohelet" and never to Solomon by name, (2) the kingly voice of the book's preliminary passages speaks, after the second chapter, as one who is outside royal circles, and (3) the book's language is unlike any known examples of Hebrew from the time of Solomon, though it *is* similar to that from a much later period. In addition, the epilogue refers to the author as a sage, rather than a king, and the author speaks more as a critic of society than as one of its architects.

Further, Qohelet gives no indication that extensive travel to Jerusalem is necessary for worship (4:17–5:6 [Engl. 5:1-7]). Items which would not befit an Egyptian setting (proposed by some) but which would fit Palestine include the almond tree (12:5) and the use of cisterns (12:6).[21]

In sum, evidence for the book's date, along with aspects of the author's self-presentation, suggest that Qohelet was an educated person of at least moderate means and at least middle age living in Palestine between the fifth and third centuries B.C.E.

As for Qohelet's audience, comments in the book suggest the circumstances of a hard-working, possibly beleaguered group. Oppression and uncertainty exist around them (4:1; 5:8 [Eng. v. 9]. They are motivated by envy of the wealthy (4:4; 9:6). The results of their labor may disappear at any time, due to a stranger or to disaster (5:12–14 [Eng. vv. 13–15]; 6:2). Yet they know no other way. So they work hard, even when it does not seem to be for any good purpose (4:7-8). Through work and wisdom they seek to establish security, for if they establish it, they expect more pleasure to be theirs. Yet it is hard for them to acquire "surpluses" such as pleasure and security (1:3; 3:9). They hang onto the hope that by exerting just a little more effort they can acquire such surpluses.

The author's relationship to his audience may be understood as follows. He sees that this group has become trapped into viewing every part of their lives, even their religious practice, as a means of manipulating their own success and security. Yet in their determination to achieve the good things in life, they are actually missing those very things. The goal of Qoheleth's instruction, then, is to persuade his audience of another way of living, a proper assessment of work, pleasure, wisdom, and worship that will allow them to make the most of both the "good day" and the "bad day" (7:14).

A Three-Fold Rhetorical Strategy

By the categories of classical rhetorical criticism, Ecclesiastes is *deliberative* rhetoric (concerned with persuading its audience to action) as opposed to *judicial* (defending or condemning a person or event) or *epedeictic* (strengthening adherence to some belief or value).[22] I will now argue that the book of Ecclesiastes demonstrates a three-fold rhetorical strategy to which I give the terms *ethos*, *destabilization*, and *restabilization*. These are complementary processes which sometimes alternate and overlap throughout the book.

---

[21] See H. W. Hertzberg, "Palästinische Bezüge im Buche Kohelet," *ZDPV* 73 (1957): 113-24; idem, *Der Prediger*, 42-45.

[22] For a discussion of these and the following categories in classical rhetorical criticism, see Corbett, *Classical Rhetoric*, 28–29, 37–94.

Yet there is an appropriate sequence to the following presentation.[23]

Kind of Argument: The Primacy of Ethos

First, Qohelet establishes ethos, the persuasive power of his own credibility as derived from the speech itself.[24] Three elements in particular constitute ethos: the speaker's *competence*, the speaker's *status*, and finally, the speaker's moral *character*, especially benevolence—a perceived concern for the welfare of his or her audience. Regarding competence, Qohelet does not appeal to special revelation for his authority, for like other sages, he finds the divine word in the creation all around him. Ethos in Ecclesiastes is enhanced through matters such as Qohelet's literary dexterity. His use of the *ṭôb*-saying, for example, accomplishes a sense of his intellectual abilities. Rhetorical questions are particularly significant in the establishment of consensus and for engaging participation by the audience with the speaker.[25] Ethos is also accomplished through the Solomon persona,[26] as well as by Qohelet's ongoing reports of personal experience.

Finally, ethos is achieved significantly through the frame-narrator's affirmations of Qohelet in all three of these aspects.[27] In sum, Qohelet puts very little emphasis on emotional appeal or logical argument while yet giving the appearance of extensive empirical data. Those who find him worthy of their trust will accept his assessments, and then his advice.

Destabilization

Second, Qohelet moves to destabilize the symbol and belief system of his audience. Here he has a delicate balance to achieve. He must accomplish a certain amount of credibility to be heard at all. To do so he must demonstrate

---

[23] Ogden (*Qoheleth*, 21–22) recognizes a different three-fold structure in the argument, but one which also ends with positive instruction: "the book . . . moves from programmatic question through response to advice grounded on the preceding evidence."

[24] In addition, deliberative rhetoric involves logos, the rational, an emphasis on logical argument, and pathos, the emotional, an attempt to motivate the audience through imagination and passion. Deliberative communication will always involve some element of all three types of persuasion, but the emphasis of Ecclesiastes is not primarily on these two.

[25] See Johnson, "Rhetorical Question," 210–13, 250–51.

[26] Gordis, *Koheleth*, 204.

[27] This third-person voice declares Qohelet to be competent: one who taught knowledge, studied and arranged proverbs (12:9). His benevolent motivation is suggested by the commendation that he sought to find appropriate words and to write words of truth rightly (יֹשֶׁר 12:10). Finally, this voice also declares him to have significant status since he is among the wise (12:9, 11). See Fox, "Frame-Narrative," 96–106, and *Time to Tear Down*, 363–77, and Seow, "'Beyond Them, My Son, Be Warned': The Epilogue of Qoheleth Revisited," in *Wisdom, You Are My Sister*, 125–41.

that he sees things in a way similar to that of his audience: he shares their frustration, their struggle, their cynicism, their values. On the other hand, there are perspectives and values concerning which he and his audience do not agree. In certain ways, he wants them to change their behavior and their orientation.

To challenge the practices of his audience directly would be to jeopardize his credibility. Therefore he adopts a strategy which is largely indirect, and which employs destabilization as its major tool.[28] As with ethos, rhetorical questions are an important means by which Qohelet accomplishes destabilization, something Johnson refers to as "audience victimization."[29] Among other issues, Qohelet uses them to take on the assumption that toil produces security or profit.

Another type of destabilization is accomplished through Qohelet's parody of King Solomon,[30] and through his parody of certain wisdom forms,

---

[28] "Destabilization" and "restabilization" are terms used by L. G. Perdue in his insightful work with metaphor in the wisdom literature. See Perdue's discussion of metaphor and destabilization in *Wisdom in Revolt*, 22–27. His work with the book of Job is most similar to the program developed in this essay—the treatment of metaphor is similar although I employ the term "destabilization" somewhat more broadly than he does. Perdue's work with Ecclesiastes, on the other hand, is significantly different from the approach to that book taken here, although his work with cosmological and anthropological metaphors within Ecclesiastes is insightful (*Wisdom and Creation: The Theology of Wisdom Literature* [Nashville: Abingdon, 1994], 193–242).

[29] Johnson, "Rhetorical Question," 251–54. Questions, even when the audience suspects they might be rhetorical, create gaps, an anticipation of resolution which Qohelet regularly delays. This delay not only engages the reader's attention, but requires that the reader engage the assumptions and values of the speaker as long as it takes to achieve the answer. In the case of 1:3 ("What surplus for toil?"), an answer (though partial) does not come until 2:11 ("There was no surplus under the sun"). Fredericks, who contends that Qohelet answers the question of 1:3 positively in the book, declares the statement of 2:11 to be "part of a temporary 'disillusionment'" (*Coping*, 53). Citing the question of 5:15 [Eng. v. 16] and its eventual resolution in 6:9, Johnson notes that such gaps "produce cognitive dissonance and destabilize the reader's frame of reference" ("Rhetorical Question," 253; cf. Good, "Unfilled Sea," 63–73, and Meir Sternberg, *The Poetics of Biblical Narrative: Ideological Literature and the Drama of Reading* [Indiana Studies in Biblical Literature; Bloomington: Indiana University Press, 1985], 235–37). Johnson also demonstrates how, in 7:23–8:1, the knowability of the world is called into doubt by the use of a rhetorical question, and then reestablished as Qohelet demonstrates the possibilities of knowledge, until, in 8:1, the importance of wisdom is reaffirmed by rhetorical questions ("Rhetorical Question," 259–62).

[30] C. L. Seow, "Qohelet's Autobiography." Solomon had become a symbol of all that was positive about wisdom. He was wise beyond all others, successful in all his toil, and consequently blessed with all variety of pleasures. Qohelet takes on this symbol, and declares all that it represents to be *hebel*. The triumphalist symbol of Solomon is torn down as the *hebel* symbol is build up.

such as the *ṭôb*-saying and example stories.[31] Sometimes Qohelet criticizes more directly certain choices and values, such as the desire for lasting fame (2:16; 9:5, 15), work for its own sake (4:7–8), individualism (4:9–12), and improper speech before God (4:17–5:6 [Eng. 5:1–7]). At other times he points out aspects of human experience over which humans have no control, such as injustice (7:15; 8:10–15), the apparent capriciousness of God (6:2; 9:1–3, 11–12), and having a fool for an heir (2:19).

Finally, Qohelet addresses certain fears of this group which relate to inherent human limitations. Old age is coming with its pain and reduced capacities. Death will follow, and perhaps there is no existence after death (3:19–21; 11:7–12:7). In these several ways, Qohelet makes use of his credibility to call into question certain values and assumptions of his audience. By destabilizing their value and belief system, he prepares them to receive his positive admonitions.

Restabilization

Qohelet's third move, woven throughout the book, is an attempt to restabilize, to advocate for the values and orientations which he desires his audience to adopt.[32] He has identified the problems, contradictions, and frustrations of his audience's world, and has an alternative to offer. He will not present this alternative by denying the realities which he has identified. The chaos and injustice are still there. He wants his audience to accept the things they cannot control, but to change their own way of being and doing over which they do have some control.

Qohelet's reconstructive efforts are first evident through his use of wisdom sentences, primarily of the *ṭôb*-saying type (e.g., 2:24–26).[33] Only after Qohelet has carefully established his credibility, and has developed a pattern of admonishment through the wisdom sentence, does he go on to use the imperative mood.[34] In addition to the use of rhetorical questions in establishing

---

[31] He presents such forms, and then gives them an unexpected conclusion, e.g., success stories of wisdom without a happy ending, or a *ṭôb*-saying in which the "better" element is shown to be limited.

[32] See Edwin Good, "Limits," 173–95, and Timothy Polk, "Wisdom of Irony," 3–17, for their treatments of an "ironic" mode of exposition in Ecclesiastes.

[33] This heightens the inevitable paradox of his position. He has questioned the credibility of the sages while playing out the role of a sage. He has questioned whether anyone can know what is good while offering hope that his audience can discern the good. Cf. Meir Sternberg's discussion of the omniscient narrator. While biblical narrative persuades the reader that human knowledge is limited, its rhetoric accomplishes a way for the reader to be confident of the truths presented in these stories (Sternberg, *Poetics*, 90–98).

[34] This is almost exclusively in connection with matters which are not preceded by a

consensus, audience contact, and audience victimization, Qohelet also uses them in the process of reconstruction. In the example just cited, 2:24–26, a rhetorical question supports the contention that God is the source of good things. In at least one instance, Qohelet also uses the parable or example story for reconstruction.[35] Reconstruction also occurs in the parody of the Solomon symbol.[36]

Qohelet applies this three-fold rhetorical strategy as his means of persuasion. He criticizes individualistic toil as a means of security (4:7–8) in order to replace it with a toil which involves cooperation and in which one can find enjoyment (4:9–12). He criticizes the failures of pleasure (2:1–2) in order to advocate a pleasure that comes through simple things: food, drink, rest, and one's spouse (2:24; 3:12, 22; 4:6; 8:15; 9:7–10). He counsels against remembering the mundane things of life (5:19 [Eng. v. 20]) and urges that the shortness of life be remembered instead (11:8).

Qohelet declares God to be sovereign, the source of bad as well as good, a deity of mystery (1:13; 3:10–11, 14–15, 17–18; 4:17–5:6 [Eng. 5:1–7]; 6:1–2; 7:13–14; 8:17; 9:1; 11:5, 9; 12:7). Yet he establishes a theology of divine gift, of appreciating the good things God gives a person without respect for their effort, knowledge, and religious activity (2:24–26; 3:13; 5:18–19 [Eng. 5:19–20]; 9:7). In place of attempts to manipulate the divine favor (7:15–18; 9:2) Qohelet enjoins a "fear of God" which respects the proper place of human beings, and receives enjoyment as part of the "portion" God has given (5:6 [Eng. v. 7], 17–18 [Eng. vv. 18–19]).

---

discussion of what Qohelet has experienced and observed. Examples include relations with God through the cult (4:17–5:6 [Eng. 5:1–7]), relations with the king (8:2–3; 10:4, 20), economic advice (11:1–6), and the call to celebrate one's youth (11:9–12:1). The exceptions are the problematic *ṭôb*-sayings of 7:9–10, the matter of righteousness (7:16–18), and the call to enjoy life in 9:7–10, also long after the wisdom sentence pattern has been established.

[35] The merits of toil in cooperative community are narrated in 4:9–12. Pieces of reconstructive narrative are also found at 2:26; 5:11 [Eng. v. 12]; 10:16–20; and 11:1–6.

[36] On the one hand, those in his audience may have held the figure of Solomon as a positive example. For these, it was important to show the problems of Solomon's career (cf. the contrast between 1 Kgs 10 and 1 Kgs 11). On the other hand, there were possibly those for whom Solomon was regarded as a disappointment. For these, the legacy of his reign was nothing less than personal failure and a divided kingdom. Qohelet allows for both of these perspectives. For the one who would venerate Solomon, he demonstrates that Solomon himself recognized the emptiness of his pursuits, and would do it differently if given another chance. For the cynic, Qohelet establishes that Solomon's activities were neither self-indulgence nor caprice, but part of a deliberate plan of exploration (James F. Armstrong, "Ecclesiastes in Old Testament Theology," *PSB* 4 n.s. [1983]: 17). Thus for both groups, Qohelet rehabilitates Solomon as a symbol of wisdom: *hebel*-wisdom. As in the *Gilgamesh Epic*, the mark of wisdom is not success, but the recognition that success is empty.

The Place of *Hebel* in Qohelet's Rhetoric

The role and rhetorical significance of Qohelet's symbolic use of *hebel* may now be recognized. Its importance is evident from the fact that it is used in each of the three rhetorical processes just described. As with other metaphors, *hebel* invites engagement by the reader. With *hebel*'s ambiguity, the effect is heightened, enhancing identification with Qohelet. This occurs because the invitation to resolve a puzzle is a form of compliment which shows respect for the audience.[37] Engagement also occurs once the puzzle begins to resolve, since author and audience now share something which is not true for everyone else. The enigma also enhances Qohelet's status, since there is a mystery to which he holds the clues. Finally, Qohelet's use of *hebel* to punctuate the assessment of his reports elevates his competence since it appears that only as a result of his extensive experience is he able to make such claims.

Destabilization occurs as the audience recognizes that *hebel* is not being used materially, then further recognizes that a single metaphor will not work for the term, and finally begins to seek out help to resolve the uncertainty.[38] Thus, the symbol actually embodies properties of the disorienting world to which Qohelet's efforts are addressed.

As the audience continues to pick up Qohelet's clues to the meaning of the symbol, *hebel*'s potential for restabilization becomes evident. A single image is able to incorporate a tremendous diversity of human experience. Thus, the *hebel*-symbol provides for unity and stability, at the same time that it describes diversity and chaos. In the process of resolving it, the reader not only achieves insight, but also gains hope for addressing life's other paradoxes and contradictions.

The purpose of this section has been to account for the apparent disparity in Ecclesiastes between Qohelet's observations and judgments concerning human experience, on the one hand, and the book's advice and injunctions on the other. It has described a three-fold rhetorical strategy and demonstrated how Qohelet's symbolic use of *hebel* partakes of this strategy.

The Nature of Qohelet's Writing

The above considerations of the book's integrity and its rhetorical strategy now make possible an assessment of the overall nature of Qohelet's

---

[37] As R. C. Van Leeuwen notes, there is in general a "puzzlelike character" to Ecclesiastes ("Ecclesiastes: Introduction," in *The HarperCollins Study Bible* [gen. ed. W. A. Meeks; New York: HarperCollins, 1993], 987). This is not a "riddle" in the formal sense (cf. Prov 1:6; 1 Sam 24:14), yet it does set forth something which the reader must make an effort to resolve.

[38] Perdue, *Wisdom in Revolt*, 22–27.

efforts. Essentially five positions have been taken on this issue.

The Repentant King

Early Jewish interpretation commonly viewed the book as Solomon's confessions of his sin.[39] The book was his warning to others not to repeat the vain pursuits of his own life. It assumes that *hebel* means "vanity"—sinful, foolish, and futile activity—and is an attempt to make the injunction to "fear God" central to the book, which is confessional and admonitory.

Problems with this approach include the disappearance of the kingly persona after chapter 2, the lack of any specific admission of sin, and the book's injunctions to "enjoy life." Also, some situations Qohelet declares to be *hebel* and "evil" (רָע) are matters outside human control, e.g., 2:21, leaving wealth to one who did not work for it. In addition, the speaker does not hesitate to implicate God for various things (1:13), notably the lack of justice in the world (6:1–6), as well as the fact that righteous and wicked, wise and fool share the same fate (2:15–16). These matters are hard to explain from one who is supposed to be repentant and calling others to repentance.[40]

Finally, Qohelet's skepticism about the prospects for discerning that which is good (6:12), and his exhortation not to be *too* righteous (7:15–18) at the least compromise the intensity of his supposed call to repentance.

The Ascetic

Advocates of a second early position understood the speaker as an ascetic who challenges those who are living superficial and materialistic lives to deny themselves in preparation for the afterlife.[41] By this understanding Qohelet cites numerous examples of the failure to find satisfaction in the

---

[39] According to Jewish legend, God punished Solomon for his apostasy by removing him from the throne and putting in his place Ashmedai, the king of demons. Eventually Solomon returned to faithfulness and recorded the book of Ecclesiastes as his testimony. See Louis Ginzberg, *The Legends of the Jews* (vol. 4; Philadelphia: Jewish Publication Society, 1913), 168–76; Étan Levine, *The Aramaic Version of Qohelet* (New York: Sepher-Hermon, 1978), 28; and (English translation only) Peter S. Knobel, *The Targum of Qohelet* (The Aramaic Bible 15; Collegeville, Minn.: Liturgical, 1991), 22–23. The story of Ashmedai is also recounted in *b. Giṭ.* 68a–68b and *y. Sanh.* 2, 6 (though the latter does not mention his name).

[40] Tg., for example, solves the difficulties with pious insertions.

[41] Notably Gregory Thaumaturgus, one of the earliest Christian commentators upon Ecclesiastes (third century C.E.), and Jerome (fourth century) among others. See Murphy, *Ecclesiastes*, xlviii–liii. There are also examples of early Jewish interpretation which emphasized the importance of the afterlife in the interpretation of the book. Note, e.g., the Tg. on 1:2–3 which emphasizes the vanity of "this world" and "under the sun" in contrast to what will come in the world to come.

present world in order to convince his readers to prepare for the *next* world. *Hebel*, in this case, refers to activity which is irrelevant or detrimental in light of eternity. Unlike the first position, it recognizes that the speaker does not simply lament his own behavior, but laments vain things about life itself.

At least three matters in the book demonstrate the difficulty of this position. First, the possibility of life beyond the grave is something Qohelet specifically declares cannot be known (3:19–22; 9:3–6). Second, Qohelet does not counsel his readers to set aside the pleasures of this life. In fact, third, he urges them to enjoy life (2:24–25; 3:12–13, 22) and goes so far as to insist that a life denied such pleasures is not worth living at all (4:1–3; 6:1–6).[42]

The Bitter Skeptic

A new respect for the seriousness with which Qohelet addresses the complexities and enigmas of life led to a third approach, a most common assessment of Ecclesiastes among scholars in the past two centuries. From this perspective, the speaker is a bitter skeptic, someone who is appalled at finding life to be less than it should be.[43] As a result, he declares everything to be *hebel* in the sense of being "absurd" or "meaningless." Qohelet by this understanding cites repeated examples of life's shortcomings and ironies in order to explain, and perhaps also to justify, his bitterness. This position views the book less as a piece of persuasion than as a venting of its author's frustrations.[44]

This assessment of Qohelet as cynic has been very attractive to those in Western culture after the Enlightenment, and it may be even more so to

---

[42] With regard to such passages, proponents often took recourse to allegory, e.g., Qohelet's admonition to take pleasure in food and drink was related by Jerome to the Eucharist (a comment on Eccl 2:24, "Commentarius in Ecclesiasten," *Patrologiae Latine* [vol. 23; ed. J.-P. Migne; Paris: Migne, 1863], 1070, cited by Longman, *Ecclesiastes*, 30–31). Another common tactic with problematic passages was to interpret the author to be in dialogue with fools or unrighteous persons whose words he was quoting.

[43] See, for example, Gerhard von Rad, *Old Testament Theology*, 1:455–58, and *Wisdom in Israel*, 226–37. This approach is taken by numerous translations today, e.g., NIV, The New Living Translation, GNB, NEB, and CEV. It is probably also assumed by others such as NRSV and REB which use forms of "vanity" or "futility" respectively throughout, although "vanity" reflects an ancient tradition for understanding *hebel* which can also fit with the first two positions described. See above, p. 3, n. 7.

[44] Duncan Black Macdonald uses the term "self-confession," which he considers the foremost concern of the work: "For the author himself . . . there can be little doubt that his book was primarily a revelation of himself to himself. . . . That he was thereby led to give practical admonitions as to life was secondary" (*Hebrew Philosophical Genius*, 68). Some, however, have concluded that Qohelet is trying to convince his audience that life is absurd in order to direct them in the best response to it (Crenshaw, *Ecclesiastes*, 28), although this is more characteristic of the following "Preacher of Joy" position.

adherents of a postmodern worldview. Here is a thinker who deeply appreciates the challenges to faith raised by life's absurdities and seeming inconsistencies. Yet the attempt to read the book consistently from this perspective raises several complications to which various responses have been given. The challenge has been to reconcile what appear to be direct contradictions in the book concerning the goodness or badness of life, the benevolence or capriciousness of God, the value of wisdom, and other matters. Some have taken the speaker's urges to enjoy life as wishful thinking[45] or as resignation.[46] The speaker's expressions of confidence in divine judgment have been assessed as insertions of a later, more orthodox editor.[47]

These are not implausible ways of dealing with such difficulties. Answers with similar virtue have been given to the problem of why such an originally unorthodox work was preserved and edited, given a positive assessment in the book's epilogue, and eventually granted canonical status.[48]

On the other hand, anyone who ascribes to wishful thinking or resignation Qohelet's positive affirmations of life does not adequately appreciate their frequency, their breadth (they address wisdom, pleasure, and toil), nor their typical placement at the conclusion of Qohelet's discussions. To resolve the book's tensions by recourse to subsequent editing raises the problem of circularity. It requires positing a message of a certain type, then declaring everything in the book which does not fit that assumption to be a later addition or modification.

In response, recent commentators have preferred a return to the received form of the text and a better appreciation for the more orthodox sentiments in the book. This requires that they somehow account rhetorically for the tensions

---

[45] William H. U. Anderson, *Qoheleth and Its Pessimistic Theology: Hermeneutical Struggles in Wisdom Literature* (Mellen Biblical Press Series 54; Lewiston, N.Y.: Mellen, 1997), 73. J. L. Crenshaw ponders but rejects the possibility that the author was essentially pessimistic yet ambivalently recognized certain good things in life that he failed to reconcile with the bad (*Ecclesiastes*, 27–28; see also idem, *Old Testament Wisdom: An Introduction* [Atlanta: John Knox, 1981], 142–44).

[46] Murphy, *Ecclesiastes*, 27: "But it is difficult to find more than the mood of a resigned conclusion in such passages. . . . He can only offer them in a mysterious and incalculable world: What else can one do? So take whatever joy one can find." Cf. also Scott, *Proverbs, Ecclesiastes*, 191, and Longman, *Ecclesiastes*, 34. Longman, however, finds the "normative theological contribution of the book" in the concluding message of the frame-narrator (36–39). This latter sage, he says, quotes Qohelet as a foil for instruction "concerning the dangers of speculative, doubting wisdom in Israel" (38).

[47] Among others, Barton, *Ecclesiastes*, 44–45.

[48] This is often explained by the association of the book with Solomon (e.g., by Barton, *Ecclesiastes*, 6), though, as noted previously, such association was not enough to grant the Wisdom of Solomon a place in the canon.

between Qohelet's emphatic observations (life is bad!) and his equally strong admonitions (enjoy life!). In the final two positions that effort is made.

The Preacher of Joy

Proponents of a fourth position agree with the Skeptic approach that the book's author viewed life as absurd or meaningless, yet they put much more emphasis upon recommendations to enjoyment which they attribute to Qohelet himself.[49] From this perspective, Qohelet was a preacher of joy or pleasure. He first had to convince his audience of all the absurdities in the world, which he called *hebel*. He did this *not* primarily to vent his own frustrations but to motivate his audience to focus on the truly important things in life despite all the absurdity. In fact, Qohelet is understood to say, it is by reflecting upon such absurdities that one is enabled to receive God's gift of joy. Thus, proponents of this position, like the previous, understand *hebel* to be a term of negative evaluation which declares human existence to be absurd or meaningless. Qohelet's positive injunctions come in spite of his discouraging assessment.

This position better accounts for the author's positive admonitions. Yet it remains problematic that Qohelet would declare life to be *totally* meaningless

---

[49] For adherents of this position, *śimḥâ* is *the* message in the book. While advocates of this approach emphasize in varying degrees Qohelet's encouraging remarks relative to his discouraging comments, they view his call to enjoyment as one of general optimism. R. N. Whybray notes that in the seven calls to enjoyment in the book, there is a progression from declarative *ṭôb*-sayings to the use of the imperative, and that Qohelet gives these admonitions to joy as a response to seven different problems of human life ("Qoheleth, Preacher of Joy," *JSOT* 23 [1982]: 87–98). Yet in his commentary Whybray hedges a bit on the question of Qohelet's optimism, calling him a "realist" (*Ecclesiastes*, 28). Robert Gordis says the book is the record of Qohelet's wandering and his sorrow, and of the peace he finally attained. Pursuit of happiness is a sacred duty for Qohelet, though he was too conservative to realize the logical implications of this conclusion. Gordis sees the theme of the book as its "insistence on the enjoyment of life, of all the good things in the world." He adds: "For Koheleth, nothing really counts if truth and righteousness cannot be attained. Yet man lives and God rules, and God's manifest will is man's happiness, not that it matters overmuch, but this at least is certain" (*Koheleth*, 124, 132). Of the five approaches to the argument of Ecclesiastes, M. V. Fox's position also fits best here. He understands *hebel* to mean "absurd" and, though he does not emphasize joy like Whybray (and clearly separates his position from Whybray's), he insists that Qohelet writes for admonitory purposes, and refuses to accept either the totally pious or the totally skeptical pictures of Qohelet (Fox, *Contradictions*, 11–13; *Time to Tear Down*, 3–4, 144–45). The kind of absurdity Fox attributes to Qohelet's teaching allows room for "values and truths" (*Time to Tear Down*, 11), and for "ways to be closer to happiness" (*Contradictions*, 77). On this position see also Edwin M. Good ("Limits," 168–95); Timothy Polk ("Wisdom of Irony," 11–15); François Rousseau ("Structure de Qohélet I 4–11 et plan du livre," *VT* 31 [1981]: 200–17); and C. S. Knopf ("The Optimism of Koheleth," *JBL* 49 [1930]: 195–99).

or absurd, both at the beginning and at the conclusion of the work, while at the same time instructing his audience how to find meaning. Other of Qohelet's positive admonitions in addition to joy also deserve more recognition, e.g., the fear of God, wisdom, and work.[50]

The Realist

Finally, there is a fifth position in which Qohelet, the book's author, may be described as a realist.[51] The term "realist" as used here means that Qohelet can allow that some things in life are bizarre, tragic, and defy explanation, yet can avoid taking a cynical or absurdist approach to the whole. Further, according to Realist advocates Qohelet does not merely allow for pockets of good in the midst of life's bleakness but actually holds together the uncertain and tragic with the good and deeply satisfying.

Proponents of this approach reject both the simple piety and the other-worldly spirituality of the Repentance and Ascetic positions. Yet they agree with them that admonitions of various types within Ecclesiastes reflect the book's *deliberative* rhetoric, designed to motivate its audience to some definite and specific action.[52]

Further, they insist that Qohelet is not using the term *hebel* to declare human experience as a whole to be meaningless or absurd. This position may therefore also be distinguished from those who view Qohelet as a "skeptic" or as a "preacher of Joy," even though adherents of the latter position also consider the book to be deliberative rhetoric. Qohelet, the Realists say, uses *hebel* to designate numerous *limitations* and *complications* in human experience with which one must reckon. This is the issue which distinguishes the fifth position and is also its major exegetical challenge.

Other advocates of the Realist approach have been content to acknowledge Qohelet's diverse uses of the term *hebel* while they make various attempts to reconcile these with the programmatic statements of Eccl 1:2 and 12:8 ("all is *hebel*"). All of them determine that Qohelet uses the term in more than one way since to identify *one* meaning for *hebel* in Ecclesiastes invariably leads to a harshly negative gloss for the term (see discussion in Chapter 1).

The present study provides a rationale for a consistent use of *hebel* in

---

[50] Fear of God (Eccl 5:6 [Eng. v. 7]; cf. 7:18; 8:12; 12:13), wisdom (7:12, 19; 10:10), work (2:24; 3:13; 4:9).

[51] Adherents include G. Ogden (*Qoheleth*; and "Qoheleth XI 7 – XII 8: Qoheleth's Summons to Enjoyment and Reflection," *VT* 34 [1984]: 27–38); Farmer (*Who Knows?*), Fredericks (*Coping*), Seow (*Ecclesiastes*), and Robert K. Johnston ("'Confessions of a Workaholic': A Reappraisal of Qoheleth," *CBQ* 38 [1976]: 14–28).

[52] Corbett, *Classical Rhetoric*, 28.

Ecclesiastes which affirms the Realist understanding of the book. It is true that Qohelet is disappointed with much of life as he finds it, and so, in addition to describing realities of life, one aspect of the *hebel*-symbol involves negative evaluation. Yet Qohelet is not merely venting his frustrations about life, nor is he simply groping for pockets or hints of goodness.

Thus, Qohelet's exhortations to enjoy life, to be wise, and to find good in one's work are not secondary to his main concern (Repentant King and Ascetic positions). They are not half-hearted, wishful thinking, later additions to the book, or inconsistencies in Qoheleth's thought (Cynic position). Nor are they ways to avoid the reality that life is actually totally absurd (Preacher of Joy). Rather, they, along with the fear of God, are at the center of Qoheleth's rhetorical program—lifestyle elements which he has been commending as gifts from a benevolent, if mysterious, deity. Though he dispels the false hope that any of these in themselves are a reliable source of security or satisfaction, they are to be received for what they can legitimately provide.

Chapter 1 summarized research in Ecclesiastes studies which has identified indicators of structure, sophisticated uses of language, and stylistic compatibilities with other Israelite and ancient wisdom literature. It is hoped that the efforts of the present study—to provide for a congruent employment of the term *hebel* in the book, and to suggest a plausible rhetorical schema—have further strengthened the case for the book as a masterful literary work.

ECCLESIASTES AND THE WISDOM TRADITION

As a result of the present study of *hebel* in Ecclesiastes, and of the foregoing analysis of the book's rhetoric, it will be worthwhile in this concluding section to evaluate Qohelet's place alongside what is known of other sages of the ancient Near East.

Qohelet as Critic of Wisdom

The book of Ecclesiastes is typically classified among the wisdom literature of its era. Yet Qohelet has some critical things to say about wisdom, so much so that his compatibility with the wisdom tradition has sometimes been doubted.[53] Some scholars have even argued that his teachings reflect a

---

[53] James Crenshaw has urged that three categories be distinguished: wisdom literature ("Prov, Qoh, Job, Sir, Wisd of Sol, and Wisdom Pss"), *paideia* ("the wisdom movement itself, its educational curriculum and pedagogy"), and *ḥokmah* ("a particular stance, an approach to reality") ("Method," 130, n. 4). Cf. Hans Heinrich Schmid, *Wesen und Geschichte der Weisheit* (BZAW 101; Berlin: Alfred Töpelmann, 1966), 7. This section explores ANE wisdom literature, observes awareness of human limitations in knowledge, and probes the consistency of Ecclesiastes with that body of literature in regard to *ḥokmah*.

"crisis" in Israelite wisdom.[54]

Qohelet points out that the wise are not remembered and die just like fools (2:16). They must pass along their wealth to someone who may be a fool (2:18–20), are rejected by the fickle masses (4:13–16; 9:13–16), have little to show for their wisdom (6:8), and have no guarantee of success (9:11). Further, they get pain and confusion for their efforts at wisdom (1:18; 7:16), find wisdom to be elusive (7:23–24; 8:1), and cannot discern the future or the activity of God (3:21; 8:16–17; 9:1; 10:14).

In terms of wisdom itself, Qohelet says that it brings vexation and pain (1:18), is fragile (9:18; 10:1, 12), and the gain it provides is suspect (cf. 2:13–14 with 6:8). Complete wisdom is unattainable (1:17; 7:23–24; 8:1, 16–17), and there is much one cannot know: God's work (9:1–2; 11:5), when bad fortune will happen (11:2), one's destination after death (3:21), the future in general (3:22; 9:12; 10:14), and the identification of what is good (6:12; 11:6). Further, wisdom cannot guarantee a number of things: the wisdom of one's heir (2:18–21), success (9:11), the respect of those whom it helps (4:13–16; 9:13–16), better advantage as more wisdom is attained (7:16, cf. 2:15), and escaping the fate of the fool (2:15–16).

Qohelet sometimes uses wisdom forms ironically, calling into question the certainty they represent. This is true of the *ṭôb*-sayings of 7:1–12 which are preceded by the question of 6:12: Who knows what is good? Even statements about the advantages of wisdom are sometimes followed by comments concerning its limitations (2:13–16; 9:16–18 also a *ṭôb*-saying).

Qohelet as Sage

On the other hand, there is also evidence of compatibility between Ecclesiastes and the greater wisdom tradition. For example, the epilogist declares Qohelet to be wise (12:9) and implies that he is among the sages (12:11). Further, Qohelet's methodology is consistent with that of ancient Near Eastern sages. He explores the situations of human experience with all its wonder and pain. He uses the forms of wisdom, such as the proverb, *ṭôb*-saying, and didactic poem.

Qohelet is highly concerned with wisdom and knowledge. Though it has limits, he commends wisdom (2:13; 7:12, 19; 9:16–18) and never recommends folly (7:25). Likewise, as demonstrated in this study, Qohelet employs

---

[54] Notably Hartmut Gese, "The Crisis of Wisdom in Koheleth," *Theodicy in the Old Testament* (ed. James L. Crenshaw; IRT 4; Philadelphia: Fortress; London: SPCK, 1983 [1963]), 141–53; Schmid, *Wesen und Geschichte*, 173–95; and Kurt Galling, *Die Krise der Aufklärung in Israel* (Mainzer Universitäts-Reden 19; Mainz: Johannes Gutenberg-Buchhandlung, 1952).

metaphor and symbol in a way analogous to that of other wisdom writings. The *hebel*-symbol serves as a puzzle and paradox which engages the reader, and incarnates the enigmas which Qohelet is exploring. The book of Ecclesiastes fits the definition of wisdom literature which was proposed earlier.[55]

Perspectives on Qohelet's assessment of wisdom have been greatly influenced by severely negative understandings of the term *hebel* (e.g., "meaningless," "absurd," etc.). Since this study has demonstrated that *hebel* does not mean "vanity" or "useless," there is more basis for recognizing that Qohelet's reservations about wisdom are analogous to those found elsewhere within the tradition. For Qohelet, a crucial aspect of wisdom is to know what one cannot know (8:5–7). Qohelet's critique of wisdom can be stated succinctly: Wisdom cannot provide what some would seek from it.

Critique of Wisdom Elsewhere in the Tradition

This recognition of human inability to achieve wisdom and of wisdom's limits puts Qohelet in good company among the sages. In the biblical material, wisdom is considered rare and hard to attain (Prov 1:28; 3:13–15; 30:1–4; Job 28:11–12). Job and his friends agree that the ways of God cannot be found out (Job 5:9; 9:10; 11:7; 36:26), and the speeches of the deity demonstrate the paucity of human understanding. Even the biblical book of Proverbs, although it does not often engage the complexities directly, reflects the sages' awareness of life's enigmas. An example is the juxtaposition of Prov 26:4–5 (NRSV):

> Do not answer fools according to their folly, or you will be a fool yourself.
> Answer fools according to their folly, or they will be wise in their own eyes.

In addition, there is the paradox of 11:24 (NRSV):

> Some give freely, yet grow all the richer;
> others withhold what is due, and only suffer want.

Such is also found in warnings against lending money: Do not borrow (Prov 22:7), yet lend to the poor (Prov 19:17). Further, lack of diligence brings poverty (Prov 10:4), but so does oppression (Prov 14:31), and not all wealth indicates divine favor (Prov 28:8, 11).[56] Finally, the sages recognized that only God could know the human heart (Prov 15:11; 21:2), and that the future was always mysterious (Prov 27:1).

---

[55] Its purpose is to persuade, its overarching theme is making the best of present human existence, and the data upon which it draws is largely that of common and repetitive phenomena.

[56] Cf. Prov 13:7: "Some pretend to be rich, yet have nothing; others pretend to be poor, yet have great wealth" (NRSV).

The complexities of human life are likewise engaged by other wisdom literature. In ancient Near Eastern prescriptive (or traditional) wisdom, the sages particularly noted those areas in which human beings reached the limits of their ability to understand. It is not possible to know what is in another's heart,[57] the time or nature of death,[58] or what will happen in the future, including one's own lifetime and the days of one's misfortune.[59]

In addition to other areas of human limitation, the ways of the deity were considered especially mysterious. Concern with the divine plays an important part in many wisdom texts of the prescriptive variety, particularly in Egypt:

> One knows not what may happen,
> What god does when he punishes.[60]

> While generation succeeds generation,
> God who knows characters is hidden.[61]

A Babylonian saying comments, "The will of a god cannot be understood, the way of a god cannot be known. Anything of a god [is difficult] to find out."[62] The author of *Papyrus Insinger* comments:

> The god gives the lamp and the fat according to the heart.
> He knows his favorite and gives goods to him who gave to him.[63]

As for wisdom:

> There is he who has not been taught, yet he knows how to instruct another.
> There is he who knows the instruction, yet he does not know how to live by it.[64]

---

[57] *Ankhsheshonq*, 11.16; *Papyrus Insinger* 12.20, of woman.

[58] *Insinger*, 17.5; *Any* 5.1; *Ankhsheshonq*, 12.5.

[59] *Ptahhotep*, 343; *Any*, 8.5ff; *Ankhsheshonq*, 12.3; *Insinger*, 4.5; 17.5; 32.18, 22; specifically the god's punishment, *Kagemni*, 2.1–2. Compared to Egyptian works, there is little direct discussion of knowledge in the Mesopotamian material. Exceptions include the *Sayings of Ahiqar*, which cautions concerning three things that humans do not know: the names of the stars, humankind itself, and what is in another's heart (James M. Lindenberger, *The Aramaic Proverbs of Ahiqar* [Baltimore: Johns Hopkins, 1983], proverbs no. 33 and no. 72). A few proverbs in other wisdom texts also refer to human limitations: "Will the early corn thrive? How can we know? Will the late corn thrive? How can we know?" And, "Should I be going to die, I would be extravagant (lit. eat). Should I be going to survive, I would be economical (lit. store)," text K 4347+16161, 4.34–45 (W. G. Lambert, *BWL*, 244–45, 250).

[60] *Kagemni* 2.1 (*AEL* 1:60).

[61] *Merikare*, 124 (*AEL* 1:105).

[62] Text BM 38486 = 80–11–12, 370, lines 7–8 (*BWL*, 264–66).

[63] *Insinger* 30.7–8 (*AEL* 3:209).

[64] *Insinger*, 9.16–17 (*AEL* 3:192).

Thus, wisdom is only of relative value.[65]

Ecclesiastes is likewise similar to texts of the existential (or reflective) type in the ancient Near East which often observe, but do not resolve, various paradoxes. In these texts, too, the mystery of the deity is a recurring theme. Voices in the text express confusion regarding personal suffering, and particularly inquire about the deity and divine ways. Sometimes the gods provide knowledge that is the key to a person's dilemma. Unlike the prescriptive wisdom texts, there is no expression of confidence in human ability to know.

The oppressed speaker in *The Eloquent Peasant* remarks, "Trust not the morrow before it has come; none knows the trouble in it," and again, "The heart's intent cannot be known."[66] The sufferer in *Ludlul bel Nemeqi* laments concerning the deity:

> I wish I knew that these things would be pleasing to one's god!
> What is proper for oneself may be offense to one's god,
> What in one's own heart seems despicable may be proper to one's god.
> Who knows the will of the gods in heaven?
> Who understands the plans of the underworld gods?
> Where have mortals learnt the way of a god?[67]

Like the biblical book of Job, *The Babylonian Theodicy* ponders the enigma of how the righteous can suffer if there exists a powerful God of justice. The speaker asks:

> Can a life of bliss be assured? I wish I knew how!
> The divine mind, like the centre of the heavens, is remote;
> Knowledge of it is difficult; the masses do not know it.[68]

The *Dialogue of Pessimism* illustrates how existential wisdom sometimes deliberately explores incompatible perspectives. It relates a conversation between a master and his servant during which the master

---

[65] With some exceptions, sages urged that the gods were omniscient, and their ways were beyond human ken. For Amenemope this was not a troubling situation. The benevolence of the deity, he believed, could be relied upon to help those who were righteous. Likewise, Merikare urged that the all-knowing deity would punish those who were destructive and plotted treason. Ankhsheshonq and the sage of *Papyrus Insinger* also trusted in the good will of the deity, and taught that the god's favor was of greatest consequence. The importance of wisdom was relativized somewhat because of this understanding of the deity.

[66] *Eloquent Peasant*, Papyrus Berlin, lines 183, 255 (*AEL* 1:177, 179).

[67] *Ludlul*, 2.33–38 (*BWL*, 40–41).

[68] *Babylonian Theodicy*, lines 33, 256–57 (*BWL*, 72–73, 86–87).

proposes several courses of action and then retracts each one. In every case, the servant is able to provide as much reason in favor as against the proposal. Among the final exchanges, the master proposes to do a good deed for his country. The servant responds to the effect that he will be rewarded by Marduk as a result.[69] But, as is his pattern, the master changes his mind, deciding not to do the good deed. The servant replies:

> "Do not perform, sir, do not perform. Go up on to the ancient ruin heaps and walk about; See the skulls of high and low. Which is the malefactor, and which is the benefactor?"[70]

In other words, everyone will die, so good deeds matter very little in terms of one's own benefit. When the master asks, "Then what is good?" the servant can offer only death for his answer.[71]

The *Gilgamesh Epic* emphasizes the stark contrast between humans and the gods, particularly the gods' immortality, power, knowledge, and inscrutability.[72] The hero, Gilgamesh, is depicted on several occasions as having inadequate understanding. His mother, Ninsun, who is credited with being versed in all knowledge, gives instructions to Gilgamesh.[73] The standard version of the work also includes a parody of *narû* literature which emphasizes the limitations of mortals. Human life, it says, is ignorant, fleeting, and achieves only wind.[74]

In conclusion, the examples cited from the preceding texts demonstrate that Qohelet's critique of wisdom's limitations is compatible with that found elsewhere within the tradition. Like Qohelet, the sages recognized the limitations of human understanding in regard to what was in another's heart, the nature of death, the future, the will and ways of the deity, and various paradoxes, especially those concerning theodicy. Qohelet's contribution is to hold such matters up to the light, to turn them around and examine their significance. Thus he takes up what the sages were already pondering and asks

---

[69] The text is broken and difficult at this point.

[70] *Dialogue of Pessimism*, lines 75–78 (*BWL*, 148–49).

[71] Ibid., lines 79–86 (*BWL*, 148–49). Lambert is correct that this reply, and the whole work, is to be taken satirically, for if death was determined by the author to be the only good, he would not have interrupted the process to write a witty piece of literature (*BWL*, 141). The Egyptian *Dispute Between a Man and His Ba* is presented as a man in debate with himself (*AEL* 1:163–69). Also similar in certain aspects is the Sumerian *Dialogue Between a Man and His God* (B. R. Foster, *From Distant Days* [Bethesda, Md.: CDL, 1995], 295).

[72] OB 2.4.35–37; OB 3.4.6–7; OB 10.3.3–5 (Thompson, *Gilgamesh*). On these issues see C. L. Seow (*Ecclesiastes*, 64–65, 305–6) and William L. Moran ("Gilgamesh," 558-59).

[73] Gilgamesh is also helped along by Enkidu, Urshanabi, and Utnapishtim.

[74] OB 3.4.3–8 (Thompson, *Gilgamesh*).

how one should live in the face of them. Qohelet's work does not reflect a despair concerning wisdom but a mature application of wisdom to the paradoxes and enigmas which others could only lament. His criticisms are not a rejection of wisdom nor of the sages' concern to make the best of human existence. As with other matters, Qohelet criticizes wisdom's inadequacies in order to allow for its legitimate role, viz., of providing a relative advantage in life for those who attain it.

CHAPTER CONCLUSION

Qohelet was a sage, a master of words, of metaphor, of symbol. This study represents an attempt to discern certain aspects of his creative, symbol-building, rhetorical process.[75] Qohelet has seen the complexities of the world—its enigmas, injustices, tragedies—and the distresses of those among his audience. He declares that some aspects of human existence, even humans themselves, are insubstantial, while other things are transient, and others are foul. He wants to offer his audience ways of coping with these realities.

As the focus of his deliberation, Qohelet holds forth *hebel* as a symbol, a stratagem which exemplifies the character of Qohelet's rhetoric. The use of the *hebel*-symbol complements Qohelet's efforts to achieve credibility and closeness to his audience, assists in his attempts to destabilize their perspectives, and, finally, serves his reconstructive purposes as it organizes and makes manageable the diversity and chaos of life which it describes.

Qohelet's rhetoric enables him to confirm the doubts and cynicism of his audience, while providing himself as a guide through it all. He points out the inadequacies of pleasure and toil, while charting true pleasure and the benefits of toil. He establishes the shortcomings of wisdom, while providing the very wisdom needed for the current situation. He attests to the fact of human weakness, while equipping his audience to change their lives for the better. He ridicules the presumptions of a false faith and warns against a triumphalist religion, while reaffirming the orthodox picture of God as just, powerful, and the source of good. Thus, Qohelet provides a rationale for faith and for appreciating the good gifts of God in the midst of life's pain, tensions, and paradoxes.

---

[75] It does not, however, presume to retrace the actual steps by which Qohelet crafted his work.

Appendix I

HEBEL TEXTS IN ECCLESIASTES (39*x*)

pericope *hebel* verses	Title of Pericope Synonym (S), Contrary (C), Extension (E) Rhetorical Question (RQ), misc. notes	verse(s) / Subject Quality: REFERENT
1:2 (5*x***)** v. 2	**Statement of Thesis** All is vapor	v. 2 Subject: All **OMNIVALENT**
1:2-11 v. 2	**The Creation is Weary** C: no surplus (יִתְרוֹן)(RQ) C: eye not satisfied (שׂבע) C: ear not filled (מלא) C: nothing new (חָדָשׁ) C: no remembrance (זִכְרוֹן) of those past	v. 2 Subject: Work of the Cosmos, Human Toil **Insubstantial**: FUTILE
1:12-15 v. 14	**Qohelet Begins His Investigation** S: evil business (עִנְיָן רָע) S: chasing wind (רְעוּת רוּחַ) #1 E: can't change what is wrong E: can't count what isn't there	v. 14 Subject: Works **Insubstantial**: FUTILE **& Foul**: DISGUSTING
2:1-11 v. 1 v. 11	**Pleasure** E: boast-less (הלל)(RQ) [txt. em.; MT, S: foolishness? (מְהוֹלָל)] E: useless (עשׂה)(RQ) S: chasing wind (רְעוּת רוּחַ) #3 C: no surplus (יִתְרוֹן)	 v. 1 Subject: Pleasure v. 11 Subject: Toil **Insubstantial**: FUTILE

181

2:12-17 vv. 15, 17	**Wisdom and Folly** E: no reason to be excessively wise (RQ) (יֹתֵר) E: I hated life (שָׂנֵא, hateworthy) S: work is evil (רָע) E: Common fate wise/fool S: chasing wind (רְעוּת רוּחַ) #4	vv. 15, 17 Subject: Wisdom **Insubstantial**: FUTILE **& Foul**: DISGUSTING

2:18-23
 	
vv. 19, 21,
23
	Toil
	E: I hated my toil (שָׂנֵא, hateworthy)
	E: I despaired concerning my toil (יָאַשׁ,
	   despair-inducing)
	S: great evil (רָעָה רַבָּה)
	E: there is nothing as result (הָיָה)(RQ)
	E: heart cannot rest
	E: days are pain (מַכְאֹבִים) cf. for wisdom 1:16-
	   18
	E: business is a vexation (כַּעַס)
		vv. 19, 21, 23 Subject:
		(Wealth from) Toil
		
		Foul: DISGUSTING

2:24-26 v. 26	**Enjoy Life!** ADVICE: Enjoy life, see good in toil S: chasing wind (רְעוּת רוּחַ) #5 E: God is arbitrary	v. 26 Subject: Toil **Insubstantial**: FUTILE

3:16-22
 	
v. 19
	God's Judgment Tests Humans
	ADVICE: Enjoy your work
	C: no advantage (מוֹתָר)
	S: dust (עָפָר)
	E: none know if human, animal "wind" differ
	   (RQ)
	E: both humans and animals die
	E: none help another know what comes after
	   (RQ)
		v. 19 Subject: Human
		Condition
		
		Insubstantial: FRAIL

4:4-6 v. 4	**Toil in Competition** ADVICE: Be content S: chasing wind (רְעוּת רוּחַ)(2x) #6,#7	v. 4 Subject: Toil from Envy **Insubstantial**: FUTILE
4:7-8 v. 7 v. 8	**Toil for No One Else** C: no end (קֵץ) to toil C: no satisfaction (שׂבע) with wealth S: evil business (עִנְיָן רָע)	vv. 7, 8 Subject: Obsessive Toil **Insubstantial**: FUTILE **& Foul**: DISGUSTING

4:13-16 v. 16	**The Oppressed Youth Abandoned** S: pursuing wind (רַעְיוֹן רוּחַ) #8 (cf. #2 at 1:17) E: fickle people do not respect the wise	v. 16 Subject: Wisdom **Insubstantial**: FUTILE
4:17–5:6 [Eng. 5:1-7] v. 6 [7]	**Words before God** ADVICE: Fear God E: caution re: words and the fool S: dreams (חֲלֹמוֹת) E: no reason to arouse God's anger (RQ)	v. 6 Subject: Foolish Activity **Insubstantial**: FUTILE
5:7-11 [Eng. 8-12] v. 9 [10]	**Money Brings No Satisfaction** C: no satisfaction (שׂבע) C: no gain (כִּשְׁרוֹן) except to see wealth (RQ)	v. 9 Subject: Money **Insubstantial**: DEFICIENT
6:1-6 v. 2 v. 4	**Wealth Easily Lost (God's Role)** S: evil (רָעָה) S: evil sickness (חֳלִי רָע) C: no good (טוֹב) E: not satisfied (שׂבע) E: darkness, no sun E: no knowledge	v. 2 Subject: Inability to Enjoy **Foul**: DISGUSTING v. 4 Subject: The Stillborn **Insubstantial**: MYSTERY
6:7-9 v. 9	**Toil Brings No Satisfaction** C: throat/self is not filled (מלא) C: no advantage (יוֹתֵר)(RQ) S: chasing wind (רְעוּת רוּחַ) #9 (cf. "toils for wind" at 5:15 [16])	v. 9 Subject: Toil/ Wisdom/Pleasure **Insubstantial**: FUTILE
6:10-12 v. 11 v. 12	**Human Limits** C: no advantage (יוֹתֵר)(RQ) E: allusion to both 4:17-5:6, and 6:8 S: shadow (צֵל) E: few days E: no one knows what is good for humans (RQ) E: no one can tell the future (RQ)	v. 11 Subject: Words **Insubstantial**: FUTILE v. 12 Subject: Human Condition **Transient**: BRIEF

7:1-12 v. 6	**Good and Better** ADVICE: It is hard to determine what is good E: the fool's ways to be avoided E: wisdom of relative value E: 6:11, words increase vapor (=insubstantial)	v. 6 Subject: Words **Insubstantial**: FUTILE

7:15-18
 	
v. 15
	Choosing Righteousness and Wisdom
	ADVICE: Keep a balanced perspective on
	    wisdom and righteousness
		v. 15 Subject: "My
		    Days"
		OMNIVALENT

8:10-15
v. 10
 	
v. 14 (2x)
	Unjust Rewards
	ADVICE: Enjoy life
	S: evil (רָע) (2x)
	E: wicked lives will be shortened like a
	    shadow (צֵל)
	E: Who is like the wise? RQ 8:1
	E: Who knows the interpretation? RQ 8:1
	E: No one can find God's work 8:17
	E: The wise don't know God's work 8:17
		v. 10 Subject: Unjust
		    Rewards
		Foul: DISGUSTING
		v. 14ab Subject: Unjust
		    Rewards
		Foul: DISGUSTING,
		Insubstantial:
		    MYSTERY,
		& Transient:
		    TEMPORARY

9:1-6
v. 2
(txt. em.
הבל ⇨ הכל)
	Same Fate for Righteous and Wicked
	E: does not know
	S: evil (רָעָה)
		v. 2 Subject: Same Fate
		    for All
		Insubstantial:
		    MYSTERY
		& Foul: DISGUSTING

9:7-10 v. 9 (2x)	**Make the Most of Enjoying Life** ADVICE: Enjoy life, work hard E: recommended lifestyle described [second occurrence of the term often deleted]	v. 9 Subject: "Your Days" **OMNIVALENT**
11:7-10 v. 8 v. 10	**Rejoice in Your Youth** ADVICE: Make the most of your youth E: dark days will be many E: command to rejoice in days of youth E: command to remove vexations	v. 8 Subject: All that Comes **OMNIVALENT** v. 10 Subject: Youth **Transient**: BRIEF

12:1-8
 	
v. 8
	Poem about the End
	E: evil (רָעָה) days
	C: no delight
	E: darkness
	S: dust (עָפָר)
	S: wind (רוּחַ)
		v. 8 Subject: Human
		  Condition & the
		  Cosmos
		Insubstantial: FRAIL,
		Transient: COMING
		  TO AN END,
		& **Foul**: DISGUSTING

12:8 (3*x*) v. 8	**Restatement of Thesis** All is vapor	v. 8 Subject: All **OMNIVALENT**

Appendix II

HEBEL TEXTS APART FROM ECCLESIASTES

This appendix is organized as follows:

Part 1: The Name "Abel" in the Bible (8*x*)
Part 2: Nonmetaphorical Biblical Texts (2*x*)
Part 3: Nonmetaphorical Postbiblical Texts
Part 4: Metaphorical Biblical Texts (35*x* + 5 verbs)
Part 5: Metaphorical Postbiblical Texts

Part 1: The Name "Abel" in the Bible (8*x*)

Gen 4:2 (2*x*), 4 (2*x*), 8 (2*x*), 9, 25

Part 2: Nonmetaphorical Biblical Texts (2*x*)

Hebel is found within two parable texts in the HB. Its use in Ps 62:10 [Eng. 62:9] suggests something light in weight, and in Isa 57:13, *hebel* involves a mild movement of air. These uses are consistent with a literal meaning of "vapor" for *hebel* which is particularly established by postbiblical texts (see below). In addition, cognate terms, the Greek translations of the Hebrew canon, and metaphorical uses of the term support rather than contradict this meaning. Thus, although the best evidence for *hebel*'s material sense comes from the postbiblical period, all indicators suggest a continuity in the meaning of the term over its period of use.

187

Part 3: Nonmetaphorical Postbiblical Texts (*hebel* and Aramaic *hablā*)[1]

3A. Heat/Steam

Text	Context	Meaning of *hebel/hablā*
Ḥul. 8a	burns caused by the *hebel* of a hot spit	heat
B. Bat. 73a	the *hebel* of a star	heat
Giṭ. 69b	a remedy for fever blisters involving *hebel* which one allows to rise upon oneself	steam
Šabb. 40b	the *hebel* of the baths	steamy heat
Šabb. 38b	the *hebel* of cooking stoves	radiant heat
Šabb. 47b	hot springs for medicinal use	heat
B. Bat. 18a; cf. 19a	*hebel* from an oven which harms a wall	heat
Zebaḥ. 113b	intense *hebel* which takes human lives	heat
y. ʿAbod. Za r. III, 42ᵈ bot.	*hebel* of the bath room is said to be injurious to the teeth	steam
Eccl. Rab. 1:2	*hebel* inside pots on a cooking stove	steam

3B. Breath

Text	Context	Meaning of *hebel/hablā*
B. Bat. 75a	the *hebel* of Leviathan causes water to boil	(hot) breath
Šabb. 88b	human *hebel* threatening due to its heat	breath
Šabb. 41a	expelling hot *hebel* from the mouth	breath

---

[1] The following are representative samples. Together, the nouns occur over one hundred times in the Babylonian Talmud in addition to occurrences in other texts. The verb הבל occurs only a few times, mostly in quotations from the HB. Talmudic references are to the Babylonian Talmud unless otherwise indicated.

3C. Vapor within a Living Being

Bek. 7a-b	thickness of ass urine caused by *hablā'* of the body	vapor
Lev. Rab. 29:8	persons are *hebel* while in the womb	vapor (or perhaps a metaphorical usage)

3D. Vaporous Perspiration

Yebam. 80b, *B. Meṣiʿa* 107b, *Šabb.* 41a.	*hebel/hablā'* given off by the body in connection with bathing	perspiration
Šabb. 17b הבל verb in Hiph stem	wet flax giving off *hebel*	vapor

3E. Noxious Vapor

Sanh. 77a-b	one who becomes asphyxiated in a sealed environment is said to be killed by its *hebel*	poisonous vapor
B. Qam. 54a	perhaps inanimate objects may also be killed by the *hebel* in a sealed environment	poisonous vapor
B. Qam. 50b, 51a,b	animal deaths caused by the *hebel* of a pit into which it has fallen	unhealthy air
B. Meṣiʿa 36b	animal killed by the *hebel* of marsh land	poisonous vapor

Part 4: Metaphorical Biblical Texts (35x + 5 verbs)[2]

4A. Insubstantiality Referents (11x + 1 verb)

Text	Synonym (S), Contrary (C), Extension (E)	subject / REFERENT
Prov 13:11	C: על־יד (steadily)	obtaining wealth WITHOUT EFFORT
Prov 21:6 [txt em]	E: scattered (נדף) E: seekers of death	one getting wealth by deceit SPOILED AND BRIEF LIFE
Job 7:1-21 v. 16	S: worthlessness (שָׁוְא) v. 3 S: toil (עמל) v. 3 S: trifling (קלל) v. 6 S: wind (רוּחַ) v. 7 E: cloud fades/vanishes v. 9 E: why should God care? vv. 17-18	human condition SPOILED
Ps 94:4-12 v. 11	S: fools (כְּסִילִים) S: stupid (בְּעָרִים) C: not wise (שׂכל) E: God's knowledge	human thoughts ERROR
Job 35:16	C: no knowledge (בְּבְלִי־דָעַת)	speech ERROR
*Job 27:12 הבל verb +	E: Job[3] refuses to agree with friends' false statements C: seen (חזה)	speech ERROR
Isa 49:4	S: emptiness (ריק) S: nothing (תֹּהוּ)	labor FUTILE
Job 9:29	E: Why have I labored? (RQ)	labor FUTILE
Isa 57:13 (a parable)	S: wind (רוּחַ) E: trusting in Yahweh (literal vapor within the parable)	(idol) collection UNRELIABLE

---

[2] The five occurrences of the verb הבל are indicated in the appropriate sections below and are marked with *. Only in Jer 23:16 is the noun not also present, although in Ps 62, the verb is in v. 11 and the noun (twice) in v. 10.

[3] The MT attributes this speech to Job; some scholars reassign to a different speaker.

| Lam 4:17 | C: גּוֹי לֹא יוֹשִׁעַ (nation which could not save) | help
UNRELIABLE |
| Ps 39:7-8
[Eng. 6-7]
v. 7 [6] | E: wait for (קוה) Yahweh
E: hope in (תּוֹחֶלֶת) Yahweh | wealth (emend: הָמוֹן)

UNRELIABLE |

4B. Insubstantiality Referents, Emphasizing Deception (6x + 2 verbs)

Text	Synonym (S), Contrary (C), Extension (E)	subject / REFERENT
Prov 31:30	S: lie (שֶׁקֶר)	beauty MISREPRESENTS
Isa 30:6-7 v. 7	C: no profit (יעל) S: emptiness (רִיק) E: sought without result	Egypt's aid DEFICIENT
Ps 62:10a [Eng. 9a]	S: lie (כָּזָב)	people as aid DEFICIENT
Ps 62:10b [Eng. 9b] (a parable)	E: balances going up E: (comparison) (literal vapor within the parable)	people as aid DEFICIENT
*Ps 62:11 [Eng. 10] הבל verb	S: trust (בטח) E: only God can help	trust in theft of wealth MISPLACED TRUST
Job 21:34	S: falsehood (מַעַל)	words FALSE CONSOLATION
*Jer 23:16 הבל verb (Hiph)	E: visions of their own minds E. words not from God	speech of false prophets IGNORANT
Zech 10:1-2 v. 2	S: deceit (אָוֶן) S: lies (שֶׁקֶר) S: false dreams (חֲלֹמוֹת הַשָּׁוְא)	divination FALSE CONSOLATION

4C. Transience Referents (4x)

Text	Synonym (S), Contrary (C), Extensions (E)	subject / REFERENT
Ps 39:5-6 [Eng. 4-5] v. 6 [5]	S: fleeting (חָדֵל) S: handbreaths (טְפָחוֹת) S: nothing (אַיִן) S: image (צֶלֶם)	human condition BRIEF AND FRAIL
Ps 39:12 [Eng. 39:11]	S: I am spent (כלה) v. 11[10] S: גֵּר (stranger) v. 13[12] S: תּוֹשָׁב (sojourner) v. 13[12]	human condition BRIEF AND FRAIL
Ps 144:4	S: passing shadow (צֵל עוֹבֵר)	human condition BRIEF AND FRAIL
Ps 78:33	S: sudden terror (בַּבֶּהָלָה)	God's judgment SWIFT

4D. Stock Metaphors (14x + 2 verbs)

Text	Synonym (S), Contrary (C), Extension (E)	subject / REFERENT
Deut 32:21 (in plural)	C: no god (לֹא־אֵל)	foreign deities
1 Kgs 16:13 (in plural)	(stock metaphor)	foreign deities
1 Kgs 16:26 (in plural)	(stock metaphor)	foreign deities
*2 Kgs 17:15 + הבל verb	E: Baal, molten images Perhaps: followers of false gods became false	foreign deities
*Jer 2:5 + הבל verb	E: Baal, things which didn't profit (יעל) v. 8 Perhaps: followers of false gods became false	foreign deities
Jer 8:19 (in plural)	S: idol (פֶּסֶל) E: foreign (נֵכָר)	foreign deities

Jer 10:1-16 v. 3	S: tree from the forest S: scarecrows (v. 5) E: cannot speak, must be carried, can't walk, can't do evil or good, not to be feared (v. 5)	foreign deities INEPT
v. 8 (in plural)	S: stupid (בער) S: foolish (כסל) E: their instruction is wood	foreign deities IGNORANT
v. 15 (=51:18)	S: idol (פֶּסֶל) S: lies (שֶׁקֶר) C: no breath (רוּחַ) S: work of delusion (תעתע) E: will be punished and perish	foreign deities DECEPTIVE
Jer 14:22 (in plural)	(stock metaphor)	foreign deities
Jer 16:19	S: lies (שֶׁקֶר) C: no profit (מוֹעִיל) E: not gods (v. 20)	foreign deities DECEPTIVE & UNRELIABLE
Jer 51:17-18 v. 18 (=10:15)	S: idol (פֶּסֶל) S: lies (שֶׁקֶר) C: no breath (רוּחַ) S: work of delusion (תעתע) E: will be punished and perish	foreign deities DECEPTIVE
Ps 31:7 [Eng. 31:6] (in plural)	S: falsehood (שָׁוְא) E: Yahweh (בטח // שמר)	foreign deities DECEPTIVE
Jonah 2:9 [Eng. 2:8] (in plural)	S: falsehood (שָׁוְא) E: those who שמר הַבְלֵי עזב, their חֶסֶד E: but I will sacrifice to you (Yahweh)	foreign deities DECEPTIVE

Part 5: Metaphorical Postbiblical Texts[4]

Text	Synonym (S), Contrary (C), Extension (E)	subject / REFERENT
Sir 41:11	C: not cut off (כרת)	human body TRANSIENT
Sir 49:2	תועבות הבל (abominations of vapor)	foreign deities (stock metaphor)
B. Bat. 16b	E: encouragement re: having a daughter is false; blessed is the father of a son	consolation UNRELIABLE
Ketub. 10b	E: debate whether lack of menstrual blood is a threat to fertility	consolation UNRELIABLE
Lev. Rab. 29	S: false (כזב) E: Abraham is worthy to atone for these	human deeds IMMORAL
Šabb. 152a	E: The things a man does in his youth blacken his face in his old age	human deeds IMMORAL
1QS 5:18	S: uncleanness (נדה)	human deeds IMMORAL
1QS 5:19	(see previous text)	pagans UNCOMPREHENDING
1QM 4:12; 6:6; 9:9; 11:9	(stock metaphor)	pagan nations
1QM 14:12	(broken text)	cj: livestock possessions?
4Q184	S: errors (תועות) S: mock flattery (חלק + קלס) S: falsehood (שוא) [reconstructed text]	harlot's speech WORTHLESS IMMORAL
1QH 7:32	S: empty (תהו) E: understand (בין)	human condition UNCOMPREHENDING
4Q511	רוחי הבלים (fragment)	(unclear)

---

[4] Texts from Ben Sira (2x) and Qumran (10x) are complete, but rabbinic texts are only representative.

Bibliography

Albertz, Rainer. "הֶבֶל *hœbel* Hauch." Pages 467–69 in vol. 1 of *Theologisches Handwörterbuch zum Alten Testament*. Edited by E. Jenni and C. Westermann. Munich: Kaiser, 1971.

Allegro, John M. *Qumrân Cave 4*. Vol. 1. Discoveries in the Judaean Desert 5. Oxford: Clarendon, 1968.

————. "'The Wiles of the Wicked Woman': A Sapiential Work from Qumran's Fourth Cave." *Palestine Exploration Quarterly* 96 (1964): 53–55, pl. xiii.

Alter, Robert. *The Art of Biblical Poetry*. New York: Basic Books, 1985.

Anderson, William H. U. *Qoheleth and Its Pessimistic Theology: Hermeneutical Struggles in Wisdom Literature*. Mellen Biblical Press Series 54. Lewiston, N.Y.: Edwin Mellen, 1997.

Archer, Gleason L. "The Linguistic Evidence for the Date of 'Ecclesiastes'" *Journal of the Evangelical Theological Society* 12 (1969): 167–81.

Aristotle. *The "Art" of Rhetoric*. Translated by H. E. Butler. Loeb Classical Library. Cambridge: Harvard University Press, 1926.

Armstrong, James F. "Ecclesiastes in Old Testament Theology." *Princeton Seminary Bulletin* 4 n.s. (1983): 16–25.

Backhaus, Franz Josef. *Denn Zeit und Zufall trifft sie alle: Studien zur Komposition und zum Gottesbild im Buch Qohelet*. Bonner biblische Beiträge 83. Frankfurt am Main: Anton Hain, 1993.

Baillet, Maurice. *Qumrân Grotte 4*. Vol. 3. Discoveries in the Judaean Desert 7. Oxford: Clarendon, 1982.

Barbour, Ian G. *Myths, Models, and Paradigms: A Comparative Study in Science and Religion*. New York: Harper & Row, 1974.

Barton, George Aaron. *A Critical and Exegetical Commentary on the Book of Ecclesiastes*. International Critical Commentary. Edinburgh: T & T Clark, 1908.

Barucq, André. *Ecclésiaste*. Verbum salutis 3. Paris: Beauchesne, 1968.

Beardsley, Monroe C. "Metaphor." Pages 284–89 in vol. 5 of *The Encyclopedia of Philosophy*. Edited by P. Edwards. New York: Macmillan; London: Collier, 1967.

Becking, Bob. "Hubal." Pages 814–15 in *Dictionary of Deities and Demons in the Bible*. Edited by K. van der Toorn et al. Leiden: Brill, 1995.

Ben-Ḥayyim, Zeev, ed. *The Book of Ben Sira: Text, Concordance and an Analysis of the Vocabulary*. The Historical Dictionary of the Hebrew Language. Jerusalem: The Academy of the Hebrew Language/The Shrine of the Book, 1973.

Berger, Peter L., and Thomas Luckmann. *The Social Construction of Reality: A Treatise in the Sociology of Knowledge*. Garden City, N.Y.: Anchor, 1966.

Berlin, Adele. *The Dynamics of Biblical Parallelism*. Bloomington: Indiana University Press, 1985.

———. *Poetics and Interpretation of Biblical Narrative*. Bible and Literature Series 9. Sheffield: Almond, 1983.

Bertram, Georg. "Hebräischer und griechischer Qohelet." *Zeitschrift für die alttestamentliche Wissenschaft* 64 (1952): 26–49.

Black, Max. *Models and Metaphors: Studies in Language and Philosophy*. Ithaca, N.Y.: Cornell University Press, 1962.

———. "More About Metaphor." *Dialectica* 31 (1977): 431–57.

Booth, Wayne C. "Metaphor as Rhetoric: The Problem of Evaluation." Pages 47–70 in *On Metaphor*. Edited by S. Sacks. Chicago: University of Chicago Press, 1979.

Boucher, Madeleine. *The Mysterious Parable*. Catholic Biblical Quarterly Monograph Series 6. Washington, D.C.: Catholic Biblical Association of America, 1977.

Braun, Rainer. *Kohelet und die frühhellenistische Popularphilosophie*. Beihefte zur Zeitschrift für die alttestamentliche Wissenschaft 130. Berlin/New York: Walter de Gruyter, 1973.

Breasted, James Henry. *The Eighteenth Dynasty*. Vol. 2 of *Ancient Records of Egypt*. Chicago: University of Chicago Press, 1906.

Bright, John. *Jeremiah*. Anchor Bible 21. Garden City, N.Y.: Doubleday, 1965.

Brock, Bernard L., Robert L. Scott, and James W. Chesebro, eds. *Methods of Rhetorical Criticism: A Twentieth Century Perspective*. 3d revised ed. Detroit: Wayne State University Press, 1990.

Brown, Francis, S. R. Driver, and Charles A. Briggs. *A Hebrew and English Lexicon of the Old Testament*. Oxford: Clarendon, 1951.

Brown, Frank Burch. "Poetry and Reality: A Critique of Philip Wheelwright." Chap. in *Transfiguration: Poetic Metaphor and the Languages of Religious Belief*. Chapel Hill and London: University of North Carolina Press, 1983.

Burkitt, F. C. "Is Ecclesiastes a Translation?" *Journal of Theological Studies* 23 (1922): 22–28.

Burrows, Millar, ed. *The Dead Sea Scrolls of St. Mark's Monastery*. Vol. 2. New Haven: American Schools of Oriental Research, 1951.

Buss, Martin J. "Form Criticism." Pages 69–85 in *To Each Its Own Meaning: An Introduction to Biblical Criticisms and Their Application*. Edited by S. R. Haynes and S. L. McKenzie. Louisville: Westminster/John Knox, 1993.

Byargeon, Rick W. "The Significance of Ambiguity in Ecclesiastes 2,24–26." Pages 367–72 in *Qohelet in the Context of Wisdom*. Edited by A. Schoors. Leuven: Leuven University Press, 1998.

Caird, G. B. *The Language and Imagery of the Bible*. Philadelphia: Westminster, 1980.

Camp, Claudia V. *Wisdom and the Feminine in the Book of Proverbs*. Bible and Literature Series 11. Sheffield: Almond, 1985.

Cazelles, Henri. "Bible, Sagesse, Science." *Recherches de science religieuse* 48 (1960): 40–54.

Ceresko, Anthony R. "The Function of *Antanaclasis* (*mṣ'* 'to Find'//*mṣ'* 'to Reach, Overtake, Grasp') in Hebrew Poetry, Especially in the Book of Qoheleth." *Catholic Biblical Quarterly* 44 (1982): 551–69.

Charlesworth, James H., ed. *Rule of the Community and Related Documents.* Vol. 1 of The Dead Sea Scrolls. Tübingen: Mohr/Siebeck; Louisville: Westminster/John Knox, 1994.

————. *Damascus Document, War Scroll, and Related Documents.* Vol. 2 of The Dead Sea Scrolls. Tübingen: Mohr/Siebeck; Louisville: Westminster/John Knox, 1995.

Clifford, Richard J. *Proverbs: A Commentary.* Old Testament Library. Louisville: Westminster/John Knox, 1999.

Clines, David J. A. *Job 1–20.* Word Biblical Commentary 17. Waco, Tex.: Word, 1989.

Cogan, Mordechai, and Hayim Tadmor. *II Kings.* Anchor Bible 11. New York: Doubleday, 1988.

Cohen, Abraham. *Midrash Rabbah: Ecclesiastes.* 3d ed. London: Soncino, 1983.

Cohen, Ted. "Metaphor and the Cultivation of Intimacy." Pages 1–10 in *On Metaphor.* Edited by S. Sacks. Chicago and London: University of Chicago Press, 1979.

Collins, John J. *Proverbs, Ecclesiastes.* Knox Preaching Guides. Atlanta: John Knox, 1980.

Corbett, Edward P. J. *Classical Rhetoric for the Modern Student.* 3d ed. New York: Oxford University Press, 1990.

Couturier, Guy P. "Sagesse Babylonienne et Sagesse Israélite." *Sciences ecclésiastiques* 14 (1962): 293–309.

Craigie, Peter C. *Psalms 1–50.* Word Biblical Commentary 19. Waco, Tex.: Word, 1983.

Craigie, Peter C., Page H. Kelley, and Joel F. Drinkard, Jr. *Jeremiah 1–25.* Word Biblical Commentary 26. Dallas, Tex.: Word, 1991.

Crenshaw, James L. *Ecclesiastes, A Commentary*. Old Testament Library. Philadelphia: Westminster, 1987.

———. "Method in Determining Wisdom Influence Upon 'Historical' Literature." *Journal of Biblical Literature* 88 (1969): 129–42.

———. "Qoheleth in Current Research." *Hebrew Annual Review* 7 (1983): 41–56.

———. "Studies in Ancient Israelite Wisdom: Prolegomenon." Pages 1–45 in *Studies in Ancient Israelite Wisdom*. Edited by J. L. Crenshaw. New York: KTAV, 1976.

———. "Wisdom." Pages 225–64 in *Old Testament Form Criticism*. Edited by J. H. Hayes. San Antonio, Tex.: Trinity University Press, 1974.

Crüsemann, Frank. "Die unveränderbare Welt." Pages 80–104 in *Der Gott der kleinen Leute*. Munich: Kaiser, 1979. Translated as "The Unchangeable World: The 'Crisis of Wisdom' in Koheleth." Pages 57–77 in *God of the Lowly*. Edited by W. Schottroff and W. Stegemann. Translated by M. J. O'Connell. Maryknoll, N.Y.: Orbis Books, 1984 [1979].

Dahood, Mitchel J. "Canaanite-Phoenician Influence in Qoheleth." *Biblica* 33 (1952): 30–52, 191–221.

———. "The Phoenician Background of Qoheleth." *Biblica* 47 (1966): 264–82.

Davidson, Donald. "What Metaphors Mean." Pages 29–45 in *On Metaphor*. Edited by S. Sacks. Chicago: University of Chicago Press, 1979.

Davila, James R. "Qoheleth and Northern Hebrew." *Maarav* 5–6 (1990): 69–87.

Diebner, Bernd J., and Rodolphe Kasser, eds. *Hamburger Papyrus Bil. 1*. Geneva: Cramer, 1989.

Douglas, Mary. *Purity and Danger: An Analysis of Concepts of Pollution and Taboo*. London: Routledge & Kegan Paul, 1978 [1969].

Driver, G. R. "Problems and Solutions." *Vetus Testamentum* 4 (1954): 225–45.

———. "Problems in 'Proverbs'" *Zeitschrift für die alttestamentliche Wissenschaft* 50 (1932): 141–48.

Ehrlich, Arnold B. *Randglossen zur hebräischen Bibel*. Vol. 7. Leipzig: Hinrichs, 1914.

Ellermeier, Friedrich. *Qohelet I/1. Untersuchungen zum Buche Qohelet*. Herzberg: Jungfer, 1967.

Epstein, Isadore, ed. *The Babylonian Talmud*. 34 vols + index vol. London: Soncino, 1935–52.

Erman, Adolf. *Die Religion der Ägypter*. Berlin: Walter de Gruyter, 1934.

Farmer, Kathleen A. *Who Knows What Is Good? A Commentary on the Books of Proverbs and Ecclesiastes*. International Theological Commentary. Grand Rapids: Eerdmans, 1991.

Fischer, A. "Beobachtungen zur Kompositionen von Kohelet 1,3–3,15." *Zeitschrift für die alttestamentliche Wissenschaft* 103 (1991): 72–86.

Fontaine, Carole R. *Traditional Sayings in the Old Testament: A Contextual Study*. Bible and Literature Series 5. Sheffield: Almond, 1982.

Foss, Sonja K. *Rhetorical Criticism: Exploration and Practice*. Prospect Heights, Ill.: Waveland, 1989.

Foster, Benjamin R. *From Distant Days: Myths, Tales, and Poetry of Ancient Mesopotamia*. Bethesda, Md.: CDL, 1995.

Fox, Michael V. "Aging and Death in Qohelet 12." *Journal for the Study of the Old Testament* 42 (1988): 55–77.

————. "Frame-Narrative and Composition in the Book of Qohelet." *Hebrew Union College Annual* 48 (1977): 83–106.

————. "The Identification of Quotations in Biblical Literature." *Zeitschrift für die alttestamentliche Wissenschaft* 92 (1980): 416–31.

————. "The Meaning of *Hebel* for Qohelet." *Journal of Biblical Literature* 105 (1986): 409–27.

————. *Qohelet and His Contradictions*. Bible and Literature Series 18. Sheffield: Almond, 1989.

————. *A Time to Tear Down and a Time to Build Up: A Rereading of Ecclesiastes*. Grand Rapids: Eerdmans, 1999.

Frankfort, Henri. *Ancient Egyptian Religion: An Interpretation*. New York: Harper, 1948.

Fredericks, Daniel C. "Chiasm and Parallel Structure in Qoheleth 5:6–6:9." *Journal of Biblical Literature* 108 (1989): 17–35.

———. *Coping with Transience: Ecclesiastes on Brevity in Life*. The Biblical Seminar 18. Sheffield: JSOT Press, 1993.

———. *Qoheleth's Language: Re-evaluating Its Nature and Date*. Ancient Near Eastern Texts and Studies 3. Lewiston, N.Y.: Edwin Mellen, 1988.

Galling, Kurt. *Die Krise der Aufklärung in Israel*. Mainzer Universitäts-Reden 91. Mainz: Johannes Gutenberg-Buchhandlung, 1952.

———. "Der Prediger." Pages 73–125 in *Die fünf Megilloth*. 2d ed. Hand-buch zum Alten Testament 18. Tübingen: Mohr/Siebeck, 1969.

Geertz, Clifford. *The Interpretation of Cultures: Selected Essays*. New York: Basic, 1973.

Gemser, Berend. *Sprüche Salomos*. 2d ed. Tübingen: Mohr/Siebeck, 1963.

Gese, Hartmut. "The Crisis of Wisdom in Koheleth." Translated by L. L. Grabbe. Pages 141–53 in *Theodicy in the Old Testament*. Issues in Religion and Theology 4. Edited by J. L. Crenshaw. Philadelphia: Fortress; London: SPCK, 1983 [1963].

Gibson, J. C. L. *Canaanite Myths and Legends*. 2d ed. Edinburgh: T & T Clark, 1977.

Ginsberg, H. Louis. "The Structure and Contents of the Book of Koheleth." Pages 138-49 in *Wisdom in Israel and in the Ancient Near East*. Vetus Testamentum Supplements 3. Edited by M. Noth and D. W. Thomas. Leiden: Brill, 1955.

———. *Studies in Koheleth*. Texts and Studies of the Jewish Theological Seminary of America 17. New York: Jewish Theological Seminary of America, 1950.

Ginzberg, Louis. *The Legends of the Jews*. Vol. 4. Philadelphia: Jewish Publication Society, 1913.

Gitay, Yehoshua. "Rhetorical Criticism." Pages 135–49 in *To Each Its Own Meaning*. Edited by S. R. Haynes and S. L. McKenzie. Louisville: Westminster/John Knox, 1993.

Goldingay, John. *Theological Diversity and the Authority of the Old Testament*. Grand Rapids: Eerdmans, 1987.

Good, Edwin M. "Qoheleth: The Limits of Wisdom." Pages 168–95 in *Irony in the Old Testament*. Philadelphia: Westminster, 1965.

————. "The Unfilled Sea: Style and Meaning in Ecclesiastes 1:2–11." Pages 59–72 in *Israelite Wisdom*. Fs. S. Terrien. Edited by J. G. Gammie et al. Missoula, Mont.: Scholars Press, 1978.

Gordis, Robert. *The Book of God and Man: A Study of Job*. Chicago: University of Chicago Press, 1965.

————. *Koheleth—The Man and His World: A Study of Ecclesiastes*. 3d ed. New York: Schocken, 1968.

————. "Was Koheleth a Phoenician? Some Observations on Methods in Research." *Journal of Biblical Literature* 74 (1955): 103–14.

Gordon, Edmund I. *Sumerian Proverbs*. Philadelphia: University of Pennsylvania Museum, 1959.

Gray, John. *I & II Kings*. Old Testament Library. Philadelphia: Westminster, 1963.

Grundmann, Walter. "κακός." Pages 469–81 in vol. 3 of *Theological Dictionary of the New Testament*. Edited by G. Kittel. Grand Rapids: Eerdmans, 1965.

Habel, Norman C. *Job*. Old Testament Library. Philadelphia: Westminster, 1985.

————. "The Symbolism of Wisdom in Proverbs 1–9." *Interpretation* 26 (1972): 131–57.

Harder, Günther. "πονηρός." Pages 546–62 in vol. 6 of *Theological Dictionary of the New Testament*. Edited by G. Friedrich. Grand Rapids: Eerdmans, 1968.

Harper, Robert F. *Assyrian and Babylonian Letters*. 14 vols. Chicago: University of Chicago Press, 1892–1914.

Hatch, Edwin, and Henry A. Redpath. *A Concordance to the Septuagint and the Other Greek Versions of the Old Testament*. Oxford: Clarendon, 1897.

Hayakawa, S. I. *Language in Thought and Action*. 3d ed. New York: Harcourt, Brace, Jovanovich, 1972.

Held, Moshe. "A Faithful Lover in an Old Babylonian Dialogue." *Journal of Cuneiform Studies* 15 (1961): 1–26.

Hertzberg, Hans Wilhelm. "Palästinische Bezüge im Buche Kohelet." *Zeitschrift des deutschen Palästina-Vereins* 73 (1957): 113–24.

————. *Der Prediger*. Kommentar zum Alten Testament 17/4. Gütersloh: Mohn, 1963.

Hillers, Delbert. *Lamentations*. Revised ed. Anchor Bible 7A. New York: Doubleday, 1992.

Historical Dictionary of the Hebrew Language Project. *Materials for the Dictionary. Series I. 200 B.C.E.–300 C.E.* Jerusalem: Academy of the Hebrew Language, 1988.

Holladay, William L. *Jeremiah 1*. Edited by P. Hanson. Hermeneia. Philadelphia: Fortress, 1986.

Horst, F. "Ecclesiastes." Pages 1336–54 in *Biblia Hebraica Stuttgartensia*. Edited by K. Elliger and W. Rudolph. Stuttgart: Deutsche Bibelgesellschaft, 1983.

Howard, David M., Jr. "Rhetorical Criticism in Old Testament Studies." *Bulletin for Biblical Research* 4 (1994): 1–18.

Isaksson, Bo. *Studies in the Language of Qoheleth with Special Emphasis on the Verbal System*. Studia Semitica Upsaliensia 10. Uppsala: Almqvist & Wiksell, 1987.

Janzen, J. Gerald. *Job*. Interpretation. Atlanta: John Knox, 1985.

Jastrow, Marcus. *A Dictionary of the Targumim, the Talmud Babli and Yerushalmi, and the Midrashic Literature*. 2 vols. Brooklyn, N.Y.: Traditional, 1903.

Johnson, Raymond Eugene. "The Rhetorical Question as a Literary Device in Ecclesiastes." Ph.D. diss., Southern Baptist Theological Seminary, 1986.

Johnston, Robert K. "'Confessions of a Workaholic': A Reappraisal of Qoheleth," *Catholic Biblical Quarterly* 38 (1976): 14–28.

Joüon, Paul, and Takamitsu Muraoka. *A Grammar of Biblical Hebrew.* 2d ed. 2 vols. Subsidia biblica 14. Rome: Pontifical Biblical Institute, 1991.

Kautzsch, Emil, ed. *Gesenius' Hebrew Grammar.* 2d ed. Translated by A. E. Cowley. Oxford: Clarendon, 1910.

Kennedy, George A. *New Testament Interpretation through Rhetorical Criticism.* Studies in Religion. Chapel Hill: University of North Carolina Press, 1984.

Knobel, Peter S. "The Targum of Qohelet," in *The Aramaic Bible.* Vol. 15. Collegeville, Minn.: Liturgical, 1991.

Knopf, C. S. "The Optimism of Koheleth." *Journal of Biblical Literature* 49 (1930): 195–99.

Koehler, Ludwig, Walter Baumgartner, and Johann Jakob Stamm, eds, *The Hebrew and Aramaic Lexicon of the Old Testament.* Translated and edited by M. E. J. Richardson. 5 vols. Leiden. Brill, 1994–2000.

Kraus, Hans-Joachim. *Psalms 1–59.* Translated by H. C. Oswald. Continental Commentaries. Minneapolis: Augsburg, 1988 [1978].

———. *Psalms 60–150.* Translated by H. C. Oswald. Continental Commentaries. Minneapolis: Augsburg, 1989 [1978].

Kugel, James L. *The Idea of Biblical Poetry: Parallelism and Its History.* New Haven: Yale University Press, 1981.

———. "Qohelet and Money." *Catholic Biblical Quarterly* 51 (1989): 32–49.

Kuntz, J. Kenneth. "The Canonical Wisdom Psalms of Ancient Israel—Their Rhetorical, Thematic, and Formal Dimensions." Pages 186–222 in *Rhetorical Criticism.* Fs. James Muilenburg. Edited by J. J. Jackson and M. Kessler. Pittsburgh: Pickwick, 1974.

Kutscher, Eduard Yecheskel. "Hebrew Language: The Dead Sea Scrolls, Mishnaic." Pages 1583–1607 in vol. 16 of *Encyclopedia Judaica.* Jerusalem: Keter, 1971.

Lakoff, George, and Mark Johnson. *Metaphors We Live By.* Chicago: University of Chicago Press, 1980.

Lambert, W. G. *Babylonian Wisdom Literature.* Oxford: Oxford University Press, 1960.

Lang, Bernhard. *Frau Weisheit*. Düsseldorf: Patmos, 1975.

———. *Wisdom and the Book of Proverbs: An Israelite Goddess Redefined.* New York: Pilgrim, 1986.

Lauha, Aarre. *Kohelet*. Biblischer Kommentar Altes Testament 19. Neukirchen-Vluyn: Neukirchener, 1978.

———. "Omnia Vanitas: Die Bedeutung von *hbl* bei Kohelet." Pages 19–25 in *Glaube und Gerechtigkeit*. Schriften der Finnischen Exegetischen Gesellschaft 38. Fs. Rafael Gyllenberg. Edited by J. Kiilunen et al. Helsinki: Suomen Eksegeettisen Seura, 1983.

Leahy, Michael. "The Meaning of Ecclesiastes 12,1–5." *Irish Theological Quarterly* 19 (1952): 297–300.

Leech, Geoffrey. *Semantics*. Harmondsworth, England: Penguin, 1974.

Levine, Étan. *The Aramaic Version of Qohelet* New York: Sepher-Hermon, 1978.

Lewis, C. S. "Bluspels and Flalansferes: A Semantic Nightmare." Pages 251–65 in *Selected Literary Essays*. Edited by W. Hooper. Cambridge: Cambridge University Press, 1969.

Lichtheim, Miriam. *The Old and Middle Kingdoms*. Vol. 1 of *Ancient Egyptian Literature*. Berkeley: University of California Press, 1973.

———. *The New Kingdom*. Vol. 2 of *Ancient Egyptian Literature*. Berkeley: University of California Press, 1976.

———. *The Late Period*. Vol. 3 of *Ancient Egyptian Literature*. Berkeley: University of California Press, 1980.

Limburg, James. *Jonah: A Commentary*. Old Testament Library. Louisville: Westminster/John Knox, 1993.

Lindenberger, James M. *The Aramaic Proverbs of Ahiqar*. Baltimore: Johns Hopkins, 1983.

Loader, James A. *Ecclesiastes: A Practical Commentary*. Translated by J. Vriend. Text and Interpretation. Grand Rapids: Eerdmans, 1986 [1984].

———. *Polar Structures in the Book of Qohelet*. Beihefte zur Zeitschrift für die alttestamentliche Wissenschaft 152. Berlin: Walter de Gruyter, 1979.

Lohfink, Norbert. *Das Hauptgebot*. Analecta biblica. Rome: Pontificial Biblical Institute, 1963.

————. "Ist Kohelets הבל–Aussage erkenntnistheoretisch gemeint?" Pages 41–59 in *Qohelet in the Context of Wisdom*. Bibliotheca ephemer-idum theologicarum lovaniensium 136. Edited by A. Schoors. Leuven: Leuven University Press/Peeters, 1998.

————. "Koh 1,2 'alles ist Windhauch'—universale oder anthropologische Aussage?" Pages 201–16 in *Der Weg zum Menschen: Zur philosophischen und theologischen Anthropologie*. Fs. Alfons Deissler. Edited by R. Mosis and L. Ruppert. Freiburg: Herder, 1989.

————. *Kohelet*. 4th ed. Die Neue Echter Bibel, Altes Testament. Würzburg: Echter, 1993.

————. "Qoheleth 5:17–19—Revelation by Joy." *Catholic Biblical Quarterly* 52 (1990): 625–35.

————. "Die Wiederkehr des immer Gleichen: Eine frühe Synthese zwischen griechischem und jüdischem Weltgefühl in Kohelet 1,4–11." *Archivo di Filosofia* 53 (1985): 125–49.

————. "Zu *hbl* im Buch Kohelet." Pages 215–58 in *Studien zu Qohelet*. Stuttgarter Biblische Aufsatzbände 26. Stuttgart: Katholisches Bibelwerk, 1998.

Longman, Tremper, III. *The Book of Ecclesiastes*. New International Commentary on the Old Testament. Grand Rapids: Eerdmans, 1998.

————. *Fictional Akkadian Autobiography: A Generic and Comparative Study*. Winona Lake, Ind.: Eisenbrauns, 1991.

Loretz, Oswald. *Qohelet und der Alte Orient*. Freiburg: Herder, 1964.

Lust, Johan, Erik Eynikel, and K. Hauspie, eds. *A Greek-English Lexicon of the Septuagint*. Part 1. Stuttgart: Deutsche Bibelgesellschaft, 1992.

Lux, Rüdiger. "Der 'Lebenskompromiß'—ein Wesenszug im Denken Kohelets? Zur Auslegung von Koh 7,15–18." Pages 267–78 in *Alttestament-licher Glaube und Biblische Theologie*. Edited by J. Hausmann and H.-J. Zobel. Stuttgart: Kohlhammer, 1992.

Macdonald, Duncan Black. *The Hebrew Philosophical Genius: A Vindication*. Princeton: Princeton University Press, 1936.

Mack, Burton L. *Rhetoric and the New Testament*. Guides to Biblical Scholarship. Minneapolis: Fortress, 1990.

Martínez, Florentino García. *The Dead Sea Scrolls Translated*. Translated by W. G. E. Watson. Leiden: Brill, 1994 [1992].

McFague, Sallie. *Models of God: Theology for an Ecological, Nuclear Age*. Philadelphia: Fortress, 1987.

McKane, William. *Proverbs, a New Approach*. Old Testament Library. Philadelphia: Westminster, 1970.

McKenzie, John L. *Second Isaiah*. Anchor Bible 20. Garden City, N.Y.: Doubleday, 1968.

Meyers, Carol L., and Eric M. Meyers. *Zechariah 9–14*. Anchor Bible 25C. New York: Doubleday, 1993.

Michel, Diethelm. *Qohelet*. Erträge der Forschung 258. Darmstadt: Wissenschaftliche Buchgesellschaft, 1988.

―――. *Untersuchungen zur Eigenart des Buches Qohelet*. Beihefte zur Zeitschrift für die alttestamentliche Wissenschaft 183. Berlin/New York: Walter de Gruyter, 1989.

Miller, Douglas B. "Power in Wisdom: The Suffering Servant of Ecclesiastes 4." Pages 145–73 in *Peace and Justice Shall Embrace: Power and Theopolitics in the Bible*. Fs. Millard Lind. Edited by T. Grimsrud and L. L. Johns. Telford, Pa.: Pandora Press U.S., 1999.

―――. "Qohelet's Symbolic Use of הבל." *Journal of Biblical Literature* 117 (1998): 437–54.

―――. "What the Preacher Forgot: The Rhetoric of Ecclesiastes." *Catholic Biblical Quarterly* 62 (2000): 215–35.

Moran, William L. "Gilgamesh." Pages 557–60 in vol. 5 of *The Encyclopedia of Religion*. Editor-in-chief Mircea Eliade. New York: Collier Macmillan, 1987.

Muilenburg, James. "Form Criticism and Beyond." *Journal of Biblical Literature* 88 (1969): 1–18.

―――. "A Qoheleth Scroll from Qumran." *Bulletin of the American Schools of Oriental Research* 135 (1954): 20–28.

208   *Symbol and Rhetoric in Ecclesiastes*

Mulder, J. S. M. "Qoheleth's Division and Also Its Main Point." Pages 149–59 in *Von Kanaan bis Kerala*. Alter Orient und Altes Testament 211. Fs. J. P. M. van der Ploeg. Edited by W. C. Delsman et al. Neukirchen-Vluyn: Neukirchener; Kevelaer: Butzon & Bercker, 1982.

Murphy, Roland E. *Ecclesiastes*. Word Biblical Commentary 23A. Dallas, Tex.: Word, 1992.

———. *The Tree of Life: An Exploration of Biblical Wisdom Literature.* Anchor Bible Reference Library. New York: Doubleday, 1990.

———. *Wisdom Literature: Job, Proverbs, Ruth, Canticles, Ecclesiastes, and Esther*. The Forms of the Old Testament Literature 13. Grand Rapids: Eerdmans, 1981.

Nielsen, Kirsten. *There Is Hope for a Tree: The Tree as Metaphor in Isaiah.* Journal for the Study of the Old Testament Supplements 65. Sheffield: JSOT Press, 1989 [1985].

Ogden, Graham S. *Qoheleth*. Readings—A New Biblical Commentary. Sheffield: JSOT Press, 1987.

———. "Qoheleth IX 1–16." *Vetus Testamentum* 32 (1982): 158–69.

———. "Qoheleth XI 7 – XII 8: Qoheleth's Summons to Enjoyment and Reflection." *Vetus Testamentum* 34 (1984): 27–38.

———. "Qoheleth's Use of the 'Nothing Is Better'–Form." *Journal of Biblical Literature* 98 (1979): 339–50.

———. "'Vanity' It Certainly Is Not." *The Bible Translator* 38 (1987): 301–7.

Ollenburger, Ben C. *Zion, the City of the Great King: A Theological Symbol of the Jerusalem Cult*. Journal for the Study of the Old Testament Supplements 41. Sheffield: JSOT Press, 1987.

Oppenheim, A. Leo. *The Interpretation of Dreams in the Ancient Near East. Transactions of the American Philological Association* 46. Philadelphia: American Philological Society, 1956.

———, editor-in-charge. *Chicago Assyrian Dictionary*. 17 vols. Chicago: Oriental Institute, 1956–.

Oswalt, John N. *The Book of Isaiah Chapters 1–39*. New International Commentary on the Old Testament. Grand Rapids: Eerdmans, 1986.

Ottosson, M., et al. "חָלַם." Pages 421–32 in vol. 4 of *Theological Dictionary of the Old Testament*. Edited by G. J. Botterweck and H. Ringgren. Grand Rapids: Eerdmans, 1980.

Patrick, Dale, and Allen Scult. *Rhetoric and Biblical Interpretation*. Journal for the Study of the Old Testament Supplements 82. Sheffield: Almond, 1990.

Pennacchini, Bruno. "Qohelet ovvero il libro degli assurdi." *Euntes Docete* 116 (1997): 57–73.

Perdue, Leo G. *Wisdom and Creation: The Theology of Wisdom Literature*. Nashville: Abingdon, 1994.

————. *Wisdom in Revolt: Metaphorical Theology in the Book of Job*. Journal for the Study of the Old Testament Supplements 112. Sheffield: Almond, 1991.

Perelman, Chaim, and Lucie Olbrechts-Tyteca. *The New Rhetoric: A Treatise on Argumentation*. Translated by J. Wilkinson and P. Weaver. Notre Dame: University of Notre Dame Press, 1969 [1958].

Perry, T. Anthony. *Dialogues with Kohelet: The Book of Ecclesiastes, Translation and Commentary*. University Park: Pennsylvania State University Press, 1993.

Plumptre, E. H. *Ecclesiastes or the Preacher*. Cambridge: Cambridge University Press, 1881.

Podéchard, Emmanuel. *L'Ecclésiaste*. Études bibliques. Paris: Lecoffre, 1912.

Polk, Timothy. "The Wisdom of Irony: A Study of *Hebel* and Its Relation to Joy and the Fear of God in Ecclesiastes." *Studia Biblica et Theologica* 6 (1976): 3–17.

Pope, Marvin H. *Job*. 3d ed. Anchor Bible 15. Garden City, N.Y.: Doubleday, 1973.

Pritchard, James B., ed. *Ancient Near Eastern Texts Relating to the Old Testament*. 3d ed. with supplement. Princeton: Princeton University Press, 1969.

Rad, Gerhard von. *The Theology of Israel's Historical Traditions*. Vol. 1 of *Old Testament Theology*. New York: Harper & Row, 1962 [1957].

————. *Wisdom in Israel*. Translated by J. D. Martin. Nashville: Abingdon, 1972 [1970].

Rahlfs, Alfred, ed. "Ecclesiastes." Pages 238–60 in vol. 2 of *Septuaginta*. Stuttgart: Würtembergische Bibelanstalt, 1935.

The Random House Dictionary of the English Language: Second Edition—Unabridged, 1987. S.v. "fume," "vapor."

Richards, I. A. *The Philosophy of Rhetoric*. New York: Oxford University Press, 1936.

Ringgren, Helmer, et al. "חָשַׁךְ." Pages 245–59 in vol. 5 of *Theological Dictionary of the Old Testament*. Edited by G. J. Botterweck and H. Ringgren. Grand Rapids: Eerdmans, 1986.

Roberts, J. J. M. "Zion Tradition." Pages 985–87 in *Interpreter's Dictionary of the Bible, Supplementary Volume*. Nashville: Abingdon, 1976.

Rossi, J. B. de, ed. *Variae lectionibus Veteris Testamenti librorum*. Vol. 3. Amsterdam: Philo, 1970 [1786].

Rousseau, François. "Structure de Qohélet I 4–11 et Plan du Livre." *Vetus Testamentum* 31 (1981): 200–17.

Rudman, Dominic. "A Contextual Reading of Ecclesiastes 4:13–16." *Journal of Biblical Literature* 116 (1997): 57–73.

Sacon, Kiyoshi Kinoshita. "Isaiah 40:1–11—A Rhetorical-Critical Study." Pages 99–116 in *Rhetorical Criticism*. Fs. James Muilenburg. Edited by J. J. Jackson and M. Kessler. Pittsburgh: Pickwick, 1974.

Sáenz-Badillos, Angel. *A History of the Hebrew Language*. Translated by J. Elwolde. Cambridge: Cambridge University Press, 1993 [1988].

Sasson, Jack M. *Jonah*. Anchor Bible 24B. New York: Doubleday, 1990.

————. "Wordplay in the OT." Pages 968–70 in *Interpreter's Dictionary of the Bible, Supplementary Volume*. Nashville: Abingdon, 1976.

Sawyer, J. F. A. "The Ruined House in Ecclesiastes 12: A Reconstruction of the Original Parable." *Journal of Biblical Literature* 94 (1975): 519–31.

Schmid, Hans Heinrich. *Wesen und Geschichte der Weisheit*. Beihefte zur Zeitschrift für die alttestamentliche Wissenschaft 101. Berlin: Alfred Töpelmann, 1966.

Schoors, Antoon. *The Preacher Sought to Find Pleasing Words: A Study of the Language of Qoheleth*. Orientalia Lovaniensia Analecta 41. Leuven: Peeters, 1992.

―――. "Words Typical of Qohelet." Pages 17–39 in *Qohelet in the Context of Wisdom*. Edited by A. Schoors. Leuven: Leuven University Press/Peeters, 1998.

Scott, R. B. Y. *Proverbs, Ecclesiastes*. Anchor Bible 18. New York: Doubleday, 1965.

Searle, John R. "Metaphor." Pages 83–111 in *Metaphor and Thought*. 2d ed. Cambridge: Cambridge University Press, 1993.

Segal, J. B. *Aramaic Texts from North Saqqâra*. London: Egypt Exploration Society, 1983.

Seow, Choon-Leong. "Beyond Mortal Grasp: The Usage of *Hebel* in Ecclesiastes." *Australian Biblical Review* 48 (2000): 1–16.

―――. "'Beyond Them, My Son, Be Warned': The Epilogue of Qoheleth Revisited." Pages 125–41 in *Wisdom, You Are My Sister*. Catholic Biblical Quarterly Monograph Series 29. Fs. Roland E. Murphy. Edited by M. L. Barré. Washington, D.C.: Catholic Biblical Association, 1997.

―――. *Ecclesiastes*. Anchor Bible 18C. New York: Doubleday, 1997.

―――. "Hosea 14:10 and the Foolish People Motif." *Catholic Biblical Quarterly* 44 (1982): 212–24.

―――. "Linguistic Evidence and the Dating of Qohelet." *Journal of Biblical Literature* 115 (1996): 643–66.

―――. "Qohelet's Autobiography." Pages 275–87 in *Fortunate the Eyes That See*. Fs. David Noel Freedman. Edited by A. Beck et al. Grand Rapids: Eerdmans, 1995.

―――. "Qohelet's Eschatological Poem." *Journal of Biblical Literature* 118 (1999): 209–34.

―――. "Rehabilitating 'The Preacher': Qohelet's Theological Reflections in Context." Pages 91–116 in vol. 4 of *The Papers of the Henry Luce III Fellows in Theology*. Edited by M. Zyniewicz. Pittsburgh: ATS, 2000.

———. "The Socioeconomic Context of 'The Preacher's' Hermeneutic." *Princeton Seminary Bulletin* 17 n.s. (1996): 168–95.

Seybold, Klaus. "הֶבֶל." Pages 313–20 in vol. 3 of *Theological Dictionary of the Old Testament*. Edited by G. J. Botterweck and H. Ringgren. Grand Rapids: Eerdmans, 1978.

Sheppard, Gerald T. *Wisdom as a Hermeneutical Construct*. BZAW 151. Berlin: de Gruyter, 1980.

Siegfried, Carl G. *Prediger und Hoheslied*. Handkommentar zum Alten Testament 2:3,2. Göttingen: Vandenhoeck & Ruprecht, 1898.

Skehan, Patrick W., and Alexander A. Di Lella. *The Wisdom of Ben Sira*. Anchor Bible 39. Garden City, N.Y.: Doubleday, 1987.

Slotki, Judah, and Jacob Israelstam, eds. *Midrash Rabbah: Leviticus*. 3d ed. London: Soncino, 1983.

Smalley, Beryl. *Medieval Exegesis of Wisdom Literature: Essays by Beryl Smalley*. Edited by R. E. Murphy. Atlanta: Scholars Press, 1986.

Soskice, Janet Martin. *Metaphor and Religious Language*. Oxford: Clarendon, 1985.

Speiser, E. A. "The Gilgamesh Epic." Pages 72–98 in *Ancient Near Eastern Texts Relating to the Old Testament*. 3d ed. Edited by J. B. Pritchard. Princeton: Princeton University Press, 1969.

———. "The Muškênum." Pages 332–43 in *Oriental and Biblical Studies*. Edited and with an introduction by J. J. Finkelstein and M. Greenberg. Philadelphia: University of Pennsylvania Press, 1967.

Sperber, Alexander. *The Bible in Aramaic*. Vol. 4A. Leiden: Brill, 1968.

Staples, W. E. "The 'Vanity' of Ecclesiastes." *Journal of Near Eastern Studies* 2 (1943): 95–104.

Sternberg, Meir. *The Poetics of Biblical Narrative: Ideological Literature and the Drama of Reading*. Indiana Studies in Biblical Literature. Bloomington: Indiana University Press, 1985.

Sukenik, Eleazar L., ed. *The Dead Sea Scrolls of the Hebrew University*. Jerusalem: Magnes, 1955.

Szpek, Heidi M. "The Peshitta on Job 7:6: 'My Days Are Swifter Than an
אר׳." *Journal of Biblical Literature* 113 (1994): 287–90.

Tate, Marvin E. *Psalms 51–100*. Word Biblical Commentary 20. Waco, Tex.:
Word, 1990.

Taylor, Charles. *The Dirge of Coheleth in Ecclesiastes XII*. London: Williams
& Norgate, 1874.

Thompson, R. Campbell. *The Epic of Gilgamesh*. Oxford: Clarendon, 1930.

Toorn, Karel van der. "Prison." Pages 468–69 in vol. 5 of *Anchor Bible
Dictionary*. Edited by D. N. Freedman and G. A. Herion. New York:
Doubleday, 1992.

Trible, Phyllis. *Rhetorical Criticism*. Guides to Biblical Scholarship.
Minneapolis: Fortress, 1994.

Van Leeuwen, Raymond C. "Ecclesiastes: Introduction." Pages 986–88 in *The
HarperCollins Study Bible*. Edited by W. A. Meeks. New York:
HarperCollins, 1993.

Weber, Robert, ed. "Liber Ecclesiastes." Pages 986–97 in *Biblia Sacra iuxta
Vulgatam versionem*. Editio minor. 3d ed. Stuttgart: Deutsche
Bibelgesellschaft, 1983.

Weiser, Artur. *The Psalms*. Translated by H. Hartwell. Old Testament Library.
Philadelphia: Westminster, 1962 [1959].

Wellek, René, and Austin Warren. *Theory of Literature*. 3d ed. San Diego:
Harcourt, 1977.

Westermann, Claus. *Genesis 1–11: A Commentary*. Translated by J. J. Scullion.
Continental Commentaries. Minneapolis: Augsburg, 1984 [1974].

———. *Isaiah 40–66*. Translated by D. M. G. Stalker. Old Testament Library.
Philadelphia: Westminster, 1969 [1966].

Wheelwright, Philip. *Metaphor and Reality*. Bloomington: Indiana University
Press, 1962.

Whitley, Charles F. *Koheleth: His Language and Thought*. Beihefte zur
Zeitschrift für die alttestamentliche Wissenschaft 148. Berlin: Walter de
Gruyter, 1979.

Whybray, R. N. *Ecclesiastes.* New Century Bible Commentary. Grand Rapids: Eerdmans, 1989.

———. "The Identification and Use of Quotations in Ecclesiastes." Pages 435–51 in *Congress Volume: Vienna, 1980.* Vetus Testamentum Supplements 32. Leiden: Brill, 1981.

———. "Qoheleth, Preacher of Joy." *Journal for the Study of the Old Testament* 23 (1982): 87–98.

———. "Qoheleth the Immoralist? (Qoh 7:16–17)." Pages 191–204 in *Israelite Wisdom.* Fs. Samuel Terrien. Edited by J. G. Gammie et al. New York: Union Theological Seminary, 1978.

Wildeboer, Gerrit. "Der Prediger." Pages 109–68 in *Die fünf Megillot.* Kurzer Hand-Commentar zum Alten Testament 17. Edited by K. Budde et al. Freiburg: Mohr, 1898.

Williams, Ronald J. *Hebrew Syntax: An Outline.* 2d ed. Toronto: University of Toronto Press, 1976.

———. "The Sage in Egyptian Literature." Pages 19–30 in *The Sage in Israel and the Ancient Near East.* Edited by J. G. Gammie and L. G. Perdue. Winona Lake, Ind.: Eisenbrauns, 1990.

Witzenrath, Hagia. *Süß ist das Licht . . . Eine literaturwissenschaftliche Untersuchung zu Kohelet 11,7–12,7.* Arbeiten zu Text und Sprache im Alten Testament 11. St. Ottilien: EOS, 1979.

Wolff, Hans Walter. *Obadiah and Jonah.* Translated by M. Kohl. Continental Commentaries. Minneapolis: Augsburg, 1986 [1977].

Wright, Addison G. "Additional Numerical Patterns in Qoheleth." *Catholic Biblical Quarterly* 45 (1983): 32–43.

———. "Ecclesiastes (Qoheleth)." Pages 489–95 in *The New Jerome Biblical Commentary.* Edited by R. E. Brown, J. A. Fitzmyer, and R. E. Murphy. Englewood Cliffs, N.J.: Prentice Hall, 1990.

———. "The Poor But Wise Youth and the Old But Foolish King (Qoh 4:13–16)." Pages 142–54 in *Wisdom, You Are My Sister.* Catholic Biblical Quarterly Monograph Series 29. Fs. Roland E. Murphy. Edited by M. L. Barré. Washington, D.C.: Catholic Biblical Association, 1997.

————. "The Riddle of the Sphinx: The Structure of the Book of Qoheleth." *Catholic Biblical Quarterly* 30 (1968): 313–34.

————. "The Riddle of the Sphinx Revisited: Numerical Patterns in the Book of Qoheleth." *Catholic Biblical Quarterly* 42 (1980): 38–51.

Wuellner, Wilhelm. "Where Is Rhetorical Criticism Taking Us?" *Catholic Biblical Quarterly* 49 (1987): 448–63.

Yadin, Yigael, ed. *The Scroll of the War of the Sons of Light Against the Sons of Darkness*. Translated by B. Rabin and C. Rabin. Oxford: Oxford University Press, 1962.

Zer-Kavod, Mordechai. *Qohelet*. Jerusalem: Mosad ha-Rab Kook, 1973.

Zimmerli, Walther. *Das Buch des Predigers Salomo*. 3d ed. Das Alte Testament Deutsch 16/1. Göttingen: Vandenhoeck & Ruprecht, 1980 [1962].

————. "Das Buch Kohelet—Traktat oder Sentenzensammlung?" *Vetus Testamentum* 24 (1974): 221–30.

Author Index

217

Text Index

Word and Form Index

General Index